Gestalt psychology and the cognitive revolution

Gestalt psychology and the cognitive revolution

David J. Murray

Queen's University, Kingston, Canada

HARVESTER
WHEATSHEAF

New York   London   Toronto   Sydney   Tokyo   Singapore

First published 1995 by
Harvester Wheatsheaf
Campus 400, Maylands Avenue
Hemel Hempstead
Hertfordshire, HP2 7EZ
A division of
Simon & Schuster International Group

Typeset in 10/12 pt Ehrhardt
by Keyset Composition, Colchester

Printed and bound in Great Britain by
T.J. Press (Padstow) Ltd, Padstow, Cornwall.

British Library Cataloguing in Publication Data

A catalogue record for this book is available from
the British Library

ISBN 0-7450-1186-1 (pbk)

---

1   2   3   4   5   99   98   97   96   95

This book is dedicated to Keir and Rachel

Contents

Preface

When I was beginning my academic career in the 1960s, focusing my energies on research on human short-term memory and, later, on some aspects of long-term memory, I had little time available for trying to formulate a 'big picture' of psychology. This was not because I lacked the interest in doing so but because so much time was taken up doing experiments and keeping up with the exploding literature on memory that followed the publications of Broadbent's *Perception and Communication* (1958), George A. Miller's 1956 paper on the question of whether information theory could be used to explain why the memory span for digits was 7 plus or minus 2, and others. In other words, I started my career just after the 'cognitive revolution' had begun and I remember how, after having taken courses on learning in animals, and having been told that scientific rigour in psychology demanded that one refer as little as possible to speculative mental processes underlying behaviour, not only I but hundreds of graduate students in the 1960s were afraid to write words like 'image', 'consciousness' and even 'memory' or 'memories' (we were supposed to talk about 'responses' rather than 'memories').

But when the mathematical modelling of memory processes began in the 1960s (some of them are summarized in Norman, 1970), we were forced to lift the rather cloudy spectacles with which we had peered at our own data and contemplate a broader view in which short-term memory, attention and long-term memory were parts of a single 'information processing' system. Paivio's book on *Imagery and Verbal Processes* (1971) broke down the barrier to talking about images, and Neisser's book on *Cognitive Psychology* (1967) was a powerful influence not only because of the originality of its contents but also because of its title. Departments of Psychology around the world soon found themselves obliged to offer courses on cognitive psychology, forcing many of us to broaden our views even further to encompass word identification processes, decision-making, problem-solving, reasoning and psycholinguistics because we had to teach those subjects. As I write this in November 1993, even the term 'cognitive psychology' is a little *passé*: we are now supposed to write about 'cognitive science' and our viewpoint has been stretched to such a wide extent that we can no longer grasp the topic in its entirety because the ideal cognitive scientist is expected to know not only the literature from experimental psychology, but also details of philosophy, computer programming, mathematics and neuroscience that simply were not demanded of my generation in the 1960s.

In the frantic effort to keep up with progress, we often have no time to look back. However, almost by accident, I found myself teaching a course in the 1970s on the history of psychology and was approached by a publisher to write the book that eventually appeared as *A History of Western Psychology* (first edition 1983; second edition 1988). One of the sections of that book that was most interesting for me to write was the chapter on Gestalt psychology. I discovered that at a time (1920–1940) when the behaviourists were busy building the prison in which the inmates could not talk about images, consciousness or memories, the Gestalt psychologists were formulating ambitious theories in which mental representations, particularly of plans and goals, played a prominent part. They discussed images (though not with the comprehensiveness that Paivio would later bring to the subject); they believed that automatic brain processes of which we were not conscious acted to 'organize' incoming inputs (and also data being retained), so as to make the world easier for the subject to understand and act in; and they wrote at length on 'memories' as opposed to 'mediated responses'. At the same time, they forced many psychologists to ask questions about the usefulness of these concepts in experimental psychology, questions which Osgood, in his famous 1953 textbook, was later at pains to emphasize.

But the Gestalt contributions to cognitive science remained little read even well after the cognitive revolution had started tearing down the walls of the behaviourist prison. It was therefore with pleasure that I received a letter from the publishers of this book asking if I would be interested in expanding the chapter on Gestalt psychology in my history text to a volume showing the relevance of Gestalt psychology to modern cognitive science. I accepted the invitation with little hesitation. In actually writing the book, however, I ran into two problems which I am not sure I have solved successfully. First, since the Gestalt psychologists made their mark on the history of psychology principally with their research on sensation and perception, how far should I try to deal with these major topics in a book ostensibly on cognition? Second, when the Gestalt psychologists used words indicative of goal-directed behaviour (and other words such as 'organization', 'Ego', 're-structuring' and 'isolation'), should this terminology be adopted in an acceptable cognitive science? Or can words like 'plans' and 'goals' be omitted from a deterministic account of human cognition, as the behaviourists had insisted? This is essentially a question in the philosophy of science.

I have dealt with these problems as follows. With respect to the first question, Chapter 2 gives an account of Gestalt contributions to perception but it is an account in which I stress the links between their theories of perception and the theories of cognition that arose from them. At the end of that chapter there are some brief remarks on the relevance of Gestalt ideas to some theories of perception in the 1990s. With respect to the second question, I introduce some notions about the usefulness of terms like 'goals' etc. in the body of the survey of the Gestalt literature (notably in Chapter 5 on problem-solving). However, in Chapter 6 I extend the discussion to include the question of the usefulness of such terms as 'distinctiveness', 're-structuring', 'goals' and 'self' in a systematic cognitive science. In an argument very similar to that put forward as early as 1969 by Simon in his book *The Sciences of the Artificial*, I argue that psychological science has to make a choice between levels of discourse in discussing its subject-matter. At a very low level, neurological events may be described; at a higher level, 'habits' consisting of motor responses to sensory or silently spoken stimuli may be described, as J.B. Watson tried to do; but at a higher level still, where images can be referred to, in particular, images of possible future events, it becomes appropriate to use such concepts as 're-structuring', 'goals', and the 'self'. That the 'distinctiveness' of stimuli *relative* to a background is more important than the absolute physical intensity of the stimuli is an argument that was spelled out by the Gestalt psychologists more than by any other group, and the relevance of this view to late twentieth century thinking on perception and memory is also discussed in Chapter 6.

Because this book is devoted mainly to the writings of the first-generation Gestalt psychologists, Wertheimer, Koffka and Köhler, I have said less than perhaps I should have said about the extensive research in the 1950s on the determination of tachistoscopic word identification and other forms of cognition by the subject's needs and attitudes. Late twentieth century research on associative priming is possibly providing the groundwork for a theory of trace activation which will include an explanation of 'selective perception', but I am more concerned in the present work in stressing how the Gestalt psychologists of the 1920s and 1930s foreshadowed the cognitive revolution. The research of the second generation of Gestalt psychologists, such as Mary Henle, Hans Wallach, and Solomon Asch, served as a bridge between the first generation and the late twentieth century cognitive scientists and deserves special treatment elsewhere.

Most of what the first generation Gestalt psychologists wrote about cognitive science concerned memory and problem-solving, so these are the issues given prominence here. The aim of the book is to persuade cognitive scientists, who have insufficient time to add the history of psychology to the many other topics they are expected to know, that back in the 1920s and 1930s there existed a group of psychologists with whom they would probably have got on well at an imaginary conference in cognitive Heaven.

The preparation of this volume was supported financially by Operating Grant 410-92-0187 from the Social Sciences and Humanities Research Council of Canada and a grant from the Advisory Research Council of Queen's University. I am extremely grateful to Peter Dodwell for reading Chapter 2 and making many helpful suggestions and to the library staff at Queen's University for their unfailing assistance whenever I needed books or articles. I particularly thank them for obtaining, through the services of University Microfilms International, a copy of Mitchell G. Ash's PhD thesis (Harvard, 1982), an indispensable source on the rise of Gestalt psychology. I understand this thesis can also be obtained through Interlibrary Resource Departments in British universities; my copy took two months to arrive in Canada, and cost $35 US. I also wish to thank two anonymous reviewers for suggestions concerning my original proposal for the book, and one anonymous reviewer for commenting on the first draft of the manuscript. But especially hearty thanks must go to Ryan D. Tweney, whose many perspicacious and scholarly remarks on that first draft led to major revisions of several sections, revisions I am now very glad I had the opportunity to make. Finally, a special word of thanks must also go to my research assistant, Maureen Freedman, whose expeditious preparation of the manuscript, preparation of photocopies, and assistance with library work greatly facilitated my task.

David J. Murray
Department of Psychology
Queen's University
Kingston, Ontario

The meanings of 'behaviourism', 'Gestalt psychology' and the 'cognitive revolution'

Introduction

As knowledge about psychology has progressed over the past hundred years or so certain words have come into and gone out of fashion. At the end of the nineteenth century, it was commonplace to find references to 'images', 'goals' (frequently related to the exercise of 'will') and the 'self' (frequently called the 'Ego'). But in 1913 John Broadus Watson (1878–1958) invented behaviourism, a viewpoint according to which such mentalistic terms, typical of the everyday speech used to communicate our thoughts, were to be banned from a scientific psychology. Instead psychologists were supposed to talk only about 'habits', sets of learned movements that would be elicited if particular stimuli appeared in the organism's environment. This language, which seemed appropriate for the description of animal behaviour, was also applied to human behaviour. As will be stated in more detail below, the behaviourism of Watson had a delayed effect. It was not until about 1930 that Anglo-American psychologists took his ideas seriously, but then, particularly under the influence of Clark L. Hull (1884–1952), behaviourism came to dominate experimental psychology until about 1956. About that time, a number of writers suggested turning the clock back and allowing words like 'images', 'goals', and the 'self' to re-enter scientific psychology. This was the beginning of the so-called 'cognitive revolution'.

The use of mentalistic terms in a scientific psychology was, however, not abandoned in Germany during this period. Following the publication in 1912 of an influential paper by Max Wertheimer (1880–1943), between about 1912 and 1933 a movement known as the Gestalt movement came to exercise a dominating influence on German psychology. Its influence then shifted to North America with the enforced emigration of the three pioneers of Gestalt psychology, Wertheimer, Kurt Koffka (1886–1941) and Wolfgang Köhler (1887–1967). Although some of their writings were translated into English, others were not and although Koffka's *Principles of Gestalt Psychology* appeared in 1935, it seemed to have little influence when compared to the ideas of Hull, Skinner and other neo-behaviourists.

It is the purpose of this book to show that many of the ideas about human cognitive psychology that have come to prominence since the cognitive revolution were actually anticipated by the Gestalt psychologists. They talked of 'images', 'goal-directed behaviour' and the 'Ego' at a time when these words were unfashionable because of the dominance of behaviourism, and they carried out many experiments on human memory and human problem-solving with implications for late twentieth century cognitive psychology that have been underestimated (possibly because they were not translated). This book is an attempt to redress the balance. At the outset it must be made clear, however, that I am not claiming that the Gestalt psychologists directly *influenced* the cognitive revolution but I do claim that they *anticipated* many findings of the cognitive revolution, and that there is thus a *correspondence* between their scientific terminology and the terminology that has become acceptable as a result of the cognitive revolution. Moreover, I shall argue in the final chapter that the scientific terminology acceptable in a system of cognitive psychology will depend on the level of discourse; at a high level, words like 'image', 'goals' and the 'self' are acceptable, whereas at the lower level 'habits' might be acceptable. However, since humans have the ability to form 'mental representations' of the world that might include images, I shall argue (as have others) that it is doubtful whether a psychological system based entirely on 'habits' will be adequate to describe the mental life or overt behaviour of humans.

In fact, the Gestalt psychologists maintained that human behaviour, and probably the behaviour of higher animals such as apes, dogs and cats, could only be described and explained *if* it were accepted that they had mental representations such as images. In particular, they argued that for behaviour to be adequately described, it was necessary that the behaving organism had mental representations of possible *future* events, thus allowing the formulation of goals, plans and intentions. And for humans it would be what Koffka called an 'Ego' that would be in charge of this planning activity. Among activities that could be planned would be the deliberate memorizing of movement sequences, strings of verbal material like words or nonsense syllables, or even meaningless drawings. With respect to list-learning, the neo-behaviourists had thought of the human memorizer as passively learning a sequence of speech-responses ('speech-habits') but the Gestalt psychologists stressed instead the active role of the subject in re-organizing and re-structuring the material that had to be memorized. The Gestalt psychologists also extended the notion of re-structuring to explain problem-solving behaviour by both the higher animals and by humans. Hence, in this book the stress will be on the Gestalt research on memorizing and problem-solving.

There are other topics of concern to late twentieth century cognitive scientists which the Gestalt psychologists discussed in less detail; these include language learning, reading, identification processes as explored through the use of the tachistoscope, and mathematical models of learning. These topics will receive only tangential mention, although on the last issue of mathematical modelling, some stress will be laid on the importance of the Gestalt psychologists in laying the groundwork for late twentieth century models according to which stimulus distinctiveness is a key measurable variable.

In this first chapter, I shall place Gestalt psychology in its general historical context with respect to the behaviourist period and the 'cognitive revolution' which overturned the behaviourist regime. However, there is a danger that in subdividing the chapter this way, the reader may get the impression that matters were more black and white than they really were. Behaviourism was a movement that was adopted by the majority of learning theorists, and the 'cognitive revolution' is an ongoing movement in which most scholars concerned with human memory, language and thought have found themselves members. But during the period of behaviourist domination, there were renegades who held out for a mentalistic description even of animal behaviour; such a person was Edward C. Tolman (1886–1959). And during our own time there have been individuals who have argued that the cognitive revolution was a misplaced endeavour, for example, B.F. Skinner (1904–1990). Particular individuals have also questioned whether there really was a 'cognitive revolution', since many of the scientific concepts used by cognitive scientists in the late twentieth century had been used widely in a general European/American tradition going back to the nineteenth century and had persisted in the German movement of Gestalt psychology. For example, Karier (1989), in reviewing Baars' book *The Cognitive Revolution in Psychology* (1986), has claimed that the 'simplification, condensation and general reduction required in order to fit a very rich complicated history' into a clear-cut division of the history of investigations into human cognition into pre-revolution and post-revolution categories is 'just too constraining. Not only is too much left out of the picture but the picture itself is marred by overgeneralizations that lead at time to distortions' (p. 78).

This argument is particularly telling if Gestalt psychology is left out of the picture, as it largely is in Baars' book. A claim can be made in fact that the Gestalt psychologists defended mentalistic traditions throughout the period of behaviourist domination; it can also be claimed that the cognitive revolution involved a re-discovery of basic mentalistic concepts that had been discussed not only by the Gestalt psychologists and the later nineteenth century psychologists but by almost all psychologists going back to Aristotle. However, the claim being made here is that the Gestalt psychologists' writings formed an important bulwark which helped to prevent the spread of behaviourism into Europe and which also provided many original ideas which have not yet been absorbed properly into cognitive science.

Historical background

The twentieth century is now drawing to a close and no doubt there will be a plethora of retrospective analyses of just what has been achieved during its span. Progress in science and technology has, of course, been extraordinary and there have been at least four growth industries which are almost entirely twentieth century – cinema, oil, computers and psychology. As a branch of science in which one could obtain a doctorate, the discipline dates back only to 1879, when Wilhelm Wundt (1832–1929) founded his Institute at the University of Leipzig in Germany and as a profession dedicated to helping people with emotional or intellectual difficulties, it can perhaps be dated to 1896, when Lightner Witmer (1867–1956) developed a 'psychological clinic' at the University of Pennsylvania for assisting children with learning problems. In the case of experimental psychology, there has persisted throughout the century an uneasy tension between conservative psychologists who are content to work on restricted problems that are susceptible to investigation by experimental methods and more radical psychologists, who look for large theories to encompass the findings of the conservatives.

When Wundt started his experimentation on psychological matters, he was strongly influenced by the pioneering work of E.H. Weber (1795–1878) on the measurement of sensory thresholds, G.T. Fechner (1801–1887) on psycho-physics, which claimed to 'measure' sensation strength, H. von Helmholtz (1821–1894) on vision and audition, and F.C. Donders (1818–1889) on reaction times. In his writings Wundt attempted to offer a synthetic model of the human mind in which individual sensations associated with a stimulus were operated on by an 'apperceptive' process in which largely unconscious events, involving the subject's long-term memory, were brought into play so that the perceiving subject was able to identify the stimulus and act on it. Wundt also wrote extensively on the way in which human behaviour was largely determined by the operation of the 'will', so that behaviour was guided by particular plans and goals, and difficult problems could be resolved mentally by a willed act of concentration on the problem. A question that particularly exercised Wundt and his followers was that of whether the contents of 'mind' could be analyzed into individual elements, such as sensations, feelings or thoughts: the name 'structuralism' was given to the viewpoint according to which this was a valid subject for psychological enquiry. At the beginning of the twentieth century this viewpoint was attacked by the 'functionalists', who argued for a broader psychology based on evolutionary theory and biology. But Wundt's system should not be bypassed in a hurry on the way to our real goal of describing Gestalt psychology. The 'apperception' mechanism was a concept in a long tradition going back to Leibniz in the late seventeenth century (see The Gestalt Movement below), a tradition that shared with Gestalt psychology the belief that what the subject is aware of in *consciousness* is only the end result of a great deal of brain processing which has no conscious correlate. The conscious perception of a brief set of letters C A T as referring to the word 'CAT', which in turn refers to an animal of which the subject may have an image, is associationistic in the sense of being non-random and mechanically caused but it is also mentalistic in the sense that reference is made to conscious perception, memories of words, and images of animals, and Wundt's system may therefore be said to be in a tradition of cognitive science.

Furthermore, he insisted that most human acts show evidence of some sort of mental representation of the future. Even speaking a simple sentence is not obviously a product of the classical laws of association (for why then should sentences not run 'cat dog bark tree. . .'?), but of a plan as to how the final words of the sentence should link up to the earlier ones. This plan is one in which some mental form of representation takes on a linguistic form as a set of words forming a coherent sentence, such as 'My cat is Siamese and is named Archimède'. By way of pre-formed mental representations (perhaps clear images, perhaps vaguer representations not easily described by self-observation), we can *will* to carry out such actions as speaking sentences. Wundt's system has been called 'voluntarism' (see Murray, 1988, pp. 199–214, for more details) and is a clear forerunner of modern theories that stress that human actions spin themselves out according to pre-arranged plans or programmes represented in the subject's experience by mental models. Wundt's views can be easily reconciled with those of many modern cognitive psychologists and, following the work of Marcel (1983), there has been a plethora of recent studies using tachistoscopes in which Wundt's claim that inputs are processed unconsciously before being identified is being verified to an extent that would probably have delighted him. I suspect that his first question if he were revived and brought to a modern laboratory would be 'Whatever happened to apperception?'

Obviously when we come to claim that the Gestalt psychologists anticipated the cognitive revolution, we do not claim also that nobody else did. Wundt's section on tachistoscopic word naming in his *Outlines of Psychology* (1896, pp. 223–44) is still worth reading and his emphasis on how the *subjective* experience of identifying a briefly exposed word involves both fuzzy and clear perceptions had its roots in even earlier studies of the task that asked for self-observations. *Because* Gestalt psychology had its roots in earlier German psychology, it is clear that many of the mentalistic concepts used by late twentieth century cognitive scientists were also anticipated by the late nineteenth century pioneers of psychology.

There was also another group of psychologists who actually irritated Wundt because they used introspection (which Wundt disliked) in studying the processes of human problem-solving; the researchers of the Würzburg school, which functioned between about 1901 and 1910, indicated that once the subject was set to solve problems, the thoughts that came to mind were determined by the nature of this set. When the solution did come, however, it often seemed to come suddenly rather than as the result of a deliberate series of conscious inferences and it often came without the accompaniment of any obvious imagery. Meanwhile, particularly in Britain and in North America, a considerable amount of research was being carried out on how animals solve problems; a particularly important set of experiments was carried out by E.L. Thorndike (1874–1949) on how cats escaped from confining boxes. He suggested that they used 'trial-and-error' behaviour initially and then learnt by success or failure how to escape from future confinements. In Russia investigations were being carried out by I.P. Pavlov (1849–1936) on how animals came to make associations between food and individual stimuli, regularly paired with the food, that had previously been of neutral emotional interest to the animal. The topics of structuralism, functionalism, the Würzburg school and early studies of animal learning are reviewed in most histories of psychology (e.g. Murray, 1988; Leahey, 1992).

By about 1910 experimentation was well under way in a variety of topics and certain general viewpoints, such as structuralism and functionalism were in competition, but (with the possible exception of Wundt's system itself) there was no systematic theoretical viewpoint that attempted to integrate these experimental findings. The greatest book on psychology in this early phase of its development was probably William James's *Principles of Psychology* (1890), which did not attempt to put forward a synthesis but discussed instead individual topics and often came to surprisingly simple conclusions that seemed to mediate *against* the construction of large theories. For example, he rejected Fechner's psychophysics as founded on error; he thought Wundt's system was self-contradictory and that 'structuralism' was doomed to failure given the stream-like continuity of consciousness; he thought associationism would ultimately be reduced to brain physiology; and he was responsible for dividing memory into short-term and long-term types, with the main difference being that short-term memory was restricted to what had just entered consciousness and not left it, while long-term memory contained information that had once been in consciousness but had left it before being retrieved again. Contemporaneously with the development of experimental psychology, psychiatrists were collecting evidence on the basis of case histories that indicated that unconscious processes frequently determined the course of conscious experiences that the patients themselves did not understand and found emotionally disturbing; the fullest history of the discovery of the unconscious during this period is given by Ellenberger (1970).

But at the end of the first decade of the century three radical movements arose, psychoanalysis, behaviourism, and Gestalt psychology, each of which tried to offer a scientific framework for encompassing the observations that had been collected from introspection, experiments, and case histories. The three schools differed in the amount of faith they placed in each of these kinds of evidence: for example, trying to explain mental phenomena by introspective analysis was disapproved of by both the behaviourists and the Gestalt psychologists. However this did not mean that subjects' reports about their own beliefs and thinking processes were necessarily ignored; the leader of the behaviourists, J.B. Watson, carried out a questionnaire survey on sexual attitudes and some Gestalt psychologists asked subjects to report their own thought-processes while problem-solving, just as the Würzburg school had done (see Chapter 5). Case histories, on the other hand, were made the basis of theories of emotional disorders as in the examples of the psychological analysis of Pierre Janet (1859–1947) and the psychoanalysis of Sigmund Freud (1856–1939); to many academic psychologists of the twentieth century, psychoanalysis has been suspect partly *because* it relies on the practitioner's interpretation of remarks made by patients and relies little on evidence derived from experimental manipulations. (It is frequently claimed that the doctrines of Freud cannot be *disproved*, but one of the major stumbling blocks to an appreciation of Freud's theory has been the fact that we cannot do experiments which might disprove Freudian theory without being unethical – one cannot deliberately raise children in unsuitable environments, nor can one test theories of repression by deliberately creating situations that are harmful to the subject's ego or well-being.) However, psychoanalysis is not our concern here and it will be mentioned only incidentally in what follows. Here we are more concerned with the remaining schools, behaviourism and Gestalt psychology.

Behaviourism

Behaviourism was first promulgated as a specific standpoint by J.B. Watson, an American who had an excellent record of publications on animal behaviour (both instinctive and learned) before he published his first article on behaviourism in the 1913 edition of the *Psychological Review*. Behaviourism has two aspects, a methodological aspect and a substantive aspect. From the point of view of methodology, Watson insisted that the introspective method had to be dropped, only observations that could be expressed in terms of distinct measurable events should be considered an integral part of the data of psychology. In stressing measurability, he was of course reaching for the same objectivity that characterized physics and biology. But at the same time the quest for measurable entities in psychology meant that mental events would have to be excluded on the grounds that they were not measurable or directly observable by a person other than the subject. That mental events were not measurable had been stressed more than a century earlier by Immanuel Kant (1724–1804), but various nineteenth century psychologists had disagreed with Kant, insisting that mental events could be given quantitative values: Johann F. Herbart (1776–1841) believed that a number could be ascribed to the strength of an 'idea' (*Vorstellung*) in consciousness, and invented a system of psychomechanics in which ideas competed in consciousness, with the stronger ones pushing the weaker ones down below a 'threshold' of consciousness; and Fechner (1860) had argued that a sensation could be said to have a certain strength that could be measured indirectly by various psychophysical methods. Watson however was not interested in these attempts to measure 'internal scalable magnitudes', as I have called such non-physical mental entities as sensations, ideas, or habits (Murray, 1987); in fact he was not interested in incorporating mental events into psychology at all. At one stroke, he asserted that the study of conscious experience was fruitless because it relied on introspection and he implied that attempts to measure internal scalable magnitudes were doomed from the start (unfortunately Watson never wrote at length on this important question). Below we shall elaborate on how he also banished from his kind of psychology the study of images, the use of the word 'memory', and the use of the word 'unconscious' as employed by Freud and his followers.

The second, substantive aspect of behaviourism was concerned with the content of psychology. Watson believed that once sensations had been processed, physical responses were released and that these physical responses included glandular reactions (as in the emotions), autonomic reactions, and reflex and voluntary motor reactions. It was on the assumption that only these reactions could be influenced by experience that Watson put forward a system of psychology in which extensive experience with particular stimuli led to an increase in the probability of the associated reactions: for example, practice at motor skills led to an increased fluency and automaticity of what were originally voluntary movements – they became 'habits'. Furthermore, by a process of association, individual stimuli could be associated with emotional reactions which would not normally be evoked by those stimuli: a loud noise causes a fear response in a 9-month old, but if a furry animal is shown just before each presentation of the noise, the child will soon 'learn' to show a fear reaction to the furry animal, a fear that will generalize to other furry objects (Watson and Rayner, 1920). By the same process of association, a stimulus can be associated with the voluntary enunciation of a sound by a child and gradually the child learns a repertory of speech movements. For Watson, as it had been for an early Russian pioneer of behaviourism, Ivan M. Sechenov (1829–1905), thinking was only talking without the final elimination of air through the mouth.

However for Watson, if thought consisted entirely of motor activity that is determined by previous motor activity and sensory inputs, it seemed that there was no room for images. Nor is the word 'memory' necessary, for the word 'habit' (referring to a learned set of motor responses) made the word 'memory' superfluous (Watson, 1928a, p. 70).

Of course, habits can become dysfunctional through the lack of use, so there will be 'forgetting', and Watson's evidence for 'forgetting' was based on the study of animals who 'forget' how to run in a maze. But in the behaviourists' world 'memory' and 'forgetting' are words that are not needed because we can encompass the same phenomena in terms of the use and disuse of motor and verbal habits.

Similarly, imagery is rejected because Watson believed that only external stimuli can elicit a sense organ process – 'the brain is stimulated always and only from the outside by a sense organ process' (p. 75). This is an absolute denial of the proposition that the brain can be stimulated from the *inside* to provide a 'sensation', or, as we call it, an image. Internally induced 'sensations' can be so real that the subject can mistakenly think they are genuine sensations; we call them 'hallucinations' or 'dreams', but Watson does not discuss these in the passage with which we are here concerned. In Watson's view, images remain 'unproven – mythological, the figment of the psychologist's terminology' (p. 76). When we recall our mother coming in to tuck us up at night when we were children, according to Watson, we are only maintaining a verbal habit, a re-play of things we put into words at the original time we saw our mother; he wrote 'all "memories" are at bottom motor memories and obey the laws of learning, disuse and releasing' (p. 77).

Watson also rejected the Freudian notion of the unconscious. However before saying why this was so it is important to note that Watson shared with Freud a profound belief in the importance of emotional experiences in infancy as determinants of later personality. Freud believed that a drive for pleasure, particularly sexual or tactile pleasure, the so-called 'libido', is the major motivating force in a child's life (later, he added a destructive drive, but we by-pass discussion of this issue here). External objects or persons become associated with libido and so do parts of the child's own body or even the child's own concept of his or her 'self', a concept which is being formed at about the age of two. Self-love was called 'narcissism'. Watson said almost the same thing in different words: he believed that there were three basic emotions in the neonate, fear (particularly of loss of support), rage (at being restrained), and love (on being fed, handled gently, etc.). These emotions can form the basis of conditioned responses, so that a child learns to associate certain things with love, including his mother and possibly even his own body; what Freud called 'libidinal cathexes' Watson called 'conditioned loves'. A full account of the importance of conditioned emotions in child development will be found in Watson's third major book, *Behaviorism* (1924).

But Watson parted company from Freud because in Watson's system where all memories are motor (including verbal memories), forgetting simply meant the disuse of motor or verbal habits. In Watson's system, however, it was perfectly possible for emotions to be associated with *un*verbalized responses, which could include habits involving motor skills which cannot be easily described in words, for example, unstriped muscular and glandular responses such as are associated with most emotions; and habits and conditioned emotional responses set up in infancy before the infant has learned to speak. Thus, to give Watson's own example, if a mother gives too much nurturance to an infant before the infant has learned to speak, a vast repertory of conditioned 'loves' will be associated with the mother which are not verbalized. If the child grows up to be over-dependent on the mother, even to the extent that 'marriage means nothing; the girl cannot break her nest-habits' (Watson, 1928a, p. 103), this is not evidence of a Freudian regression or of an 'unconscious' fixation on the mother, it is evidence of a system of conditioned loves that have never been verbalized. Later, in his widely read book on child-rearing (Watson, 1928b), he discouraged over-affection on the part of the mother towards her infant child on the grounds that it would stifle independence in the adult personality. For Watson, Freud's unconscious was as 'mythological' as images.

The study of human memory in Anglo-American academic circles was dominated by the discipline known as 'verbal learning', in which subjects acquired habits consisting of the rote learning of lists of nonsense syllables; and 'forgetting' was viewed as competition between habits, so that if habit *B* (say, the habit of being able to reel off a list *B* of syllables by heart) was learned after a habit *A* (a reeling off of a different list *A*), then the *B*-habit would dominate the *A*-habit because the *B*-habit had been acquired more recently, and responses in the *A*-habit would be produced with difficulty. Sometimes 'habits' would be studied in miniature, as when pairs of syllables such as fut-nar, jeb-wis, etc. were studied with a view to memorizing that 'nar' went with 'fut', 'wis' with 'jeb' and so on. If fut-nar had been learned and then fut-dax had to be learned, there was some 'forgetting' of fut-nar. In this model, 'forgetting' is viewed as the temporary dominance of one habit over another at a particular point in time.

There was little mention in this neo-behaviourist ambience of the use of imagery, strategies (plans) for memorizing, strategies for re-organizing the list material, or strategies of search in retrieving the material. Before behaviourism, items to be memorized were indeed items that could be the subject of conscious mental representations; during behaviourism, one was no longer supposed to memorize or forget items; instead one acquired verbal habits that were essentially sequences of speech-movements. We shall see that the Gestalt psychologists of this time-period offered a countervailing opinion and so did the adherents of the 'cognitive revolution' after 1956. My thesis is that the Gestalt work requires better recognition than it has so far received.

However, it must not be imagined that the behaviourist empire was founded easily. Samelson (1981, 1985) has closely examined the degree of acceptance of Watson's writings among academic psychologists of the period 1910–1940, and has discovered that Watson was at first treated very much as an extremist whose views were considered to be peripheral in the history of psychology.

But the roots of the movement did take hold in the 1920s, as Samelson (1985) describes. The word 'behaviorism' was being dissected by Tolman in his courses in 1921 and two of Watson's books had appeared by then, giving a stronger scientific underpinning to his views. But Watson himself had also left academia by this period and was writing pro-behaviourist articles on education and child-rearing which the public read eagerly, assuming that there was a large corpus of scientific proof to attest to the acceptability of Watson's advice, and the Social Science Research Council, with large sums of money to spend on psychological research designed to be of benefit to the public, was founded in the early 1920s. In turn the Council received cash support from the Laura Spelman Rockefeller Memorial, directed by an ex-psychologist named Beardsley Ruml. Among their other ventures, the Memorial funded a conference at Hanover, New Hampshire, in 1925, designed with a view to finding agreement amongst psychologists as to the future of the science concerned with human behaviour, it supported the research of Mary C. Jones on the removal of children's fears, research directed by Watson, and, possibly most important, it funded the establishment of a Centre for the Study of Human Behaviour (after 1929 the Institute of Human Relations) at Yale. As Samelson (1985) describes it:

> In one of its first moves, the Institute brought Clark Hull out of the wilderness at
> Wisconsin to the East Coast and provided him with the setting (and the Rockefeller

money) for the development of neobehaviorism and another attempt to integrate the social sciences. The revolution was on the march. (p. 43)

To summarize, even though Watson's 'radical behaviorism' was received with scepticism by most of the psychological establishment in the first decade after the 1913 article, in the second decade it was given a boost by the fact that it was so well known to the general public and in the late 1920s money was available for the massive programme of research dominated by Hull, who clearly accepted Watson's views. It is therefore dangerous to speak of a behaviourist domination of experimental psychology before the late 1920s, but it becomes more appropriate to do so for the period 1930–1956.

The Gestalt movement

It is generally recognized that the first major paper of the Gestalt movement was that of Wertheimer (1912) on the perception of apparent movement. The Gestalt movement thus began at about the same time as behaviourism, inaugurated by the paper of Watson (1913). Like behaviourism, Gestalt psychology represented a rebellion against trends that had been current in the German psychology departments of the previous decade, but the rebellion was not focused predominantly against the use of introspection, although Köhler (1929, Chapter 3) had many objections to make to introspectionism. Instead it was focused against a tradition of thinking that went back to the empiricism of the eighteenth century, a tradition that said that the starting point for a valid psychology was the assumption that the brain took simple sensations, and by a process of association, identified and evaluated those sensations. Instead, the Gestalt psychologists stressed that the total process of sensing, identifying and evaluating took place in an immediate way, so that the perceiving subject was presented with a representation of reality that was *instantly* 'clear' in the sense that he or she could take action on the basis of valid information about the environment. By a similar token, Gestalt psychologists objected to the goals of the structuralist psychologists, represented particularly by E.B. Titchener (1867–1927), who had claimed that mental experiences could be analyzed into units called 'sensations', 'feelings', and 'thoughts'. The word 'structuralist' was also associated with the work of Wundt, who in his *Outlines of Psychology* (1896) discussed the analysis of mental experiences. But it is also in this work that Wundt writes about 'creative synthesis', as Boring (1950) notes,

> Wundt's discussion was contradictory. He talked about elements and their combination as if he were expounding a straight mental chemistry and then argued about creative synthesis, seeming to believe that it is by emergence that the *psychische Verbindungen* [psychical compounds] get their special characteristics. (p. 608)

But the Gestalt psychologists were not concerned with unravelling Wundt's inconsistencies. It was the notion that individual sensations could be isolated from the total context that worried them. The whole thrust of their intellectual endeavour, insofar as sensation and perception were concerned, was to stress the predominance of the whole over the parts (or, rather, the *difference* between the whole and the parts); individual parts are always judged by the subject, in a manner that depends on automatic functioning of the subject's brain, within their global context. The Gestalt psychologists had an identifiable foe in extreme structuralism and any other movement claiming to extract sensations from the flow of the mind. One such movement was that of the philosopher F. Brentano (1838–1917), whose goal was to analyze mental experience into its constituents (Brentano, 1874), and Sullivan (1968) has argued that Gestalt psychology partly arose in reaction to his theories.

However the notion that the nervous system acts automatically to present us in consciousness with clear percepts that have already been to some extent organized so that the parts are subsumed into comprehensible wholes is a notion that has a long history in German psychology. The first major German philosopher of modern times, Gottfried W. Leibniz (1646–1716), in a critique of the writings of the empiricist philosopher John Locke (1632–1704), contended that the human mind is aware of the details of the external world only *after* a certain amount of unconscious processing has taken place (Leibniz, 1765). Leibniz's views were based on the notion that consciousness is present in *degrees* both in different objects (e.g. humans have more consciousness than plants) and within the same object (e.g. within humans the degree of consciousness varies from wide-awake self-awareness to states in which one is hardly aware of anything, such as when one is sleeping). The case of sleeping represents an instance where a small degree of consciousness is present, but it can be augmented if we are woken up and the amount of sound it might take to waken us up would vary with the depth of sleep. Even when we are fully awake, the mind is presented with a clear picture of reality, a unitary reality which is the end result, or emergent phenomenon, of what we would nowadays call unconscious processing. Leibniz conceived of the sensory system as receiving countless '*petites perceptions*', little perceptions which taken unprocessed would be chaotic but the mind perceives a clear picture from these *petites perceptions*, such as, when we are walking by a lake in a breeze, we hear a unitary roar of the waves that is made up of countless little perceptions of splashing sounds. From the mass of minute, barely conscious perceptions emerges that strong perception of which we are certainly conscious through a process for which Leibniz coined a new word, 'apperception', although he may have got this idea from the writings of a French mathematician named Pardies (Diamond, 1972).

The topic of apperception, a word used relatively infrequently in the literature in English in the eighteenth and nineteenth centuries, was widely discussed in the German literature of that period. Leibniz's influential successor, Christian Wolff (1679–1754) divided psychology into two kinds, empirical and rational. Empirical psychology involved the description of mental experience and of behaviour, the accumulation of the *facts* of psychology; rational psychology was the attempt to make sense of these facts, to explain them under a general theory (which included discussion of the mind/body question). In his book *Psychologia Rationalis*, Wolff (1734) claimed that the purpose of sensation is to provide us with *evidence* of the external world, whereas the other faculties, such as attention, memory and imagination, allow us to build up a clear picture or *representation* of the external world. These intellectual faculties combine with the act of sensation to allow us to identify and evaluate objects. Leibniz had talked of apperception as a device allowing 'obscure' ideas to become 'clear', and this conceptualization was taken over by Wolff. Later when Kant developed his vast philosophical system he qualified Leibniz's views by dividing apperception into two kinds. He believed that the human had an innate capacity for understanding certain things, such as the fact that sensations are ordered in space and time, the fact that causes led to effects, and others. (He called these 'categories' of understanding, and used the word 'intuitive' to indicate that these ideas were not acquired by experience, contrary to the arguments of Hume (1739–1740) and other empiricists.) The grasping or the understanding of how sensations were related in space he believed to be the result of intuition (or 'transcendental conscious-ness' or 'pure apperception') but since it is only experience that allows us to name, recognize or identify sensations, and since this happens very quickly and not necessarily as the result of a conscious process of mental analysis, he claimed that the identification stage of perception was the result of 'empirical apperception' (Kant, 1783, p. 170; see also Lange, 1894, pp. 250–255). For Kant, pure apperception and empirical apperception operated to ensure that we had a clear representation of the external world at any instant, and memory then allowed us to form what modern psychologists, such as Johnson-Laird (1983), have called a 'mental model' of the external world. In this mental model 'space' would be understood as an abstract concept, even though we are equipped innately with the ability to relate spatial sensations to each other. Incidentally, Kant's five arguments in favour of our innate ability to order sensations in space have each been criticized by Bertrand Russell (1945, Book 3, Chapter 20).

Kant had been sceptical of the possibility of ever developing an acceptable rational psychology because he claimed that we have no intuition for understand-ing the nature of the mind (or the 'soul', as he called it) and, as a consequence, we could not use mathematics to describe mental events in a way that events in space and time can be described in mathematics. He was even sceptical about the likelihood of developing a successful empirical psychology, because he argued it would have to be based on introspection, which he considered to be unreliable. However he did admit that one could observe the behaviour of other people and describe, for example, how children developed their abilities. To this almost behaviouristic kind of psychology he gave the name pragmatic anthropo-logy (Kant, 1798). Leary (1980) has shown that Kant himself, however, did not adhere rigorously to these notions and in fact prepared the way for his successor in the professorship of philosophy at Königsberg, Johann Herbart, to offer an extraordinary detailed mathematical model of mental processing in which a mental 'presentation', 'idea', or 'concept' (*Vorstellung*) could be ascribed a 'strength' depending on how far it occupied consciousness (Herbart, 1816).

In this model, ideas competed for conscious attention, with weak ideas being inhibited by strong ideas and pushed below the threshold of consciousness. Apperception played a part in the model, thanks to one of Herbart's postulates that argued that the *quality* of an idea, as well as its quantity, could influence the ebb and flow of ideas in and out of consciousness. If two ideas were related and not in opposition to each other, one idea could help the other into consciousness, and if the two ideas were both present in consciousness, they could both recede into consciousness but in such a way that if one were brought up again into consciousness it would bring up the other as well. This was the basis of the act of apperception: a given idea presented by the senses could evoke a related idea currently in the unconscious, an idea which would rise to consciousness with little resistance. As Boring (1950) noted,

> As with Leibniz, any idea that rises into consciousness is apperceived, but Herbart meant more by the word, for no idea rises except to take its place in the unitary whole of the ideas already conscious. The apperceiving of the idea is therefore not only the making of it conscious, but also its assimilation to a totality of conscious ideas, which Herbart called the 'apperceiving mass'. (pp. 256–257)

Although Herbart's mathematics were not widely accepted, in part because Wundt (1874) thought some of his assumptions about inhibitions were unreasonable, his doctrine of the apperceptive mass influenced the work of both Fechner and Wundt. Fechner developed his science of psychophysics on the assumption that one could measure the strength of a sensation by indirect means but Scheerer (1987) has shown how Fechner believed that before a sensation was given to consciousness, the neurological substrate of the sensation went through a series of transformations that had no counterpart in consciousness. Wundt encouraged experimentation into apperception itself; one of his students, Friedrich (1883; see Behrens, 1980), attempted to show that the more items in consciousness there are, the less clear is any one item as reflected in the time elapsing before a response can be given to it. (This work foreshadowed the research of Hick (1952), who showed how the reaction time to respond to one of n stimuli varies directly with the logarithm to the base two of $n + 1$.) Wundt also reported research on how quickly subjects could identify stimuli that were briefly exposed and proposed that there was a short period in which the perception of the stimulus was confused (because unconscious processing was being carried out) and then the percept became clear to the extent that it could be responded to (Wundt, 1896; see also Boring, 1950, pp. 338–339).

We seem to have wandered far from the Gestalt movement but the above was a preliminary to the statement that Gestalt psychology represented the culmination of this tradition because from the outset its goal was to explain *how* perception became clear in the first place. The details of the development of

Gestalt psychology will be spelled out in more detail in Chapter 2, but here we might reflect upon almost the final words that Köhler (1969) published:

> Why do brain processes tend to produce perceptual organizations of remarkable clearness of structure? (p. 164)

This was the question to which the three great exponents of Gestalt psychology, Max Wertheimer, Kurt Koffka and Wolfgang Köhler devoted their lives.

They were anticipated in this endeavour not only by the writers we have just discussed, but also by a group of psychologists writing mainly in Austria. Once it was accepted that conscious perceivers perceived what they did only *after* a process of apperception or synthesis, it made sense to distinguish between the sensory content and the result of the later process. Furthermore, the question was narrowed down so that not only the process of sensation was studied, but also the *relationships* between the raw sensations themselves: four lines can be arranged to form a square, and the Austrian psychologists claimed that the perceived 'squareness' was something over and above the mere presence of the 'four lines'. Being able to *call* it a square was a separate ability. That relationships between sensations of various qualities and intensities have a certain autonomy in experience was indicated by Ernst Mach (1838–1916) in his widely read *Analysis of Sensations* (1886); for example, a melody such as 'Twinkle Twinkle' is recognized as the same melody no matter where on the piano it is played; a photograph is recognized as representing the same scene whether it is viewed in brilliant sunshine or in gloomy twilight. That relationships between stimuli exert a direct influence on the nervous system was also demonstrated by Mach (1866) when he showed that if a disc is divided into two equal parts, one black and one white, yet the border between them is not a straight line but has an abrupt 'jag' in it, then when it is rapidly spun round, it looks grey (the fusion of black and white), except at the point where the jag exists where a black band is seen. This 'Mach band' is a sensation that results from a sudden discontinuity in the relationship between the black and white segments.

The fact that relationships can be preserved no matter how the individual sensations may vary, as with the melody or photograph, was discussed in detail by Christian von Ehrenfels (1859–1932) of Vienna, who invented the term 'form quality' or 'Gestalt quality' to refer to the squareness aspect of the appropriate combination of four lines (von Ehrenfels, 1890). Because his main paper is not available in English, I shall examine his ideas on the meaning of Gestalt more carefully. After having discussed the logical problem of whether *any* whole can be said to be more than the sum of its parts, and the biological problem of whether the brain in some way processes the relationship between parts in a manner independent of the processing of the parts themselves, von Ehrenfels defined Gestalt quality as follows:

> By Gestalt qualities we understand such positive contents of ideas that are connected together with the presence of complexes of ideas in consciousness, these complexes in

turn consisting of individual divisible elements – by divisible, we mean that they can be conceptualized as existing without one another. Those complexes of ideas that are necessary for the presence of Gestalt qualities we shall name the *Grundlagen* [foundations] of the Gestalt qualities. (pp. 262–263)

That is, when stimulus elements that can be mentally conceptualized as discrete are related in some way in a stimulus complex that can be sensed, the ideas (*Vorstellungen*) that are aroused by the stimulus complex have a quality of wholeness or independence of form (*Gestalt* quality) that can be separated from the raw stimulus complex (the *Grundlagen*) itself.

Von Ehrenfels distinguished between relationships in time and relationships in space (e.g. a melody is a Gestalt in time; a square is a Gestalt in space), but a Gestalt can also exist in a set of sounds produced simultaneously, a Gestalt based on a sense of harmony. (Readers interested in music may consider, for example, the main section of Schubert's song 'Death and the Maiden', in which the singer sings the same note repeatedly, but each note is given a different harmony by the piano, so that apart from the melodic Gestalt of the piano part, there is also a Gestalt quality to each separate note repeated by the singer.)

In discussing how far a Gestalt was more than the sum of the parts, von Ehrenfels stressed that the answer probably depended on an analysis of *attention*: we normally attend to the squareness of the four lines as opposed to some mental concatenation or assemblage of the lines, but von Ehrenfels avoided any extensive analysis of the attention process. He stressed that Gestalt qualities contain no contradictions (a square cannot also be round) and that the presence of a Gestalt quality reduces ambiguity. Gestalt qualities also serve easily as the basis for higher-order thought, as in geometry, where the concept of a square simplifies theoretical treatments that would be cumbersome if expressed only in terms of straight lines. This fact in turn depends on the fact that Gestalten can be similar to each other, and the ease of memorizing Gestalten (e.g. the ease of memorizing a theorem such as Pythagoras's which involves mentally making each side of a triangle also the side of a square) indicates that the basic units of memory are as likely to be Gestalten as they are individual sensory elements. These examples from geometry are mine but they help to conceptualize ideas that von Ehrenfels expressed in more abstract terms. Gestalten also form the basis of imagination, combining old memories to yield new thoughts. It was von Ehrenfels's belief that, in perception, the Gestalt quality appears automatically:

We therefore arrive at the conclusion that Gestalt qualities are given psychologically simultaneously with the *Grundlage* without any special activity devoted to them. (p. 287)

Von Ehrenfels anticipated the later work of Rubin (1915) on figure-ground perception when he stressed that, if Gestalt quality is to emerge, the *Grundlage* itself must stand out from the background: a square will only show 'squareness' if it is in a different colour from the background and is not camouflaged in any way.

Just before his death in 1932, von Ehrenfels dictated a short article (von

Ehrenfels, 1937) in which he stated that both Meinong and he thought that it was possible for some assemblages of elements *not* to yield Gestalt quality, but that Wertheimer and Köhler considered that all *Grundlagen* yield Gestalt qualities as a direct by-product of being observed. For von Ehrenfels the normal contents of memory, such as memories for words and images of persons, were themselves associated with Gestalt quality. Other writers elaborated on von Ehrenfels's view, including Alexus Meinong (1853–1920), Stephan Witasek (1870–1915) and Vittorio Benussi (1878–1927). One account of their work is given by Boring (1950, pp. 441–447), Boring's verdict however is that the Gestalt school was new and different enough from the work of these authors to be considered a movement in itself. It was less devoted to philosophy and more devoted to experimental demonstration.

This is also the place to mention the doctoral thesis of Mitchell G. Ash (1982) entitled *The Emergence of Gestalt Theory: Experimental psychology in Germany, 1890–1920.* Ash traces out, in considerable detail, the early history of the Gestalt movement. Among the influences on its development were the attempts by the above authors to determine whether Gestalt quality was an irreducible given in human cognition, or whether it could be reduced to associations to raw sensations. Other contributions to the controversy were made by Carl Stumpf (1848–1936) and Friedrich Schumann (1863–1940), both of whom were teaching at Berlin when Wertheimer was a student there in 1902–1904. Stumpf also supervised the doctoral theses of Koffka and Köhler. Even though Stumpf's ideas on Gestalt quality were eventually criticized by Köhler, Stumpf respected him enough to nominate him in 1920 as his successor.

In his description of the rise of Gestalt psychology, Ash discusses not only the issue of Gestalt quality (pp. 206–40), but also stresses how the research of Helmholtz, Mach, Stumpf and others on sensations had given rise to the general question of how the brain processes sensations before the subject experiences a conscious percept. He stresses how the phenomenological movement led by Edmund Husserl (1859–1938) was prevalent in German university circles in about 1910, a movement that insisted that psychology should take as its ground material the actual *experiences* of the perceiving subject. He also points out that Gestalt psychology attempted to provide a general answer to the question of how far psychology should be related to physics and biology. Since many of these issues were discussed in philosophy departments many philosophers felt that it was inappropriate that philosophy chairs should be held by experimental psychologists. Around 1910 there was a major dispute as to where experimental psychology fitted in – should it continue to be a branch of philosophy, or an independent scientific discipline? The upshot of this controversy was that psychologists were no longer welcomed as occupants of chairs in philosophy but it became easier for experimental psychologists to obtain university positions independent of philosophy departments. The academic success of Wertheimer, Koffka and Köhler in the 1920s was, according to Ash, a direct outcome of this resolution of the controversy (see also Ash, 1981).

It is obvious, however, from this analysis of its predecessors, that Gestalt psychology was focused on the question of *perception* and its neighbour *consciousness*. So long as the Gestalt psychologists were writing about perception, they co-existed peaceably with the behaviourists who were writing about learning. But it was only a few years after Watson's 1913 paper on behaviourism that Köhler (1917a,b, 1918) published some studies of behaviour in chimpanzees and chickens which demonstrated that *relationships* between sensations did not only affect perception, but also behaviour. These animals, for example, could learn to choose between two stimuli to get food when the *lighter* of the two stimuli was associated with food (for example, a chimpanzee could choose grey in a choice between black and grey, and white in a choice between grey and white). Moreover there was a direct clash between Köhler and Thorndike on the issue of whether animals learn to receive rewards *only* by trial and error (as Thorndike seemed to suggest in the case of cats), or whether they can form cognitive insights in order to obtain rewards (as Köhler claimed in the case of chimpanzees). As Gestalt psychology matured, Wertheimer applied some of its concepts to human problem-solving and Köhler and Koffka applied some of its concepts to human memory, a word they freely used in direct opposition to Watson. Moreover it became clear that the Gestalt psychologists believed the behaviourists to have produced a desiccated psychology in which no references to imagery or cognitive elaborative organizational processes were allowed in the description of how apes and humans learned. More details on these matters will be amplified in Chapter 2. But behaviourism continued to dominate North American psychology (and Russian psychology under Pavlov, who disliked Gestalt psychology), between 1930–1956. It was only after the erosion of the power of behaviourism in the 1950s, an erosion due directly to the onset of the cognitive revolution, that the writings of the Gestalt psychologists came to be more appreciated.

The cognitive revolution

The cognitive revolution is agreed upon by many to be a phenomenon dating from the 1950s. According to Gardner (1985, p. 29), G.A. Miller fixed the exact date as 11 September 1956. At a Symposium on Information Theory held at the Massachusetts Institute of Technology on 10–12 September 1956, the 11th was outstanding for two particular papers: one by Allen Newell and Herbert Simon demonstrating that a proof of symbolic logic could be carried out on a computer; the other by Noam Chomsky who offered a new theory of language based on the idea that natural language has certain formal properties (that make it akin to mathematics) including transformations such as the transformation of an active sentence into a passive sentence. Miller also described his work on the limitations of memory: humans can only hold about seven 'categories' of sensory dimensions in mind, so that if one had to assign each of a large set of greynesses to one of seven memorized labels, the task was manageable, but became difficult if more than seven labels had to be borne in mind. At the same time, Miller discussed whether this had anything to do with the familiar fact that the memory span for digits is also about seven. He concluded that the connection between the two kinds of experiments was questionable, because by acquiring the cognitive skill of re-coding small sets of digits into larger memory 'chunks' one could increase the memory span beyond seven.

Furthermore there was extensive discussion of the mental attributes of conscious experience, a literature that was given a particular impetus by the publication in 1958 of Broadbent's *Perception and Communication*. In this book, the human was still seen as an organism that had learned many motor habits (Broadbent referred frequently to Hull's theory), but now these habits were conceptualized as residing in a long-term store. Items entered long-term memory usually by entering consciousness. While an attention process filtered out the important from the unimportant material, the more the individual 'processed', or thought about, or rehearsed the material in consciousness, the more likely was it that the information would enter the long-term store. These processes were represented by a flow-chart, including feedback systems, which was at the time a novelty for the scientific representation of psychological functioning. Also important in retrospect was the use of the word 'item' to refer to the material memorized; in behaviouristic terms, when a string of digits such as 5487601 was to be memorized, a verbal motor habit was set up which could be ingrained by rehearsal, whereas in the cognitive-type model 5,4,8,7,6,0, and 1 were seven 'items' to be put in a 'store'. From that time on analogies between human memory systems and other physical storage systems became popular (Roediger, 1980, has an extensive list). Only very recently, with the rise in popularity of neural network models and 'connectionist' models with their emphasis on activation flowing between input neurons and output neurons via 'hidden' neurons, does there seem to be a return to older ways of representing stored memories as 'habits'.

Of course the cognitive revolution had its predecessors in the 1930s and 1940s. The Gestalt psychologists were among them and the main thrust of this book is to emphasize this. Another important predecessor was E.C. Tolman, who had actually spent some time in the early 1920s studying with Koffka in Germany. In his book *Purposive Behaviour in Animals and Man* (1932), Tolman laid out evidence that had convinced him that no account of learning in rats could properly omit reference to the rat's goals in solving the problem: a rat put in a maze was not a mere machine that, having by random processes reached the goal-box, then repeated its steps in mechanical fashion. The rat was conceived to form what Tolman (1948) later called a 'cognitive map' (whether the word 'image' is appropriate here is not easy to decide), a symbolic representation of the whole or most of the maze even when the rat was in the start-box, and the maze represented a sign-gestalt (Tolman's word) for the rat which led to the development of a 'means-end-readiness', or plan to navigate the maze in order to repeat the pleasurable experience of obtaining the reward. By a series of ingenious experiments, Tolman showed that even when there is no food reward in the goal-box, rats acquire a visually-based knowledge of the layout of the maze; for example, rats given a few experiences in the maze with no food will then learn to run the maze very quickly to get food when it is available, far more quickly than rats put into the maze for the first time. Much later, one of Tolman's students, Henry Gleitman, wrote a best-selling textbook, *Psychology* (1980) in which he collected evidence that even animal learning can involve what humans would call 'expectations'. Even in classical conditioning, when a dog learns to salivate to a metronome associated with food, experiments by Rescorla (1967) and others reveal that the metronome has to be paired with the food in such a way that the metronome is a reliable signal that the food will appear. Countless undergraduates in the 1980s have learned from Gleitman's text and others that dogs form 'expectations' that they will receive food when they hear metronomes and that rats form 'expectations' that they will receive food when they press the lever in a Skinner box. The words 'purpose' and 'expectation' had no place in Watson's or Hull's accounts of animal learning, or, by analogy, human learning. In his use of the term 'cognitive map', Tolman was twenty years ahead of the cognitive revolution.

Also ahead of the cognitive revolution were various attempts in the 1940s to represent the human subject, not as a machine filled with habits, but as a machine that was perpetually comparing its own performance to some abstract standard, a machine that made use of feedback. Following Wiener's invention of the term 'cybernetics' (1948), feedback mechanisms became commonplace in psychological models such as that of Broadbent and robot-like mechanical models such as those built by Ashby (1952). Moreover it was shown that certain logical processes, such as implication, could be modelled in terms of electrical circuits *or* by neurons: as Gardner (1985, p. 18) puts it, you can represent the fact that entity A plus entity B implies entity C either by a set of switches (as in a computer) or by a set of synaptic events (as in a brain). A key paper in the evolution of this idea was that of McCulloch and Pitts (1943). All of these notions served as a background to the 'cognitive revolution', whose early history in the 1940s and 1950s can be traced through a set of conferences bringing together cyberneticists, psychologists, physiologists, electrical engineers, mathematicians and others during these decades. The history of these conferences is spelled out in more detail that we need give here both by Newell and Simon (1972, addendum) and by Gardner (1985).

Apart from the works mentioned, 1956 was also the year of publication of Bruner *et al.*'s *A Study of Thinking*, in which the authors stressed the role of different cognitive strategies that are used when a human subject must figure out what unifying 'concept' is illustrated by a set of various objects or drawings that have something in common.

From the 1950s onwards writings on cognitive psychology have proliferated to the extent that behaviourism has come to be seen as providing an historically important but old-fashioned and unhelpful vocabulary for describing the myriad-faceted aspects of human conscious experiences associated with memorizing, retrieving, decision-making, problem-solving, concept-forming, recognizing, attending, identifying, imaging, skill-learning, language-learning, and creative imagining. Key landmarks in the revolution after the 1950s include Neisser's *Cognitive Psychology* (1967) which christened the discipline and was notable for contrasting top-down processing models (such as the Gestalt models) with bottom-up processing (of the kind indulged in by those who begin with individual sensations as the building-blocks of mental experiences); Paivio's *Imagery and Verbal Processes* (1971) which re-introduced the topic of imagery into psychology after a fallow period of almost five decades and raised the question of the sensory modes whereby objects are *mentally* represented to the subject; Newell and Simon's *Human Problem Solving* (1972) which summarized the evidence on machine simulation of human problem-solving but also stressed how humans operated to solve problems using units called 'production systems', sequences of planned actions that were often susceptible of being re-phrased as steps in a computer program; Anderson and Bower's *Human Associative Memory* (1973), one of the first attempts to use computer simulation as a means of testing a theory of how humans learn and retrieve sets of facts ('propositions'); Tulving's *Elements of Episodic Memory* (1983) in which long-term memory was divided into several kinds on the basis of experimental and neurophysiological evidence, and in which it was also stressed that no theory of memory could do without a theory of retrieval as well as a theory of storage; the compendium *Parallel Distributed Processing* (1986) by McClelland, Rumelhart and other members of the Cognitive Group at the University of California at San Diego, a book that re-introduced the notion of modelling learning processes by representing psychological action as involving the activation of units arranged in a network, this activation being influenced by feedback as to the success of each action; Newell's *Unified Theories of Cognition* (1990), a book that summarized much of the previous evidence within the context of a model that considers human learning as the acquisition of the ability to handle larger and larger 'chunks' of data with experience; and the paper by Anderson (1991) entitled 'Is human cognition adaptive?' in which various phenomena of memory, categorization, inference making and problem-solving are integrated into a rational scheme. Other important individual contributions have included various mathematical models of the memory process such as those of Atkinson and Shiffrin (1968), Raaijmakers and Shiffrin (1981), Murdock (1982) and Anderson (1983); analyses of the types of errors made by humans in reasoning and probabilistic problems (Kahneman *et al.*, 1982; Gigerenzer and Murray, 1987); analyses of the evidence on how reaction times vary with the nature of the cognitive task (Luce, 1986); and many detailed studies of the detection and identification of very briefly exposed visual stimuli (many reviewed by van der Heijden (1992)). Excellent accounts of the experimental evidence on human memory, but without too much detail on the mathematical models, are provided by Baddeley (1990) and Parkin (1993), while the experimental evidence on psycholinguistics, a scattered literature that has been lacking in good summaries, has recently been reviewed extensively and clearly by Kess (1992).

In almost all of these books, there is mention of imagery and short-term memory; it is recognized that 'unconscious' processing occurs, the term 'unconscious' now being more popular than it was in the early and middle years of the cognitive revolution; researchers on thinking revived the introspectionist method of the Würzburg school; and throughout there is the feeling that the human subject's cognitive experiences cannot be described in a psychological science *without* the use of a guiding force, an executive, a 'self', a planner. This topic is still controversial, but has been given a new importance because new evidence has surfaced concerning the relationship of speech to thought. According to Watson, thinking was nothing more than inner speech, but since Paivio (1971) and others showed that visual imagery can be the subject of experimental investigations, many people now believe that visual imagery co-exists with inner speech as a vehicle for 'thought'. At least one case has been found of a person with temporary but almost complete aphasia who could nevertheless plan actions, operate machines, and carry out certain complex actions such as booking into a hotel (Lecours and Joanette, 1980). Merlin Donald, in his recent book, *Origins of the Modern Mind* (1991), believes that the ability to experience imagery evolved before the ability to speak. In such a proto-human, the planning of actions in advance using symbolic visual or other representations of the external world would be feasible to the extent that such an organism could reasonably be said to be self-aware, or have a 'self'. We shall explore this issue in greater detail in Chapters 3, 4 and 6, but note now that the question of the existence or otherwise of a 'central executive' (perhaps, 'homunculus') is a key issue in modern cognitive psychology.

Yet if we consider the above list – imagery, short-term memory, the unconscious, self-observation, the question of a controlling planning agent – we find that each of these issues was also an important aspect of Gestalt psychology, particularly in the period of their later writings, that is, from Köhler's *Gestalt Psychology* (1929) to Wertheimer's *Productive Thinking* (1945). They accepted that thinking involves images; they did some of the first experiments on short-term memory; they went to great lengths in trying to determine how far perception was determined by unconscious processes, and certainly argued that insights in problem-solving could be the result of unconscious processes; they studied 'thinking aloud' as a means for investigating problem-solving; and above all, the subject was represented as an active processor of information, using strategies, plans and feedback not only in perceiving, but also in memorizing, retrieving, problem-solving, and decision-making. In all of these respects the Gestalt psychologists anticipated the 'cognitive revolution'.

Nevertheless this fact is underknown, and it is the purpose of this book to make it better known. In the two most widely read histories of the cognitive revolution, the contributions of the Gestalt psychologists are somewhat under-played because it is probably true that the pioneers of cognitive psychology in the 1956 period were not directly influenced by Gestalt psychology. For example, Newell and Simon (1972) admit explicitly that the North American knowledge of non-behaviouristic work on thinking and problem-solving was sparse until the 1940s:

> The European work on thought processes was just beginning to be made available to Americans through translation and migration. The translations of Duncker's *On Problem Solving* and Wertheimer's *Productive Thinking* appeared in 1945; Humphrey, in *Thinking* (1951), provided the first extensive English-language discussion of Selz's research and theories; Katona's *Organizing and Memorizing* and a number of Maier's papers on problem solving had already appeared in 1940 but had almost been lost in the distractions of the war. (p. 881)

Moreover, Baars (1986), in his account (through interviews) of the origins of the cognitive revolution, has only 13 scattered references to Gestalt psychology in his book of over 400 pages; none of his interviewees discuss it in depth although George Mandler and Ulric Neisser mention their interest in it at the outset of their careers. Furthermore, in the comprehensive history of the cognitive revolution by Gardner (1985), Gestalt psychology is given a mere four pages (pp. 111–114). Gardner stresses the importance of the Gestalt contributions to the study of perception, mentions their discoveries about problem-solving which we shall discuss in depth in Chapter 5, but concludes on a somewhat negative note:

> In the view of most contemporary observers, the particular theoretical program of Gestalt psychology was not well founded. Principles of perception such as *proximity* and *symmetry* do provide a rough-and-ready guide to how information is organized, but there are too many exceptions or indeterminate cases; speculations about the operation of the brain, and its effects upon phenomenal perception, have been undetermined by neurological findings; the major explanatory concepts are too vague to be operational-ized. (p. 114)

Gardner's remark about Gestalt speculations on the brain refers to the belief expressed by Köhler (e.g. Köhler and Wallach, 1944; Köhler, 1969) that events in the brain do not depend only on synaptic transmission from neuron to neuron but by the spread of 'currents' in the brain tissue. Other Gestalt speculations included the notion that motion perception is related to neural transmission from the neurons encoding the stimulus at a specific time to the neurons activated at a later time when the stimulus has moved; modern research however indicates that there are specialized motion detectors that are activated by movement in its own right. There is little doubt that Gestalt psychology has acquired a reputation for being over-speculative in the area of neural networks (or non-networks, if the theory of currents is considered). The same point has been made by Neisser (1993), who has argued that the Gestalt psychologists caused their own downfall by speculating more about physics than about biology. But that is not a good reason for rejecting its other claims, and since the present work is not particularly concerned with sensation and perception, but more with memory and thought, we shall continue with the argument.

Incidentally, Neisser's comment was made at a conference entitled, 'Reassessing the Cognitive Revolution', organized by the Philosophy Department at York University, Toronto, in October 1993. I attended the conference and counted the number of references made to Gestalt psychology in a total of about 15 hours of talks. Neisser made three references to it, Jerome Bruner (1993) made a reference to Köhler's concept of requiredness (to be discussed on p. 49), but seven other references were merely in passing. The main impression I got from the conference was that the re-introduction of mentalistic concepts into psychology in the 1950s was seen by *psychologists* as the main characteristic of the cognitive revolution, but many *philosophers* think of the main innovation of the cognitive revolution as being the introduction of computer simulation of cognitive processes, a topic to be discussed in Chapters 5 and 6 (Johnson, 1993).

Of course the cognitive revolution did not give rise to a unified school of cognitive scientists. In his recent book, *Unified Theories of Cognition*, Newell (1990) discusses several competing models as well as his own particular model (one that will be discussed later). Previously we mentioned several contemporary mathematical models concerned with memory; these are essentially in competition. So there is not yet a 'unified' system of cognitive psychology that can simply be compared with Gestalt psychology. The cognitive revolution, it seems to me, has been most characterized by a negative attribute: it does *not* restrict itself to talking about 'habits' but uses instead all the verbal paraphernalia that Watson tried to get rid of, images, memory, expectations, plans, decisions, and other words descriptive of conscious experience. Since the Gestalt psychologists adopted the same stance in the 1930s, it is clear there is room for an appreciation of their work. The plan of this appreciation will be as follows: Chapter 2 will discuss the development of Gestalt psychology in more detail; Chapter 3 will focus on Gestalt views on memory and learning; this will be a prelude to Chapter 4, which will discuss theories of memory and learning following the cognitive revolution, with the aim of drawing parallels and comparisons between Gestalt and late twentieth century views. Chapter 5 will discuss thinking, problem-solving, and reasoning and relate Gestalt contributions on these issues to contributions that have arisen in the course of the cognitive revolution. Chapter 6 will be less historical and more theoretical. It will be devoted to a discussion of whether certain terms used by the Gestalt psychologists, notably 'distinctiveness', 're-structuring', 'goals' and 'self' should be adopted into the terminology of 'cognitive science'. I hope that it will give readers a more optimistic view of the possibility of a future unified psychology than they will have gained from the present chapter.

Chapter 2

Gestalt psychology as a general approach to psychology

This chapter consists largely of an introduction to the general nature of Gestalt theory, with the particular object of showing how a viewpoint that was at first restricted to the study of human perception was extended to include the study of animal perception and to the general problem of cognitive processing both in animals and humans. It is generally agreed that the Gestalt school started with the publication of Wertheimer's paper on apparent movement in 1912 and that it reached its culmination in Koffka's *Principles of Gestalt Psychology* in 1935, a space of twenty-two years. But Wolfgang Metzger (1899–1979) continued the tradition in Germany until well after the war and in North America Köhler, Hans Wallach and Harry F. Helson extended Gestalt investigations into sensation and perception in a manner that has had a permanent influence on those fields. The main purpose of this chapter is to prepare the way for a more detailed look at Gestalt theories of memory and problem-solving.

A brief history of the development of Gestalt thought

There are several histories of the Gestalt movement, including Ash's doctoral thesis (1982), the book-length work of Hartmann (1935) and a useful article in German by Metzger (1963). A general critical survey of the movement was provided by Katz (1942). An essay on sources of information about the Gestalt movement is given in Ash (1982, pp. 521–535). A number of important papers are translated in abridged versions in Ellis (1938) and some later Gestalt papers have been reprinted in Henle (1961). Among the histories of the movement included in comprehensive histories of psychology, we may single out that of Boring (1950), which clearly relates the thought of the Gestalt movement to that of von Ehrenfels (and other members of the Austrian school) and other writers on perception. Boring is particularly good on the issue of why a Gestalt such as 'squareness' should be conceived of as a conceptual entity to be isolated from the simple system of a closed configuration of four lines lying at right-angles to each other. If one simply enumerates sensations – Wertheimer (1922) noted that if he heard a sequence of 17 tones played along with an accompaniment of 32 tones, he did not hear 49 tones, but a tune along with an accompaniment – this enumeration represents a *sinnlose Und-Verbindung*, a meaningless summing of 'ands'; as Boring phrased it,

> The construction of a perception by the mere accumulation of elements in congeries is what [Wertheimer] named the *bundle hypothesis*. Gestalt psychology was, of course, a protest against such a mere addition of parts to parts. The whole is almost certain to be more than a collection of its parts. It is not a bundle, and its integration is more than an *Und*. (p. 607)

As a philosophical background, I have always found Boring's summary on the above matter helpful, but Ash has criticized Boring's account on the grounds that he overemphasizes the impact of Kantian nativism on the genesis of the Gestalt movement; underemphasizes the fact that Husserlian phenomenology forced German psychologists about 1912 to re-evaluate subjective experience as a datum for psychological discourse; and does not say enough about the reaction of Stumpf's students, Wertheimer, Koffka and Köhler, to Stumpf's own ideas (Ash, 1982, pp. *xvi-xix*).

More detail on the actual experiments themselves will be found in the chapter on Gestalt psychology in Murray (1988), who lists many of the various discoveries of the Gestalt school in chronological order. On the other hand, Leahey (1992) has asserted that 'the Gestalt psychologists' almost mystical theory did not travel well. It was far too German to do well in England and America, where psychology has been most studied since World War II' (p. 73). The amount of space devoted to Gestalt psychology in his book, *A History of Modern Psychology*, is only four pages apart from casual references. However in the *History of Psychology* by Viney (1993), and also in *The Story of Psychology* by Bolles (1993), Gestalt psychology receives a generous treatment.

Since this review is predominantly about Gestalt psychology as applied to areas other than perception, we shall here introduce the history of Gestalt psychology in the context of short biographies of the three major writers of the school, Wertheimer, Koffka and Köhler. Their primary interests were concerned in the first instance with perception, but Wertheimer's later research was mainly on problem-solving, Koffka's interests turned extensively to memory, and Köhler wrote not only on memory but also on the role of psychology in the broader context of science.

Max Wertheimer (1880–1943)

Max Wertheimer was born on 15 April 1880 in Prague in Czechoslovakia but at that time German was frequently used in the schools and universities. After finishing his *Gymnasium* training at the age of 18, he studied law in Prague for two and a half years and also attended lectures on philosophy. He so enjoyed these that he gave up law and studied philosophy (and psychology) at Prague (where he took courses from Christian von Ehrenfels). It seems that later, in

1907, von Ehrenfels lost his hold on Wertheimer when Wertheimer read some essays by von Ehrenfels advocating eugenics (Ash, 1982, p. 248).

Wertheimer then moved to Berlin, where he avidly read the new psychology experiments and listened to Stumpf's lectures but, possibly because he wished to continue some work he had started in Prague with a law school friend, Julius Klein, he did not actually do his doctoral dissertation under Stumpf. Instead, he went to Würzburg where, under the supervision of Oswald Külpe (1862–1915), he developed the argument that word association tests could be used for the detection of criminal guilt, an argument that Carl Jung would later claim antedated his own similar (and better known) idea (Ash, 1982, pp. 250–3).

For the next five years Wertheimer travelled to various laboratories working on a variety of problems, including the study of primitive music (Stumpf at Berlin had formed a collection of phonograph records of music from various parts of the world), and an investigation on how people from different societies formed number concepts. It was in the context of the former research that he asserted that a melody is a kind of Gestalt (Ash, 1982, p. 254). At the same time he read extensively in the new journals of psychology that had sprung up in the late nineteenth century, and since he was at Würzburg at the time the Würzburg school was getting under way it is a reasonable question to ask whether he was influenced by the school. However, Newman (1944), who knew him well, stated:

> Where did Gestalt psychology come from? Certainly neither from Prague, nor Berlin, nor Würzburg. Details of what Wertheimer later wrote came from each but the basic plan was apparently his own. (p. 431)

Newman points out that at this time there was dissatisfaction with the elementarism and associationism of the Leipzig school under Wundt and certainly there was a growing respect for phenomenology, a philosophical approach that stressed the usefulness of directly reporting what one saw or felt (without necessarily trying to analyze it by 'introspective' guesswork).

The event that is supposed to have spurred Wertheimer into action was a realization that, in the phenomenon of apparent movement, we have a case where what is *seen* (phenomenologically) is determined, not by stimulation of the retina by an external object, but by a relationship between two separate stimulations of the retina by separate objects. If at one moment t_1, you see a stationary horizontal line A and very shortly afterwards at t_2 a stationary horizontal line B is presented, in a location lower than A:

then *what* you see depends on the time elapsing between t_1 and t_2. If this interval is extremely short, you see a flickering display of two lines. If the interval is longer than about a fifth of a second, you see two separate lines, A then B. But if the interval is timed just right (in Wertheimer's experiments a typical time delay was about one-twentieth of a second), you see line *A* apparently 'move' to the position of line *B*. The 'movement' of *A* to *B* is not really there in the external world, but you see it, and it is determined by the spatial and temporal relationships of *A* and *B*. It is determined by the *spatial* relationship because if *B* had been in a different location, say standing upright at the end of *A*, the direction of this apparent movement would have been different; and it is determined by the *temporal* relationship, being only manifest when *A* and *B* are presented successively at a particular range of time intervals.

Wertheimer's article, of which an extended summary in English is available (Shipley, 1961), mentioned von Ehrenfels's theory of Gestalt-quality and noted that Schumann had adopted the view that apparent motion represented a 'centrally produced content of consciousness' which Exner had called a 'sensation of motion' and which had Gestalt-quality. However Wertheimer rarely used the word 'Gestalt' in what followed, he was more concerned with discovering the variables that influenced the phenomenon – these included studies of the changing appearance of the stimuli as the interstimulus interval varied, the influence of the colour, shape and distance apart of the stimuli, the effect of attention or set (*Einstellung*) on the appearance of the movement, the effect of introducing a stationary third object between the stimuli and after-effects. Many of the stimuli used in the first series of experiments, on the effect of the interstimulus interval, used two lines as stimuli, sometimes arranged one above the other, sometimes at angles to each other. For example, with two stimuli inclined to each other at angles of 45 degrees, touching at the vertex, each exposed for 5 milliseconds, he found that with interstimulus intervals of 35 milliseconds both lines were seen simultaneously; the optimal apparent motion was found at a 59 milliseconds interval; at 116 milliseconds a sort of 'slow motion' was seen; and at 178 milliseconds one saw first one line, then the other, with no apparent motion. These short exposures probably precluded eye movements. If the lines are called *A* and *B*, what one sees phenomenally may be represented as *AϕB*: ϕ has a phenomenal context that is given by the 'subjective supplementation of the between positions which are not objectively manifest as spatially and temporally continuous' (Shipley, 1961, p. 1050). This kind of apparent movement came to be called the 'phi phenomenon'.

In the theoretical summary, Wertheimer was a little dismissive of Gestalt-quality or attentional processes as offering satisfactory explanations of his data, and instead preferred a physiological hypothesis according to which

> If the point *a* is stimulated, and within some specific short time, the neighbouring point *b*, then there would occur a kind of *psychological short-circuit* from *a* to *b*. A specific passage of excitation occurs in the span between the two points. If, for example, the amount of circular disturbance from *a* has reached the peak of its time process course and the circular disturbance from *b* now occurs, then excitation flows over (a physiologically specific event), the direction of which is given by the fact that *a* and its circular disturbance occurred first. (p. 1085)

This penchant for physiological explanations of perceptual phenomena would influence all later writings of the Gestalt psychologists, particularly those of Köhler. Wertheimer thought of 'neighbouring parts' in the brain as being *functional* rather than *geometric* neighbours, although he found it difficult to believe that the brain areas serving adjacent points on the retina would not also be close to each other in a geometric sense.

Wertheimer wrote this article at Frankfurt; his colleagues there included the young Wolfgang Köhler and the young Kurt Koffka, both of whom had recently received PhDs from Berlin under Stumpf and were now appointed as research assistants to Fredrich Schumann (1863–1940) at Frankfurt. Schumann was a fine inventor of psychological apparatus, best known for his memory drum and the superior tachistoscope that Wertheimer had employed in his studies of the phi phenomenon. Also present at Frankfurt was Gabriele Gräfin von Wartensleben (1870–1953); she studied the identification of 6- or 9-letter displays presented on the tachistoscope (von Wartensleben, 1913) but also wrote in 1914 a brief outline of Gestalt opinions (see Ash, 1982, pp. 300–30 and Harper, Newman and Schwab, 1985).

Shortly afterwards Köhler left Frankfurt to go to the Canary Islands to do research with animals, and Koffka went to the University of Giessen, where he expanded into writing the theoretical principles of the Gestalt psychology that Wertheimer had been promulgating in his lectures at Frankfurt.

When the First World War broke out in 1914, Köhler remained in the Canary Islands for the duration of the war, and got on with the work on the mentality of apes which was to make him famous. He also carried out the work mentioned in Chapter 1 on relational responding, showing that both hens and chimpanzees can learn to respond to the darker or lighter of two stimuli in order to obtain a food reward. Koffka continued to teach in Giessen but turned his energies to the study of brain injuries. Wertheimer spent the war with his friend the musicologist Erich von Hornbostel (1887–1936). Von Hornbostel worked in Berlin where Stumpf had started the collection of phonographic records related to ethnomusicology which Wertheimer had also studied in his wander-years before the work on apparent movement. But now the energies of von Hornbostel and Wertheimer were turned to the development of devices that could detect the direction of underwater sounds, such as those made by submarines. All this work resulted in only one 8-page paper (von Hornbostel and Wertheimer, 1920). They were among the first to demonstrate that sound localization in part depends on the difference in time with which the sound from the source arrives at the two ears. However, von Hornbostel continued to be a minor contributor to Gestalt psychology after the war.

When the war ended in 1918, research on Gestalt psychology was reinvigorated, particularly following the publication of the new journal *Psychologische Forschung*, which was founded in 1921 under the editorship of Wertheimer, Köhler, Koffka, Kurt Goldstein and Hans Grühle. It ran uninterrupted until

1938, was not published during the Second World War, but started again in 1948 and in 1974 took the name *Psychological Research* (a testimony to the widespread, though often reluctant, adoption of English as the language of international science).

As had been the case in Frankfurt, Wertheimer's presence in Berlin stimulated a number of younger people to work on Gestalt questions. This work included the experiments by Ternus (1926) on the question of how a stimulus can be said to have a phenomenal 'identity' when it undergoes apparent movement, and by Duncker (1929) on 'induced' motion – a beam of sunlight is focused via a mirror onto a large piece of cardboard (66 by 48 cm) so that the light is 2 centimetres in diameter. Viewed from a distance of one metre, the stationary spot of light seemed to move as the cardboard was moved back and forth: the spot seemed to move in the opposite direction. When Köhler became director of the Psychological Institute at Berlin in 1922, others joined the group, but further details of this will be given in the section on Köhler. (Wertheimer was probably not offered this position of director, partly because he was Jewish, and partly because his publication list was less impressive than Köhler's (Ash, 1982, pp. 509–510).)

Wertheimer's own contributions became particularly famous, in two papers published in *Psychologische Forschung* in 1921 and 1923. The second laid out the philosophical principles of Gestalt psychology, including his opposition to theories of perception based on *Und-Verbindungen*, and stressed that from a phenomenological point of view the visual field is naturally *organized*, by automatic lawful brain-processes, into a structure in which figures stand out on backgrounds (an adoption of views that had been put forward by the Danish psychologist E. Rubin in 1915, translated into German in 1921); individual stimulus elements become fused into unitary wholes. It is here that we read about the spontaneous arrangement that we make of

OO   OO   OO   OO   OO

into five pairs of dots; they are arranged ab/cd/ef/gh/ij and not a/bc/de/fg/hi/j or some other arrangement.

Wertheimer believed that this stressed the influence of the factor of *proximity*; other factors involved in natural groupings included the factor of *similarity*. Thus in

the larger circles are grouped together because they are similar (apart from their shape, they may have had the same colour). There is also the factor of *uniform destiny* or 'common fate' where a sequence of stimulus dots might be lifted up at an angle to a sequence of dots lying along a straight line; the former will be mentally grouped together. The factor of *continuity* is where a picture that looks like a wavy line superimposed on an array of battlements is so organized because we naturally follow the continuity of the line and the continuity of the battlements. The factor of *closure* is where self-enclosed units, such as the circle or our familiar square, take on Gestalt quality. There is always a tendency for these organizational processes to culminate in a 'simple' or 'clear' picture. We usually attempt to organize diagrams that do not possess Gestalt quality because of their diffuseness or complexity in terms of one or another organization that does have figural stability (*Prägnanzstufen – Prägnanz*, according to Ellis, 1938, p. 79, cannot be translated, and *Stufen* means steps or stages. Ellis suggests that the best translation of *Prägnanzstufen* would be 'regions of figural stability').

In the first of these papers Wertheimer himself had enunciated the key principles of Gestalt psychology; he wrote

> The given is itself in varying degrees 'structured' [*gestaltet*], it consists of more or less definitely structural wholes and whole-processes with their whole-properties and laws, characteristic whole-tendencies and whole-determinations of parts. 'Pieces' almost always appear 'as parts' in whole processes. (Wertheimer, 1922, condensed by Ellis, 1938, p. 14)

The expansion of this view into a principle that applied not only in perception but in science in general was undertaken by Köhler (see below).

In 1920 Wertheimer also published a monograph on productive thinking; by 'productive' thinking was meant thinking that was devoted to the solution of a problem, and was not merely day-dreaming, reminiscing, or fantasizing. This was to augur for a future in which he devoted his intellectual energies mainly towards the issue of problem-solving. As mentioned earlier, at Berlin he also supervised many students. His method was to insist on extreme care in the making of an observation; he usually let the student write the research up himself, without Wertheimer appearing as a co-author.

One of his colleagues at this time in Berlin, and then in Frankfurt, was Wolfgang Metzger, who was later to uphold the Gestalt tradition in Germany through and after the Second World War. When Hitler came to power in 1933, Wertheimer fled almost immediately with his family to Prague and then to the United States, where he accepted a position at the New School for Social Research in New York City. Metzger succeeded him at Frankfurt.

It should be noted that the work of the Gestalt psychologists was by this time quite well known in North America. Much of the credit for this must go to Robert M. Ogden (1877–1959), who had studied with Titchener at Cornell and Külpe at Würzburg and had taught at the University of Missouri, the University of Tennessee and the University of Kansas before becoming Chairman of the Education Department at Cornell in 1916. He stayed at Cornell until 1945, shifting to the Psychology Department in 1939. He had corresponded with Koffka since 1911 and he gave Koffka the opportunity to write the first article in English on Gestalt psychology (Koffka, 1922a), published a translation of Koffka's *Growth of the Mind* in 1925, and arranged for Koffka to be the first

Gestalt psychologist to visit the United States in 1924. Koffka had settled into a permanent position at Smith College in 1927, and in that year Ogden travelled to Berlin, where he met Wertheimer. Ogden did his best to persuade Wertheimer to visit Cornell for the academic year 1929–30, but Ogden could not raise enough money to bring both Wertheimer and his family over, and in the meantime, Wertheimer had accepted the offer of an appointment at Frankfurt. However, Köhler did come to Cornell for about a month in 1929. But when it became necessary in the Nazi era the way had been paved for Gestalt psychologists to emigrate to the United States. A fuller appreciation of Ogden's sponsorship of Gestalt psychology is given by Henle (1984), including an account of Titchener's scepticism of Ogden's efforts to encourage a movement that Titchener, in a letter to Helson, thought 'erected a whole system of psychology on a single dictum in the form of an inverted pyramid' (p. 14).

At the New School, Wertheimer gave seminars which were more in the nature of discussion groups than formal classes where facts were taught, and it was here that his interest in the processes of problem-solving came to supersede his work on perception. Fortunately, we have a record of these seminars as they took place between 1936 and 1941, because one of his students, Abraham S. Luchins, in the late 1960s, collected verbatim notes that had been made by himself and others, and, in collaboration with Edith M. Luchins, reconstructed the course of these seminars and some of Luchins's own (Luchins and Luchins, 1970). Luchins himself had been developing the notion of *Einstellung*, the 'set' or 'fixed path' a person may bring as a first approach to a solution of a problem on the grounds that the approach has been successful in the past. Blinded by this fixation, he or she may miss more obvious or faster routes to the solution of the problem. Luchins developed this theme in the third volume of the reconstructed seminars, but the first two volumes concentrate on Wertheimer's own ideas. Wertheimer eventually published a book entitled *Productive Thinking* in 1945, but the reconstructed lectures gave as good an insight into Wertheimer's methods for analyzing the processes of problem-solving as does this book. Moreover they show Wertheimer's preoccupation with a concept that arises naturally out of the Gestalt goal of analyzing the clarity of perception: when we perceive, we naturally seek to *structure* the world in a meaningful way. Wertheimer felt that the same was true in the thinking processes of everyday life. He remarked to some students that 'men sometimes found it unbearable to live in a mental fog, in situations in which they could not obtain some sort of structural clarity. Man seemed to have a desire for a simple structuring of the cognitive field and for a clear-cut orientation' (Luchins and Luchins, 1970, Vol. I, p. 193). We shall discuss Wertheimer's contributions to our understanding of reasoning and problem-solving in Chapter 5, but note that for Wertheimer the most interesting kinds of problems were scientific or mathematical ones, and that in analyzing successful solutions to problems he made use not only of his classroom experience but also of the first-person accounts of eminent scientists.

Wertheimer, still in the office of Professor in the Graduate Faculty of the New

School, died of a heart attack on 12 October 1943. His colleagues and students remembered him not only as a stimulating seminar leader but also as a pianist, chess player, and friend (Newman, 1944). In a paper written in his memory, Köhler (1944) noted that, once Wertheimer had his insight that psychological phenomena should be regarded 'from above', rather than 'from below', as was the wont in many of the experiments emanating from the early psychological laboratories, he immediately also saw that the same attitude should determine the psychologist's attitude to behavioural phenomena.

More generally, Wertheimer's distinction between perspectives 'from above' and 'from below' foreshadows the popular late twentieth century distinction between 'top-down' and 'bottom-up' processing in the perceptual and cognitive realms. Wertheimer may have been the first to enunciate the distinction explicitly.

Kurt Koffka (1886–1941)

Koffka was born in Berlin on 18 March 1886, and it was his uncle, a biologist, who first turned the adolescent's mind to science and philosophy, even though his family had traditionally included a fair proportion of lawyers. After finishing his *Gymnasium* years in 1903, Koffka spent a year in Edinburgh where he improved his facility in English, a gift which stood him in good stead in later years. He did a great deal of reading to familiarize himself with Anglo-American culture. When he returned to Germany in 1904, he decided however to study psychology rather than philosophy and at Berlin he studied his own kind of colour blindness – according to Harrower-Erickson (1942), the monograph that resulted from this work in 1908 included studies of colour contrast and figure-ground phenomena that would continue to intrigue him for the rest of his life. It was also in 1908 that he received his doctorate in philosophy with a dissertation directed by Stumpf on the psychological perception of rhythm. However, the 'rhythm' in question was not a property of a series of sounds but of projected lines and circles on a screen; Stumpf had suggested the study of 'visual rhythm', and following the collection of objective measures (reaction times, foot tapping) and subjective measures (self-observations) from twenty subjects, including Mira Klein, who later became his wife, Koffka concluded that rhythm was a result of a mental 'grouping' of the stimuli by the subject. He tried to describe this psychical grouping in terms that would please Stumpf but was clearly headed towards his own independent view of this Gestalt-forming process. However, he probably obtained his first position, an assistantship in Freiburg with Johannes von Kries (1853–1928) because of his work on colour blindness. Von Kries was best known for his rounding out of Helmholtz's physiology of vision with the 'duplicity theory' of the differing functions of the rods and the cones. But von Kries (1882) had also been responsible for a fierce attack on Fechner's theory that sensation strength could be 'measured' with the same validity as that possessed by spatial distances and temporal durations. It would be extremely interesting to know whether Koffka was in any way influenced by von Kries's scepticism about traditional psychophysics. Koffka then went to Würzburg where, according to Köhler (1942), he became disillusioned with the writings of Külpe and other members of the Würzburg school because, although they showed the importance of mental set in determining the flow of thoughts in a problem-solving context, they did not abandon mosaic-type analyses of sensory processes and 'automatisms in memory'.

So it was as a well-established young psychologist that Koffka joined Wertheimer and Köhler at Frankfurt. In particular, he followed up on Wertheimer's research on apparent movement, along with a group of co-workers, including Adolph Korte, a Gymnasium teacher, and Friedrich Kenkel, a student. For example, Korte (1915) worked out by experiment the exact details of the optimum timing of the two stimuli for obtaining apparent movement, given their luminance and distance apart, while Kenkel (1913) showed that apparent movement could be demonstrated in the Müller-Lyer illusion. If the 'arrows' at the end of a single horizontal line were changed rapidly from outwardly directed to inwardly directed and back again, the line seemed to contract and expand along with the changes in arrow-direction. However Benussi (1914) believed that the kind of apparent movement shown in the Müller-Lyer illusion was not the same kind of movement as had been studied by Wertheimer, using two lines. Benussi, who had written many papers on perceptual phenomena and illusions, believed that perception involved, first, the evocation of sensory contents by the stimuli, followed by an extra-psychical process which brought the contents into a dynamic relationship. So-called Gestalten are the result of sensations plus psychical activity. Koffka (1915) took active issue with this account, which he believed did not go far enough in treating Gestalt as 'givens' in themselves that could not be reduced to sensations plus 'relating' processes. Gestalten are descriptively no less immediate than their parts, so they are functionally no less primary. Furthermore, according to Koffka, Gestalt theory treats the brain process correlated with an experience not as the individual excitation of a particular brain area plus association, but as a whole process with its whole properties. In asserting these claims, Koffka left behind him the apparatus of the Austrian school according to which there were 'founding' sensory contents and accessory 'founded' perceptual contents. The foundation of a Gestalt is a unitary process. The controversy between Koffka and Benussi on apparent motion is described in detail by Ash (1982, pp. 327–360).

In Germany progress up the academic ladder involves writing a second thesis, a *Habilitationsschrift*, which will allow one to lecture at a university in the capacity of *Privatdozent*. Koffka's thesis, which gave him this position at the University of Giessen in central Germany, was his work done at Würzburg on mental 'ideas' (*Vorstellungen*) and according to Harrower-Erickson (1942) this research fore-shadowed the theory of memory to be developed in Koffka's later years.

R.M. Ogden had been at Würzburg at this time and had been a subject in this research. The task Koffka set his subjects was that of describing their mental experiences on perceiving a word; frequently an image would arise, and Koffka classified the images into as many as six different kinds. According to Ash (1982, p. 262), it was Koffka's supervisor, Külpe, who had described images as 'centrally excited sensations', and Koffka indeed preferred to think of images as being different from sensations because they arose from cognitive activity as opposed to excitation through the sense organs. At Giessen he carried out a great deal of research on perception, ultimately published in a long series of articles in the *Psychologische Forschung*, and was promoted to the first level of Professor (*ausserordentlicher Professor*). During the war years (1914–1918) he worked on brain injuries, especially cases of aphasia, and later did work on sound localization with military aims in mind, related to the work Wertheimer had done with von Hornbostel. It was at this period that Koffka also wrote his first major book on Gestalt psychology, *The Growth of the Mind* (published in German in 1921, translated into English by R.M. Ogden in 1925).

Prior to Koffka's book, a number of widely read books on child development had appeared – these included the first classic on the subject, Preyer's *Mind of the Child* (1882) and the more recent book by William Stern entitled *Psychologie der frühen Kindheit bis zum sechsten Lebensjahre (Psychology of early childhood up to the age of 6)* (1914). More theoretical were the works of Thorndike (e.g. *Educational Psychology*, 3 vols, 1913–1914), who applied to children's learning his theory that learning was mainly based on reinforcement. Shortly before Koffka wrote, the behaviourists were insisting that descriptions of even child behaviour should avoid reference to conscious experience, and both Thorndike and the behaviourists were stressing environmentalism, giving the impression that the baby's mind was initially chaotic, with sensations and actions leaving traces some of which would be remembered better than others because they were associated with reward or punishment.

Koffka attacked these notions head on. He claimed that a behaviourist's description of a child's behaviour would be psychologically 'empty' because it did not refer to the goal-directedness of even a child's behaviour. He claimed that the baby's mind is not 'chaotic' because (a) the baby might be genetically pre-programmed (to use a modern term) to attend selectively to some stimuli more than others (notably human voices and human faces), and (b) because the baby's phenomenal experience of sensation is organized into figure/ground relationships. Taking up the issue of behaviourism in more detail, he argued that the cats in Thorndike's puzzle boxes were not responding movement-by-movement in a reflex mechanistic manner, but showed evidence of selective attention to details that was apparently determined by the animal's understanding of the goal of its actions, namely the goal of escaping from the box. He argued that the higher animals showed evidence of 'intelligent' learning as revealed by Köhler's experiments with apes, and he stressed that Köhler's work on relational responding showed that even organisms of lower 'intelligence' than adult humans are not responding piecemeal to individual stimuli but in a more holistic manner to total situations.

Koffka therefore described the growth of the child's mind over the first few years of life in terms that were not behaviouristic: children were assumed to have goals that directed their actions, to be adaptive and versatile in their learning of motor skills and language, to be selective in what they attended to particularly with respect to their observations of other persons, and to be capable of 'ideation', including image-formation. These images permitted them to form a mental representation of reality. In particular, being able to mentally represent what somebody else has done facilitates the imitation by the child of the action in question. In learning language, the child was argued to make considerable use of imitation of adult speech, and Koffka also suggested that the child make use of self-imitation at the earlier babbling stage. By imagination, the child can form what Koffka called 'configurative conjunctions' between perceptions of other people's behaviour and movements produced by himself in imitation of those behaviours. This approach to child development gave the child considerable credit for adaptiveness and ingenuity. According to Koffka, there was a danger that Thorndike's tendency to underestimate the intelligence of his cats, and Thorndike's emphasis on reinforcement as increasing the probability that an *action* will be repeated, would serve badly if adopted into the framework of a theory of human development. Children's behaviour is determined not only by the immediately preceding stimulus but by a goal to which each stimulus is related (and attended to or ignored accordingly); and the behaviour of a child cannot be described solely in terms of actions, because the child has an intense mental life which a purely behaviouristic psychology fails to describe. Throughout the book, in discussing the development of specific sensory abilities and motor activities, Koffka referred to the available evidence in works such as those of Preyer and Stern, as well as the results of more recent experiments by members of the growing profession of child psychology.

At about the same time, Ogden persuaded Koffka to write an article in English presenting Gestalt psychology to Anglo-American readers. This article appeared in 1922 in the *Psychological Bulletin* and its title, 'Perception: An Introduction to the Gestalt-theorie' reveals that it was limited to that topic. According to Köhler (1942), Koffka

> attempted to explain the difference between Gestalt principles and other views in a discussion of perception. Now it is true that *initially* the difference could best be clarified through reference to instances from perception. But masterful as Koffka's presentation was it probably led to the erroneous belief that Gestalt psychologists unduly overrate perception and have little to offer in other parts of psychology. A second article by which this impression might have been destroyed was planned but never actually written. (p. 100)

In discussing perception, Koffka first expanded on his belief that the 'bundle hypothesis' was misleading, as was the 'constancy hypothesis', a term that had been popularized by Köhler (1913) and that referred to the hypothesis that every sensation is a definite and direct function of a stimulus. Moreover Koffka insisted that the new Gestalt psychology was not simply an elaboration on von Ehrenfels's term 'Gestalt-quality': the new Gestalt theory sought to get rid of theories that combined sensations, associations, and attention, as if they were unitary elements, and replace them with a view that stresses that every sensation is the result of a complex process that takes account of relationships between stimuli. Even a simple experiment on differential thresholds does not involve the 'comparison' of two separate, slightly different, stimuli but instead involves the detection of a 'step' in sensation as one surveys the total field in which the two stimuli are displayed. Moreover since instructions can influence performance in this task, the stimuli can never be judged without there being some prior attitude on the subject's part – the attitude must itself be a part of the scientific description of the phenomenon. As examples of the role of attitude, Koffka referred to some of Wertheimer's experiments on apparent movement, for example, if after numerous presentations of a vertical line *A* and a horizontal line *B* at right-angles to each other so that *A* seems to rotate down to *B*, the subject is confronted with *B* alone, there is still perceived an apparent 'movement' from where *A* had been located on the previous trials.

Koffka then went on to say that the various factors of grouping that Wertheimer discussed should be complemented by more extensive discussions of work on figure-ground organization. He criticized the analysis of Titchener (1910) of figure-ground articulation, which attributed the effect to the possibility that the ground was perceived at a lower level of consciousness than was the figure – this was an example of the false constancy-hypothesis. Figure-ground articulation for Koffka involved a total activity of the system, including the effect of prior attitudes: in an ambiguous or reversible figure, instructions to see one particular figure could lead to that figure's appearing dominant even when the instructions were changed to neutral. A number of little known phenomena about figure-ground organization were stressed by Koffka. A shadow on a ground looks darker than on a figure (Katz, 1911). Koffka (1922b) studied figure-ground effects in the phenomenon of retinal rivalry, where a display presented to one eye looks as if it alternates with a display presented simultaneously to the other eye. He took a reversible figure (see Figure 2.1) that could be seen as a yellow Maltese cross on a blue octagonal ground or as a blue Maltese cross on a yellow octagonal ground and presented it to one eye, with an empty blue octagonal field presented to the other eye. If the subject made the yellow cross the figure, it persisted in view; there was little alternation with the blue ground. But if the blue cross were made the figure, so that the yellow formed the ground, retinal rivalry occurred between the yellow ground presented to that eye and the blue ground presented to the other eye. In an unpublished experiment by Hartmann, flicker fusion was studied: identical displays were presented in succession. At slowish rates, the subjects saw the same stimulus

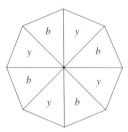

Figure 2.1 The Maltese cross in an octagon used by Koffka in his experiment on binocular rivalry. *b* means blue, *y*, yellow. (Source: reprinted from K. Koffka (1922a), *Psychological Bulletin*, **19**, p. 564.)

flashing on and off. At faster rates, there was fusion: the display seemed stationary in time, although with some flickering at certain rates. But if the display contained a figure on a ground, the figure seemed to become stationary at a slower rate of presentation than did the ground. Koffka also referred to a section in his *Growth of the Mind* in which he claimed that figure-ground organization is the first perceptual phenomenon to be experienced by newborn children.

Finally, Koffka summarized evidence from experiments on colour and brightness, experiments on the viewing of lines with the head tilted, experiments on sound localization, and experiments on psychophysical judgments that indicated that there is no 'absolute' in perception. In any perceptual task, individual details are interpreted in the context of the total display. In particular, a general 'level' is adopted by the perceiver and standard for judging the details of the display. Without such a standard level, perception is unstable: in a totally dark room with no spatial areas inside that could serve as a standard against which to judge individual display elements, a single point of light seems to wander about (the autokinetic effect). If a mirror is set at an inclined angle on a table, vertical lines look inclined, but if one looks at the mirror through a tube so that the rest of the room is invisible, vertical lines look vertical because the display is not being judged against the 'level' set by the appearance of the whole room. Koffka also went into considerable detail on how colours were perceived in relation to their background, and reported some data from experiments on how well the magnitude of arm movements could be reproduced that indicated that the accuracy in reproducing magnitudes tended to be maximal for items in the middle of the range of magnitudes used in a particular experiment (Hollingworth, 1910). It was the range of magnitudes, not the absolute value of a single magnitude, that determined accuracy. Poulton (1989) has an extensive review of range effects that have been discovered by psychophysicists writing since Koffka's time. From all of this research, Koffka concluded that the effect of any single stimulus in a display is a function of a general 'level' which is related to the range of stimuli in question. Clearly this statement is a direct foreshadowing of the 'adaptation level theory' of Helson (1964), according to which all perceptual judgments are a function of figure quality, spatial and temporal background quality, and the physiological state of the observer.

Two years after the publication of this important article, Koffka made his first visit to the United States, spending a year as a visiting professor at Cornell University, and a year at the University of Wisconsin, and many of his publications in this period were theoretical rather than experimental. In 1927 he was appointed William Allen Neilson Research Professor at Smith College in Northampton, Massachusetts. He went back to experimentation on visual perception, publishing the research as papers in later articles in his long series of 25 contributions to the Gestalt theory (*Beiträge zur Psychologie der Gestalt*); the first three papers had appeared between 1913 and 1919 in the journal that had been founded by Ebbinghaus and others, the *Zeitschrift für Psychologie*, the remainder were published in *Psychologische Forschung*, the last appearing in 1932. It was also in this year that he did some anthropological research in the field in Uzbekistan in Central Asia, which at that time had recently been absorbed into the Soviet Communist empire. Nothing was apparently published of this work, but it brought Koffka ill health from relapsing fever. It was while he was in that country, recovering from the illness, that he wrote the first chapter of what was to become his *magnum opus*, *Principles of Gestalt Psychology*. He originally conceived it as a work for the layman (Harrower-Erickson, 1942) but it turned out to be a work of 700 pages, discussing a large number of experiments in detail and extending the Gestalt theory to almost all areas of experimental psychology (Koffka, 1935a).

Since we shall be dealing in detail with Koffka's ideas on cognitive psychology in later chapters, we rest content to note here that the book itself expands on a notion that Köhler (1920, 1929) had developed, the notion that the elements in a visual 'field' are subject to 'forces' operating on the field. The word 'field' was extended from referring only to the area that one saw, the visual 'field', to the notion that behaviour itself takes place in a general 'field' provided by the environment. In physics, if a magnet is placed under a sheet of paper on which lie iron filings, the iron filings will be acted upon by a magnetic force and they will 'jump' so as to align themselves along lines of force determined by the shape and intensity of the magnet. The area over which the magnet has influence comprises the 'field' of the magnet. Previous Gestalt writers had extended the analogy to the visual field: in an area covered by a 'look', certain stimulus elements, notably figures, would be grouped by such 'forces' as similarity or given 'good figure' by the principle of closure. Köhler had extended the notion of 'field' to cover the functional activity of the brain: in the brain the relationship *between* elements in the stimulus field was mapped 'isomorphically' by elements in the brain field, although this is not to be taken as arguing that a 'brain field' necessarily comprised a topographical area of the brain; it was more of an abstraction representing a faith in the notion that Gestalt forces were operative in the brain that led directly to the Gestalt phenomena experienced in conscious perception.

Koffka went on to talk about the human organism as subject to an 'environmental field' (the stimuli impinging on his sense organs) and a 'physiological field' (determined by his present physiological state) and argued that the subject over the years had built up what Koffka called an 'Ego', also subject to field forces. This 'Ego' allowed the subject to form cognitions concerning environmental stimuli, cognitions that were coherent with the subject's past experience; essentially the Ego is a composite of many memory traces, a topic that will be discussed in more detail in the following chapter.

The chapter headings of the *Principles* reveal its scope. The first chapter is entitled 'Why psychology?' The second, which includes the above ideas, was called 'Behaviour and its field: the task of psychology'. The next five chapters are entitled 'The environmental field', and deal respectively with general issues, visual organization and its laws, figure and ground, the perceptual constancies, and three-dimensional space and motion. Chapters 8 and 9 are on action, including discussions of reflexes, the 'Ego', the 'executive' that exceeds pre-planned movements, attitudes, emotions and the will. The next four chapters are on memory; Chapter 14 is on society and personality, followed by a final concluding chapter. Readers will note the remarkable comprehensiveness of Koffka's extension of Gestalt theory from perception to other areas. It was this aspect of Koffka's work that Henle (1987) stressed in an appreciation of Koffka's book as viewed in retrospect fifty years later.

After the publication of the *Principles*, Koffka published six articles (listed by Harrower-Erikson, 1942) on a variety of topics including learning theory, art and the ontological study of value (Koffka, 1935b). He visited Oxford in 1939 to study brain injuries (a revival of an old interest) and at Oxford gave a series of lectures which he planned to make into a book but did not complete. He died of a heart attack while back at Smith College, on 22 November 1941.

The paper on value came out at about the same time as Köhler gave the William James lectures on the same topic, eventually published as a book (Köhler, 1938). In the nineteenth century, struggling to formulate the differences between the natural events described by physics and the mental events described by psychology, Wundt (1894) had come to the conclusion that mental events differed from physical events partly insofar as mental events had 'values' associated with them, hedonic, moral, aesthetic, stimulating, and so on. When Koffka discussed the 'ontological status' of values, which he did in an imaginary dialogue between a psychologist, a scientist, and a philosopher, he stressed that values should be accepted as scientific data in their own right. When Köhler wrote his book *The Place of Value in a World of Facts*, he elaborated on this theme in detail, as we shall see.

Wolfgang Köhler (1887–1967)

Born of German parents in Estonia on 21 January 1887, Köhler moved to Germany with his family when he was six, and then studied at Tübingen, where he studied philosophy, history and natural science, at Bonn, where he was taught experimental psychology by Benno Erdmann, and finally at Berlin, where at the same time as he commenced his PhD research on psychoacoustics under Stumpf, he attended lectures on physics from Walther H. Nernst (1864–1941) and Max K.E.L. Planck (1858–1947). It was Nernst who had worked out the mathematical rules underlying the diffusion of ions in liquids and the resulting electrical currents that could arise, and Max Planck was the founder of quantum mechanics, a revolutionary way of looking at the behaviour of atoms and their particles. Köhler's thesis, which was published in two parts (1909, 1910), involved a study of the reaction of the eardrum to tones of different frequency; he was able to affix a tiny mirror onto his own eardrum. A beam of light could be reflected off the mirror as it moved with the eardrum; the beam of light then activated a recording apparatus. He made the surprising discovery that the eardrum's response to particular pitches corresponded quite closely to its response to spoken vowels, and later checked this discovery phenomenologically by presenting a series of differently-pitched tones to three subjects, asking them to 'judge the tones for their similarity to vowel sounds ... the correspondence was confirmed' (Ash, 1982, p. 268). Stumpf had already noticed that pitch perception did not seem to represent a pure one-to-one correspondence between physical frequency and psychological sensation, and had tried to explain the perceptual effect in the context of a theory of 'clang colour' (or timbre, the perceived difference between middle C on a piano and middle C on a violin). Köhler was forced to disagree with Stumpf, but his findings confirmed his growing conviction not only that phenomenological observations could illuminate sensory psychology, but also that the psychical contents of experience could not be predicted simply from a knowledge of the physical stimuli. For more details on this controversy, the reader is recommended to consult Ash (1982, pp. 264–274). Ash makes no mention of any discussion by Köhler of the possibility that the auditory system might have evolved to be specially attuned to the sounds of human speech (vowels), although we noted above that Koffka would later suggest this in the *Growth of the Mind*.

After he was hired as Schumann's assistant at Frankfurt and met Wertheimer, Köhler pursued his questioning of perceptual doctrines of the past. A year after Wertheimer had published his paper on apparent movement, Köhler (1913) wrote an article for the *Zeitschrift für Psychologie* in which he attacked what he called the constancy assumption, the notion that to every sensation there corresponds a particular stimulus event. He agreed that the apparent dominance or intensity of a sensation depended on the degree of attention devoted to the stimulus, but denied that shifts in attention were responsible for every perceptual experience in which there seems to be a discrepancy between the observation and the constancy assumption. In the illusions, such as the Müller-Lyer illusion, it is only by an abnormal effort of attention that we can isolate the two straight lines from their total content (lines plus arrowheads) and reduce the illusion. Attempts to explain illusions in terms of 'unnoticed sensations' were of little value for Köhler: they did not lead to further scientific progress. In this article Köhler did not offer a particular alternative that would be more useful than the constancy assumption for thinking about the psychology of perception, but he was clearly paving the way for the Gestalt view that operations in the central nervous system that depended on the total configuration of the stimulus would determine what the stimulus looked like.

Also in 1913, Köhler was appointed Director of an Anthropoid Station on Tenerife, the largest of the Spanish Canary Islands off the west coast of Africa. This Station had been funded by the estate of a rich banker, Albert Samson, and its purpose was to conduct research on the 'natural, biological bases of individual and social morality' within the aegis of experimental psychology among other disciplines. The same fund had provided financial support for Stumpf's archives of phonograph records of ethnic music, and was later to fund the publication of Köhler's book on physical Gestalten (Köhler, 1920). The board of the Station included Max Planck and Carl Stumpf; its first director, Eugen Teuber, was in charge for only a year before Köhler took over in 1913. When the war broke out in 1914, Köhler was conscripted for German military service, but no ships from countries friendly to Germany would take off the 60 Germans on the islands who fell into this category for fear of attacks from Allied shipping. So Köhler stayed there throughout the war. He was able to receive books, mail and money and even corresponded with Robert M. Yerkes (1876–1956) in the United States, who was also busy establishing ape colonies for research purposes in that country. Köhler was suspected (by the British consul, among others) to be spying for the Germans, feeding information to a German fuel-ship offshore about what British ships were in the offing, or coming into Tenerife for re-fuelling (Ash, 1982, p. 408 says this was a 'rumour'; Ley, 1990, claims he has evidence from an old man who worked at the Station during the war that the rumour was true). At any rate, Köhler eventually left the Station in 1920 following a series of ill-timed coincidences; the funding for the Station was running low partly because of the collapse of the German mark, the land it stood on was sold to an English firm in 1918 and the Station had to be moved, and Köhler and his family suffered a series of illnesses. The Samson foundation funded his living expenses when he moved back to Germany to look for an academic post and he eventually obtained the highly desirable position of Professor at the Berlin Institute, succeeding Stumpf, who had been obliged to retire at the age of 73. (Before being able to accede to the Berlin position, Köhler had to act for a short time as Chairman at Göttingen, succeeding G.E. Müller, who also had to resign for reasons of age – the Berlin position demanded that the holder had already held a chairmanship elsewhere in Germany.)

But during his long stay on Tenerife, Köhler carried out extensive experiments on chimpanzee behaviour (the colony contained about seven individuals at any given time) and also studied chickens. His research was focused on three types of question, the question of whether size and brightness-constancy can be demonstrated for chimpanzees and chickens, the question of how the animals made choices between stimuli in order to obtain food rewards, and the question of how they solved problems in which the solution demanded a detour or roundabout pattern of behaviour. The results on constancy were reported in a paper in 1915; the results on choice responses were published in 1918 in a monograph (summarized in Ellis, 1938, pp. 217–227); and the results on problem-solving appeared as a long article in 1917, translated in 1925 as a book *The Mentality of Apes* (Köhler, 1917).

It was in the monograph on choices that Köhler reported the evidence for relational responding. The first work was done with chickens who had learned to respond to grey for a food reward, given a choice between grey and black; what would they do if confronted with the original grey and a much lighter grey? Sometimes the chickens would choose the original grey, but more than twice as often they would choose the lighter grey. In describing this result Köhler used the word 'Gestalt' to refer to the fact that the two stimuli were perceived in a 'togetherness' relation at the moment of choice. Köhler then demonstrated relational responding in his chimpanzees, and in prefacing his account of the results, noted that relational responding involved a non-analytic attitude that was probably common to all species, whereas only species that had evolved a high level of intelligence could adopt the analytical attitude that could concentrate on absolute qualities of the stimulus. Humans, by adopting an analytical attitude to the Müller-Lyer illusion, might reduce the illusion by deliberately separating the straight lines from the arrowheads in imagination, but this in a sense is going against nature: under normal circumstances humans adopt a 'structural' response to stimulus configurations, and apes will naturally adopt a 'structural' response to the totality of two greys between which a choice has to be made.

There was an interesting methodological aspect to the experimentation. In one experiment, two boxes were shown simultaneously at a distance of 75 centimetres to the chimpanzee Chica, who indicated her selected box by tapping it with a stick: to one box was affixed a card of grey that was lighter than the grey of the card affixed to the other. The 'correct' choice was the box associated with the lighter grey. After 232 trials, of which the last 75 were correct but for one error, 20 control trials were carried out in which the originally rewarded grey was used for one box, and a still lighter grey for the other. In these control tests *both* boxes contained food and the animal was therefore rewarded at every choice whether correct or not. On the first two trials, the animal chose the original grey, but thereafter she chose the new grey, the lighter of the two. Ellis (1938) summarizes this result as emphasizing 'since the animal received food even at the first two choices, one might have expected that she would continue to prefer that colour, but the structural influence was apparently strong enough, once the strangeness of a new pair diminished, to permit the pro-structural response to dominate' (pp. 224–225). Köhler had noted that when the ape was first confronted with her first critical trial, it appeared from her behaviour that the situation was new and strange, and even at the moment when the choice was made, she could be observed to be looking at the other box (the lighter grey).

Köhler went on to demonstrate relational responding by his three-year-old son, and observed once again that there were a few selections of the previously rewarded grey before the subject settled down to an unbroken sequence of 'correct' choices of the 'lighter' grey. The final half of the monograph was devoted to the study of relational responding when instead of greyness, rectangle size or colour lightness was used as the stimulus dimension of interest. Some criticisms were made by others of his experimental techniques, and these he answered with experimental evidence in a separate paper (1917b).

Köhler's work on the mentality of apes is associated, of course, with the introduction of the term 'insight' as a descriptor of a form of problem-solving behaviour where the solution seems to occur to the animal at a particular instant and the animal carries out the required behaviour smoothly and not in a trial-and-error manner. But, as defined in the *Mentality of Apes*, the criterion of insight is broader: it is 'the appearance of a complex solution with reference to the whole lay-out of the field' (p. 164). At the outset of the work, Köhler said that it was his purpose to explore a particular kind of problem, one in which the animal was given all the elements of a solution to a problem, but which required activity on the animal's part to put the elements together. The problems ranged from detour behaviour, where the animal had to go round an obstacle to get food that he could see but not reach, to implement-using behaviour, such as when the animal could climb on boxes to get food that was visible but too high to reach, or put sticks together to knock down the food or push the food off a rod from which it hung. There was even the now classic case of the chimpanzee Sultan who used a short stick to pull a long stick inside the cage, and then used the long stick to knock down the fruit from where it hung on the ceiling. This case is important because Köhler said that, 'after an unsuccessful attempt to reach the fruit with the short stick, the animal gazed about him, then suddenly carried out the correct reactions in one consecutive whole' (Köhler, 1917a, p. 150).

Köhler was extremely critical of the earlier work of Thorndike (1898) on problem-solving: Köhler claimed that cats in puzzle-boxes were forced to resort to trial-and-error behaviour *because* they could not clearly see how to get out. To demonstrate insight, the 'whole lay-out of the field' had to be clearly visible; Gestalt theory recognized wholes which are something more than the 'sum of other parts' and in the tasks the 'wholes' determine the course of action. As an example, Köhler discussed the behaviour of Sultan when he could not use a stick to pull fruit in through the bars of his cage from the outside because wire-netting covered the lower part of the bars. However Sultan took the stick and pushed the fruit sideways towards a hole which existed under the wire-netting. As Köhler states, it is difficult on a trial-and-error account to explain how Sultan, 'after he has begun to shove the fruit most carefully towards the hole, lets go of the stick, goes to the hole, stretched out his arm for the fruit, and, when he still cannot reach it, immediately returns to the stick, and shoves the fruit a little closer to the hole, so that he can get hold of it from the opening' (p. 195).

Of course, it hardly ever happened that an 'insight' solution unwound smoothly the moment a problem was set. The apes often tried solutions that did not work, but Köhler claimed that many solutions involved what he called 'good' errors. Sometimes a solution occurred to the animals that *ought* to have worked but did not for some practical reason, for example, to make a box higher, the animals sometimes inverted it diagonally so that it stood on one of its corners; the top of the box was now higher, but of course, it toppled over if the animal tried to climb on it. There were also 'bad' errors, and of these one of the most common was to resort to old habits that had been successful in previous situations, but were unsuited to the present situation. This topic formed the basis for the extended research on human problem-solving by Luchins and others that was mentioned above in the section on Wertheimer. For example, when Sultan was tired, he once put one box on top of the other underneath the position where fruit had previously hung, but not where it hung now.

The essence of Köhler's argument was that 'chance' or 'trial-and-error' played minor roles in the problem-solving behaviour of the apes. Even unsuccessful efforts at solutions could be seen to arise from repetitions of past habits, failure to take account of all of the elements of the situation, or fatigue. Moreover the conceptual link had been made between perception, choice, and problem-solving. In perception 'structural' responding determines how stimuli will appear; in choice tasks, the subject responds to a total 'structure' containing the choice-stimuli; in a detour problem, the subject must combine the elements of the problem into a new 'structure' in which the reward is obtained. The last kind of problem requires a kind of 'conceptualization' of a situation extended both in space, and because actions take place in a sequence, in time; only species of high native intelligence, such as dogs, apes or humans, may be capable of this kind of behaviour (as well as of 'absolute' responding, where the stimuli are isolated from the total situation). In work to be explored in more detail in Chapter 5, problem-solving will be considered to involve a mental 're-structuring' of the lay-out of stimuli.

It was also while he was on Tenerife that Köhler wrote a theoretical work that was meant to serve as a scientific foundation for Gestalt theory, *Die physische Gestalten in Ruhe und im stationären Zustand (Physical Gestalten at rest and in the stationary state)*, 1920; summarized in Ellis, 1938, pp. 17–54). This work introduced the analogy between events in physics, such as the diffusion of ions when one fluid is added to another, or the rearrangement of equilibrium distribution when a new electrical charge is added to an already charged and insulated conductor, and events in psychology such as the spontaneous grouping by the subject of separate elements in the visual field. The theory was developed into a speculative schema concerning neuropsychology; neural events were related to concentrations of ions in the nervous substance which in turn gave rise to electrical currents. Köhler worked fervently on this theory all his life (e.g. Köhler, 1958), but most neuropsychologists of the late twentieth century have ignored it, particularly following critical papers by Lashley, Chow and Semmes (1951) and by Osgood and Heyer (1952). We shall not stress the theory in what follows.

Köhler returned to Germany in 1920 when he became Acting Director at the Psychological Institute at the University of Berlin. Eventually he succeeded Stumpf to become Director of the Institute and Professor of Philosophy in 1922 (after the short appointment at Göttingen). The Institute was housed at one end of what once had been an emperor's palace, although it has long since been destroyed. His colleagues included Wertheimer, von Hornbostel and Kurt Lewin (1890–1947), who later applied Gestalt notions such as 'forces' and 'fields' to social situations. Other colleagues included Karl Duncker, Otto Lauenstein, Hedwig von Restorff and G.J. von Allesch. We shall mention all these individuals again. The first issue of *Psychologische Forschung* appeared in 1922, and subsequent issues included Wertheimer's papers on the laws of perceptual grouping, the series of papers on perception by Koffka, a series of papers by Gelb and Goldstein on brain injuries, and after 1926, a long series of papers by Lewin.

In the 1920s Köhler began a series of studies on the memory trace (1923) and also began developing his view that mechanical models of mental processing should be replaced by dynamic models; in a dynamic model behaviour is influenced by the ultimate goal the organism sets itself in accordance with its biological needs. Towards the end of the 1920s he gave a series of ten lectures in America which appeared in English in 1929 in a book entitled *Gestalt Psychology*. This book did a great deal to promulgate Gestalt teachings. The first three chapters included attacks on behaviourism and introspection; the next chapter stressed his new work on dynamic systems as opposed to machine theory; the next two chapters were on organization in sensation and perception; the next three chapters were on behaviour, association and recall; and the final chapter was on insight. The attack on behaviourism focused on what Köhler called their two commandments, 'Thou shalt not acknowledge direct experience in psychology' and 'Thou shalt not conceive of other functions but reflexes and conditional reflexes'. Köhler extensively attacked the first commandment and argued that we use direct experience in making physical measurements, yet nobody denies the validity of our measurements on that ground only; physics would not be possible without the assumption that all the other individuals doing the measuring have certain ideas and concepts in common.

Köhler also felt that to study behavioural events only by controlled measurement would often lead to important facts being overlooked; his observation on spontaneous behaviour in his chimpanzees did not involve carefully controlled quantitative measurement but were, in his view, valid contributions to science and

Everything that is valuable in these observations would disappear if 'results' were handled in an abstract statistical fashion. Under these circumstances, a warning against glorification of quantitative procedures alone still seems indicated. Quantitative research, I repeat, presupposes qualitative analysis in which fruitful problems are discovered. (p. 33).

He also felt that the second commandment provided an over-simplistic view of the complexity of the nervous system in humans – 'a person who looks without prejudice upon human and animal behaviour will hardly find that reflexes and conditioned reflexes are the most natural concepts to be used in an explanation of the facts' (p. 33). It was at this point that Köhler asked how far we can add to the narrow world of the behaviourist, based on his narrow measurements, by adding the information provided by direct experience. He insisted that the introspective *analysis*, after the fact, of a given direct experience, was not necessarily of much scientific value; but he also insisted that, if we make a certain assumption, the data of direct experience can give us some insight into the connection between the physical world and the mental world. The assumption, which Köhler claimed had been foreshadowed by K.E.K. Hering (1834–1918), is that direct experiences can be systematically ordered if their various kinds and nuances can be put together according to their similarities. So, experienced loudnesses can be ordered from the lowest to the highest, all sharing the general characteristic of being auditory and perhaps being of the same frequency. We can then go on to assume that whatever the physiological characteristics underlying the perception of loudness, they too can be ordered in a similar fashion.

However the chief attack on behaviourism was focused on the doctrine that human learning, particularly of verbal material, was entirely a function of use and disuse. This attack appeared in the chapter on associationism and will be dealt with in more detail in Chapter 3 below.

In the early 1930s Köhler's voice was raised among those who feared the growing rise of Nazism. He published a criticism of the regime in a newspaper, a criticism that Henle (1971, p. 9) states was the last anti-Nazi article to be published openly under National Socialism. When storm-troopers once patrolled around the Institute, he complained fiercely to the Minister of Education, who nevertheless did nothing. His courage at this time was exemplary (Pratt, 1967; Crannell, 1970; Henle, 1978). After Hitler came to power in Germany in 1933, Köhler and many other German scientists felt it necessary to emigrate. Many went to the United States, where Koffka already resided. Köhler was appointed Professor of Psychology in 1935 at Swarthmore College in Pennsylvania, a small college that had been chartered by the Society of Friends in 1864. In 1934–35 he had given the William James Lecture at Harvard and these were published in 1938 as a book entitled *The Place of Value in a World of Facts*.

However it will be appropriate to mention at this juncture that the lectures at Harvard in 1934–35 did not go over very well with many of Köhler's colleagues in America. Prior to these lectures, Köhler's work on problem-solving by apes had been well received and he had visited the United States for a number of short visits, with his cause being enthusiastically supported in the early 1920s by one of Harvard's most influential psychologists, Edwin G. Boring (1886–1968). But after about 1925, Boring increasingly felt that Köhler was losing sight of the experimental foundations of psychology and becoming too philosophical. Many Americans felt that in his *Gestalt Psychology* of 1929 Köhler had adopted too one-sided a view of associationism and behaviourism, and when he actually gave the William James lectures in 1934–35, Boring and many others complained that he was too preoccupied with epistemology and metaphysics at the expense of psychology. The upshot of this growing disillusionment with Köhler was that he did not receive a prestigious position at Harvard, one about which he and Boring had been negotiating for several years; the job went to Karl S. Lashley (1890–1958), eminent for his studies on the effect of brain lesions on learning in rats. However, Köhler's position at Swarthmore was well renumerated and it is clear that during the period 1920–1940 Gestalt psychology was being discussed at length by North American psychologists.

At Swarthmore, Köhler became the nucleus of a group of psychologists intrigued by the implications of Gestalt psychology for various areas of investigation. Karl Duncker and Hans Wallach also joined Köhler at Swarthmore and among younger Americans who carried out research there during Köhler's period of tenure were David Krech, Claude E. Buxton, Richard Crutchfield, W.D. Neff, J.C.R. Licklider, H. Witkin, Mary Henle, Richard Held, Jacob Nachmias, and Ulric Neisser. It will be recalled that it was Neisser's book of 1967 that was one of the main catalysts of the cognitive revolution. A detailed description of the interactions between Americans and Wertheimer, Köhler, Koffka, Kurt Lewin, Fritz Heider, Egon Brunswik, Karl Bühler and other eminent German psychologists who had been forced to emigrate because of Hitler has been provided by Mandler and Mandler (1969), while Sokal (1984) has written a detailed account of Köhler's negotiations with Harvard and of the reception of Gestalt psychology in North America in general.

The other two centres of Gestalt psychology in the United States were Smith College and the New School in New York City. Koffka at Smith College taught Mary Henle, who graduated there in 1934 before doing graduate work at Bryn Mawr (where she met Helson) and then obtained her first job at Swarthmore with Köhler, Wallach and Duncker; later she moved to the New School, where Wertheimer reigned. Also at Smith College were Eleanor and James J. Gibson, who would later make major contributions to the psychology of perception. But much of the research carried out by the second-generation psychologists was on personality, cognitive processes as a function of personal needs, and thought processes; little was done on animal learning or the theory of memory. The Gestaltist network also included many social psychologists influenced by Kurt Lewin (Bolles, 1993, pp. 288–289).

The most important features of *The Place of Value in a World of Facts* were (a) its stress on the idea that mental experience provides data that are just as important for science to describe as are the data for which physics and biology attempt to account (that is, data about physical objects that may or may not be living); and (b) its introduction of the concept of 'requiredness'. It was Köhler's belief that most mental experiences involve a striving or a desire for completeness; if we are hungry, we imagine food and are driven to actions that will lead to the obtaining of food; if we hear somebody expound on a proposition, we wish to know whether that proposition is true or false. In both of these cases there is a feeling by the subject that something is required that is either already provided (as in a true statement, a fulfilled desire, or a perfect perceptual Gestalt) or needs to be provided (as in a questionable statement, an unfulfilled desire, or an irregular figure). Köhler drew analogies between the 'requiredness' associated with mental experience and the 'forces' of physics. He noted also that requiredness includes the variable of 'value' – the goodness or rightness or wrongness of what we perceive and think – and was thus able to relate value, which has no place in physics but plays an essential part in thought, to the world of facts with which the non-psychological sciences had been concerned since antiquity.

The remainder of Köhler's life unfolded in relative tranquillity. He stayed at Swarthmore until 1958, when he retired to a house he had bought, and had used as a summer home, at Enfield near Dartmouth in New Hampshire. During his stay at Swarthmore, he gave a series of lectures at the University of Virginia in 1938. These he expanded into his book *Dynamics in Psychology* (1940). His research at Swarthmore was mainly on figural after-effects (see below) and on elaborating his theory of the brain events underlying perception. In 1958 he gave the Gifford lectures at the University of Edinburgh, and in 1966 he gave the Herbert S. Langfeld Memorial series of lectures at Princeton. These were published as *The Task of Gestalt Psychology* (1969), his last book. He received many honours including honorary degrees from six universities and the Distinguished Scientific Contribution Award of the American Psychological Association in 1957; he was president of the Association in 1958. He died at Enfield on 11 June 1967. A complete listing of his works is provided by Henle (1971), who has edited a collection of Köhler's papers.

His last two books show parallel courses and therefore will be treated together. In both books the opening chapters are on the need for a Gestalt approach to the problem of perception, both books expand on the brain current theory, and *Dynamics in Psychology* has a chapter on memory, some of which is mentioned again in *The Task of Gestalt Psychology*, which finishes, however, with material on thinking that is not mentioned in the earlier book.

Dynamics in Psychology began with a reference to a number of experiments on perception that had been published in *Psychologische Forschung* and are still not very well known. For example, Brown (1928, 1931) demonstrated that if a series of large circles was seen moving at a constant speed inside a large rectangle, and then the observer moved his eyes to a series of small circles moving at the same speed inside a small rectangle, the latter seemed to move much faster than the former. This illusion is not present when the same displays are viewed simultaneously. This research led to further work by Duncker (1929), Koffka (1935a, pp. 288–291) and Cartwright (1938) which indicated that the illusion is based on the fact that judgments of movement seen in an opening depend upon judgments of the distance between the moving object and the contours of the opening (Köhler, 1940, pp. 14–18). Köhler stressed that this phenomenon would not have been discovered without special experimentation, nor would his second group of phenomena, which indicated how viewing text, objects, or faces upside-down can lead to losing certain qualities of meaning which were apparent when they were viewed right-side up: an upside-down face, for example, seemed to lack facial expression. These examples illustrate that important facts in psychology might be hidden if we rely on the data of direct experience alone; experimentation must reveal the parameters that determine everyday direct experience. Köhler talked about the 'functional relationships' that determine the course of mental events, and claimed that in doing psychology, the task was to hypothesize the existence of such functional relationships and then verify them by theory and experiment. In *The Task of Gestalt Psychology*, Köhler extended the list of perceptual phenomena to be explained to include camouflage and some particularly striking illusions reported by Fraser (1908) where concentric circles in a context of radiating lines could be seen to look square-like or spiral-like (Figure 2.2). Morgan and Moulden (1986) have since explained these phenomena in terms of events in the visual processing of the contours of the circles.

Moreover, in both *Dynamics in Psychology* and in *The Task of Gestalt Psychology*, as well as in a long monograph by Köhler and Wallach (1944), Köhler applied his theory of brain currents to the phenomenon of figural after-effects. These phenomena arise when, if one fixates a geometrical figure for some time and then it is removed, subsequent figures displayed in the same location can appear to be fainter and displaced in space.

One of Köhler's dreams was to clarify the relationship between perception and memory, and this was the topic of the final chapter of *Dynamics in Psychology*. For example, two circles in a surround filled with disconnected straight lines and zigzags will stand out as a group more than will two circles in a surround filled with ellipses and other curved closed figures. Köhler stressed that, just as the nature of the background determines how distinctive and groupable particular stimuli seem to be, so in memory items standing out from a temporal background that were also similar to each other would be grouped together. More will be said on this in Chapter 3, but it was his research assistant, Hedwig von Restorff (1933), who carried out experimental studies showing how the isolation of to-be-remembered elements from their surround facilitated later recognition or recall; in 1969 Köhler described the results as being 'caused by organization and articulation within the sequence, the series as a whole' (p. 126); he asserted that he and von Restorff had taken a specific hypothetical step from organization in simultaneous perception to the study of the organization and articulation of successively presented items for memory purposes.

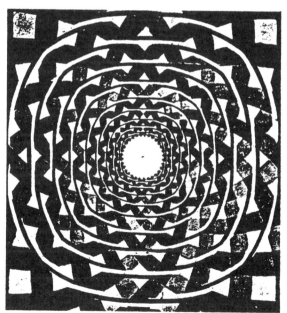

Figure 2.2 Two illusions that Köhler (1969) stressed needed explanation. (Source: reprinted from J.B. Fraser (1908), *British Journal of Psychology*, **2**.)

At the end of *The Task of Gestalt Psychology*, Köhler brought together problem-solving and perception in the following way. Insight solutions, as mentioned, often result after a great deal of mental work. In matters of science, such insights can be given by 'an abrupt reorganization of given materials, a revolution, that suddenly appears ready-made on the mental scene' (p. 163). Köhler's final words were

> Why do such revolutions which occur in certain brains tend to be the right revolutions? This is the same question we asked ourselves: why do brain processes tend to produce perceptual organizations of remarkable clearness of structure? At least this part of nature, the human brain, seems to operate in a most selective fashion. It is the *direction* of its operations which is truly remarkable. (p. 164)

The overwhelming impetus in late Gestalt psychology was to unify cognitive psychology by stressing the *non*-random, non-chance operations of the brain, a brain in which contextual relationships in the environment were mapped by isomorphic relationships between events in the neuron substance, mappings which in turn were the result of evolutionary processes that have taken place over millennia.

Conclusion

Gestalt psychology is viewed by late twentieth-century sensory scientists with a mixture of respect and disdain; they admire the laws of grouping, figure-ground organization and perceptual constancy, but feel that recent developments in sensory neuropsychology have made the neurological theorizings by Köhler and the other Gestalt psychologists obsolete. That the Gestalt laws of perception are still a major focus on research is attested to by the success of edited volumes such as *Perceptual Organization* (Kubovy and Pomerantz, 1981) and *Organization and Representation in Perception* (Beck, 1982); Epstein (1988) has argued that the time has come to rehabilitate Gestalt theory in perception, minus the field theory of currents; Hoffman and Dodwell (1985) have described a mathematical model of how the brain processes figural inputs that leads directly to prediction of the Gestalt laws of symmetry, closure, similarity, continuity, proximity and Prägnanz; and the 'adaptation level theory' of Helson (1964), a direct offshoot of Gestalt psychology, is persistently being successfully applied, as in the theory of Dodwell and Humphrey (1990) concerning the McCollough effect, a pattern-contingent colour after-effect. But the Gestalt theory of brain currents has received a major blow from the discovery that individual neurons in different cortical areas respond *separately* to the colour, figural and movement aspects of a visual stimulus (Zeki, 1992). But the present book is about cognition rather than perception, so in the next chapter we shall focus on Gestalt writings on memory and, in the following chapter, indicate that those writings, far from being obsolete, are very relevant to late twentieth-century memory theory.

Chapter 3

Gestalt views on memory

Introduction: the memory trace

Prior to the first Gestalt writings on memory there had been a considerable amount of research on the subject. Ebbinghaus (1885/1964) had invented nonsense syllables, shown that the amount retrievable of lists of nonsense syllables or of poetry was high immediately following learning but fell rapidly to an asymptote as time progressed, and demonstrated that practice at memorizing carried out in a number of short bursts led to faster memorization than did a single extended period of practice receiving the same amount of time. G.E. Müller and Friedrich Schumann (1893) had shown how rhythmizing and grouping facilitate memorizing and Müller and Pilzecker (1900) had introduced the term 'retroactive inhibition' to refer to interference with retrieval of some target item X, interference that seems to be caused by events (which may or may not involve memorizing) intervening between the time of learning X and the time of its retrieval. Moreover, in a series of articles, Müller (1911, 1913, 1917) claimed that different 'ideas' or images related to a particular context tended to 'converge' over time so that distinctive differences between the ideas or images tended to disappear. Running counter to this 'convergence principle' was another principle, that of 'affective transformation', which allowed the subject to accentuate or emphasize certain details of the stimulus material at the same time as learning. However, the second principle only came into action if the subject deliberately focused his attention on the stimulus details, whereas the principle of convergence was a general law of memory. This early research is reviewed by Murray (1976).

There was also considerable speculation about the nature of the memory trace. Richard Semon (1904/1921) preferred to call the trace the 'engram' but added another automatic process he believed to be inherent in the brain tissue underlying the trace. This process he called 'synergistic ecphory', by which he meant that whenever a stimulus X excited the nervous system, it had a tendency automatically to excite an engram left by a previously perceived stimulus identical to or very similar to X. Recognition was not a case of sensation-plus-association; it happened directly and automatically. The Gestalt psychologists referred respectfully to Semon's work (e.g. Lauenstein, 1933, p. 148; Koffka, 1935a, p. 598) but never adopted it *in toto*; indeed Lauenstein thought that Semon's engrams were too static, and argued that the trace is forever being changed in a manner that was not properly captured in Semon's theory.

This tendency for memory traces to be 'fluid' or to melt into each other was given support by a literature started by Köhler (1923). In the early days of psychophysics Fechner (1860, Vol. II, p. 142) had noticed that how easily a second weight was judged heavier than one that had just been lifted depended on the order of the weights. If the light weight was lifted before the heavier, the judgement was easier (there was a smaller 'just noticeable difference') than if the heavy weight was lifted before the lighter. The 'error factor' influenced by this order was called the 'time-error'. Fechner thought it had two components: at very short time intervals between the weights, the second weight would be lifted by a hand still excited by sensory after-effects of the first stimulus. Hence, responsivity to the second stimulus would be decreased. But he hinted that there might also be a memory factor: if a light weight were picked up first, the memory of the weight might decline, so that when the second weight was picked up, it was judged against the fading trace of the light weight and seem even heavier in contrast. That is, responsivity to the second stimulus would be enhanced. According to Hellström (1985), this 'memory' theory of the time-error was stressed by Boas (1882) rather than by Fechner.

Köhler elaborated on this opinion considerably. He demonstrated that if two bangs of *equal* intensity were sounded, whether or not the second sounded louder than the first depended on the time interval between them. At intervals below about three seconds, the second could sometimes sound fainter, whereas at intervals longer than three seconds, the second usually sounded louder, presumably because it was being compared with the fading trace of the first bang. Lauenstein (1933) altered Köhler's theory somewhat: he said that the trace of the second weight was *assimilated* to the trace of the first weight and that this assimilation process depended also on the background sound level. For reasons of space I shall only briefly note that Pratt (1933) did an experiment that confirmed Lauenstein's views but obtained some paradoxical results that were later neatly explained by Helson (1947) in terms of adaptation-level theory. Hellström (1985) has elaborated on Helson's explanation but still makes use of adaptation-level theory. There is also a noncommittal review by Tate and Springer (1971), while Laming and Scheiwiller (1985) have concluded that there is no one equation which satisfactorily predicts the curve of fading of the trace of nonverbal stimuli. But the notion that the trace is not an entity that can simply be teased apart from other traces has received considerable support from the late twentieth-century models of memory such as that of Murdock (1982), as we shall discuss in more detail in Chapter 4.

In his 1923 paper on the time-error, Köhler had stated, more or less as an aside, that

> if a trace corresponds to a previously perceived structure, the trace will possess identical structural characteristics, and because of this will also possess inner structural *forces* including an inner tendency to be transformed in a direction of increasing Prägnanz . . . Traces of the kind being discussed here are not dead entities (*Massen*) that 'can be united to perceptual components', but are rather relatively fixed pre-conditions for future events. (p. 146)

According to this picture, traces cannot be divorced from the end-results of the Gestalt process involved in setting them up, moreover they are subject to Gestalt forces still operating within themselves. The person who did the most influential work on the topic of whether the memory trace tended to change over time in the direction of good Gestalt was Friedrich Wulf (1922), who in the first issue of *Psychologische Forschung* published a study of memory for visual forms. His experiments sparked off a lively discussion of whether, when memory errors occurred, these could be ascribed to interference from or assimilation to, other memories, or whether, on the other hand, it was necessary to ascribe automatic Gestalt processes to trace retention as well as to perceptual organization.

Wulf showed a total of 26 simple nonsense shapes drawn on cards for 5 to 10 seconds to six adults. Their task was to reproduce the drawings after time intervals that varied from 30 seconds to as long as 8 weeks. Sometimes the same drawing was reproduced by the same subject several times. He found that in nearly all cases the subject reported that they first categorized the shape as a particular real-life object or they analyzed it in terms of geometrical figures, for example, Figures 3.1 (a) and (b) show a pattern which was characterized by one subject as 'three peaks' (objects), by another as 'three equilateral triangles'. In both cases, their reproductions of the figure showed an accentuation or sharpening of the points, but the subject who thought of the drawing as representing three peaks also made the peaks less symmetric, as mountains would be in nature (Figure 3.1(a)), while the subject who thought of the drawings as representing equilateral triangles heightened the peaks to conform with the notion of equilaterality (Figure 3.1(b)). Other examples were provided by Wulf: an asymmetrical figure that reminded a subject of an envelope was reproduced with greater symmetry, such as is found in a real-life envelope (Figure 3.1(c)) and a subject who thought of a pattern with unequal 'steps' as a staircase came to reproduce it, over the course of four reproductions, as having more equal steps as a staircase would in real life (Figure 3.1(d)). That subjects will try to remember 'nonsense' material by relating it to 'meaningful' material was not a new discovery. Kuhlmann (1906) had discussed a tendency towards standardization in an earlier study of memory for drawings. But in Wulf's study, the tendency to reproduce a figure in line with the way the nonsense drawing had been interpreted in the time of perception was all-pervasive.

Nevertheless Wulf suggested that an analysis of the errors indicated that not all of the errors were the result of 'assimilation to an object'. In addition to these 'normalizing' errors (*Normalizierung*), as he called them, there were also errors of 'emphasizing' (*Pointierung*) where the observer notices some particular detail in the nonsense drawing and exaggerates it in subsequent reproductions, and errors that were due to attributes of the nonsense form itself. Such a structurally conditioned change (*struktive Veränderung*) is not due to normalization or exaggeration of detail but comes about because of the form in itself. For example, the shape shown in Figure 3.2 is asymmetrical; if it had been subjected to a normalizing process in the direction of a 'flask', there would have been an accentuation of the differences between the two bulbous portions of the drawing,

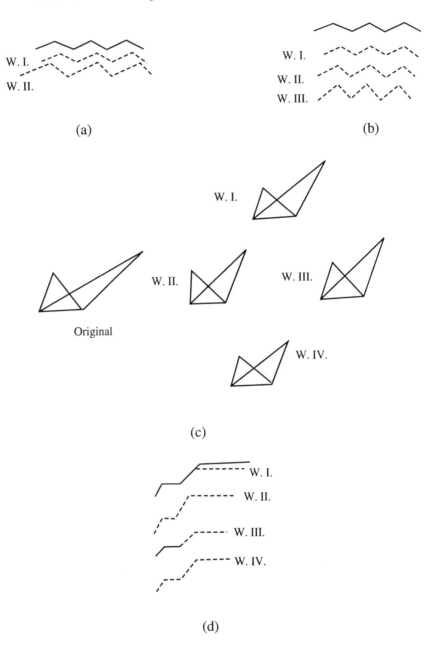

W. I.
W. II.

(a)

W. I.
W. II.
W. III.

(b)

W. I.

W. II.

W. III.

Original

W. IV.

(c)

W. I.
W. II.
W. III.
W. IV.

(d)

Figure 3.1 Some of the figures used by Wulf to study memory for form – the drawings labelled W.I. etc. are successive reproductions by the subject of the figure. (Source: reprinted from Wulf (1922) as translated in W.D. Ellis (1938), *A Source Book of Gestalt Psychology*, Routledge & Kegan Paul. (*a*) and (*b*) are from p. 143, (*c*) is from p. 142 and (*d*) is from p. 139.)

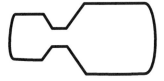

Figure 3.2 An asymmetrical random shape used by Wulf. (Source: reprinted from Wulf (1922) as translated in W.D. Ellis (1938), *A Source Book of Gestalt Psychology*, Routledge & Kegan Paul, p. 141.)

but in one subject the two portions were reproduced as more nearly alike. A tendency towards greater symmetry might result as a function of autonomous changes toward better 'Gestalt', given an asymmetrical form.

Wulf characterized all errors as being either 'sharpening' or 'levelling', but this distinction was criticized by Gibson (1929) as being of little practical use – it comprises all *possible* changes that could occur anyway. A sharpening might be reflected in the exaggeration of the mountain peaks in Figure 3.1(a), and a levelling might be reflected in a tendency to reproduce asymmetrical drawings with greater symmetry, but the *causes* of these tendencies to sharpening or levelling – are they based on normalization, emphasizing, or structurally conditioned changes? – are more important for the psychologist to know. I suspect that Wulf's distinction between sharpening and levelling is sometimes taken to represent a belief he is supposed to have had that these are just two directions of change toward better Gestalt, but in his summary (Wulf, 1922, p. 373), not quoted in Ellis (1938), Wulf makes it clear that Gestalt laws are supposed to operate to determine either sharpening or levelling, the only two possible outcomes. According to Wulf's own statement of his position, the changes categorized as 'normalizing' are themselves changes toward a better Gestalt, because a concept such as 'mountain peaks' or 'staircase' already has good stability in the memory system. This stability, however, was not necessarily a function of how often the stimuli had been experienced.

In this context, we should bear in mind an important demonstration later reported by Gottschaldt (1926), also published in *Psychologische Forschung*. Figures such as the lozenge shown in Figure 3.3(a) were presented three times to three subjects or 520 times to eight subjects. Then a figure such as Figure 3.3(b) was shown to the subjects who were asked to describe the figure in detail. Analysis of the stenographic records of the subjects' descriptions of figures like that of Figure 3.3(b), showed that no mention was made of the lozenge by 93.4 per cent of the subjects who had seen three prior exposures of figures like the lozenge, or by 95 per cent of the subjects who had seen 520 prior exposures of the figures like the lozenge. What determined whether or not the lozenge was detected in Figure 3.3(b) was not the number of times the lozenge had been experienced but the total Gestalt of Figure 3.3(b), in which the lozenge is effectively camouflaged. Similarly, Wulf claimed that what determined memory

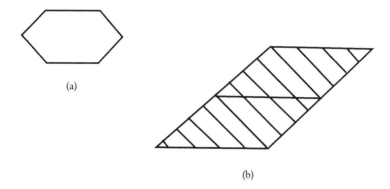

(a)

(b)

Figure 3.3 The lozenge shape shown in (a) was exposed for many trials, but when (b) was exposed, subjects did not report seeing the lozenge, which is sufficiently camouflaged in (b). (Source: reprinted from Gottschaldt (1926) as translated in W.D. Ellis (1938), *A Source Book of Gestalt Psychology*, Routledge & Kegan Paul, p. 116.)

for nonsense forms was not how often it had been experienced (although his only data on amount of 'experience' was his data on repeated reproduction) but how far the form could be related (assimilated to?) a more stable form in memory, be it a simpler geometrical form such as a triangle or an object like a range of mountains or a staircase.

Wulf's work was received with considerable interest outside Germany. In the United States, James J. Gibson (1904–1979), who was later to make his name with his emphasis on the importance to be placed on the preservation of invariants in any theory of perception, carried out an extensive survey of memory for nonsense shapes (Gibson, 1929). He used a total of 28 shapes shown to six adults and reproduced (by the same subject) immediately, after 5 weeks, or after 1 year. But there was an important change from Wulf's design. At the start of the experiment, Wulf had shown one drawing, followed by immediate reproduction, followed by another drawing. Gibson showed a series of 7 or 14 designs before asking for immediate reproduction. As a result Gibson was able to show that the errors in reproduction were, as Wulf had said, frequently errors of normalization or exaggeration; but there were a large number of errors in which details from one design in the exposed series of 7 or 14 designs were merged with details from another design. What Wulf had called errors of normalization, Gibson called errors of 'object assimilation'; the errors due to confusion between figures in the series exposed were called errors of 'figure assimilation'. Figure 3.4(a) shows how a nonsense shape was interpreted by one subject as 'half a doughnut' and reproduced with an error in the direction of this concept. Figure 3.4(b) shows how the same figure was confused with another shape leading to a reproduction which combined elements of both.

He also noted three other kinds of errors. There were errors of verbal analysis

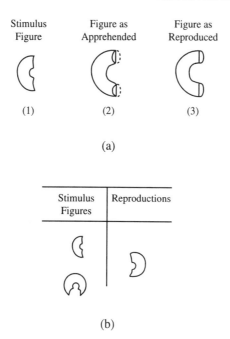

Figure as
Reproduced

(a)

(b)

Figure 3.4 In (a) the stimulus figure (1) is reproduced (3) in a manner influenced by the way the figure is apprehended (2). In (b) two stimulus figures from the same list are confused. (Source: reprinted from J.J. Gibson (1929), *Journal of Experimental Psychology*, **12**, (*a*) is from p. 17, (*b*) from p. 24.)

where subjects verbally analyzed a figure into words such as 'irregular, medieval, jutting out' – clearly this is close to object assimilation; errors of completion or dissimilation, in which figures with gaps either had the gaps closed up (completion) or exaggerated (dissimilation); and errors of rectilinearity, in which curved lines were made straight. Wulf's drawings had consisted of straight lines only, so he could not have discussed this last class, and he had not used figures with gaps, so he had not discussed errors of completion or dissimilation. Nevertheless, Wulf might have ascribed these classes of errors to structurally conditioned changes, and later researchers were to explore them in more detail. Gibson, however, did not see them as such. For him, all the errors could be ascribed to the assimilation of new percepts to old ideas in the memory of the subject, whether the new ideas were of objects, figures that had been recently seen, or well-learned, simple figures, such as circles, squares, etc.

A long literature on memory for nonsense forms ensued following from these two papers. It has been thoroughly reviewed by Riley (1962), who agreed with Gibson that Wulf is having the best of both worlds by saying that, if a shape is recalled as a 'set of mountains' this is a change in the direction of good Gestalt because mountains form a Gestalt-like content in memory. Detailed experiments

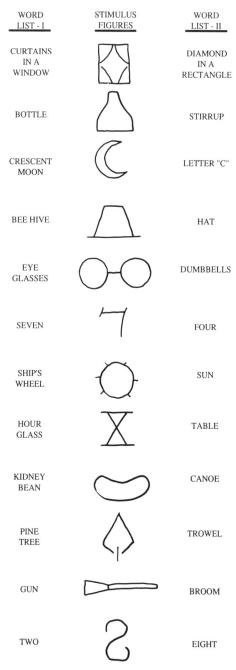

WORD LIST - I	STIMULUS FIGURES	WORD LIST - II
CURTAINS IN A WINDOW		DIAMOND IN A RECTANGLE
BOTTLE		STIRRUP
CRESCENT MOON		LETTER "C"
BEE HIVE		HAT
EYE GLASSES		DUMBBELLS
SEVEN		FOUR
SHIP'S WHEEL		SUN
HOUR GLASS		TABLE
KIDNEY BEAN		CANOE
PINE TREE		TROWEL
GUN		BROOM
TWO		EIGHT

Figure 3.5 The stimulus figures used by Carmichael *et al.*, (1932). Each figure was associated with two labels, shown in word lists I and II. (Source: reprinted from L. Carmichael *et al.* (1932), *Journal of Experimental Psychology*, **15**, p. 75.)

in which, for example, a circle with a gap in it then has to be picked out at a later time from many circles with varying sizes of gaps have yielded inconsistent results. For example, Hebb and Foord (1945) found that adults showed no tendency to pick a circle that had a gap narrower than that of the to-be-retrieved circle, but teenagers showed a statistically significant tendency at retention intervals of both 5 minutes and 24 hours to pick a circle that had a gap *wider* than that of the to-be-remembered circle. A similar apparent widening of the gap was found by Irwin and Seidenfeld (1937) using the same subjects tested at varying retention intervals, and by Crumbaugh (1954) and Karlin and Brennan (1957) using different subjects tested at various retention intervals. Perhaps a resolution of the issue is provided by Walker and Veroff (1956). Subjects shown a circle with a narrow gap of 20 degrees drew the circle 2 weeks later from memory with a wider gap; but a circle with an 80-degree gap was drawn narrower. Perhaps subjects verbally coded the stimulus as having a gap that was 'narrow' or 'wide' with something like an adaptation level determining the direction of error when reproducing the circle. At any rate, this literature is generally neglected at the present time. The sheer difficulty of drawing reliable conclusions about the memory trace from successive reproductions of forms was, however, well attested to by the extensive variability of such reproductions in an experiment by Zangwill (1937).

But it was also in the thick of the literature surrounding Wulf's paper that Carmichael *et al.* (1932) performed their classic experiment on the importance of verbal encoding at the time of presentation for later purposes of retrieval. Subjects each saw a total of twelve nonsense figures; the shapes are shown in Figure 3.5. Just before each figure was shown, the subject was told 'The test figure resembles …' For example, for the first figure in Figure 3.5 some subjects were told it resembled 'curtains in a window'. Other subjects were told it resembled a 'diamond in a rectangle'. Immediately after presentation subjects reproduced by drawing as many of the twelve figures as they could. A rating was given to each drawing based on its approximation to the original drawing, but special attention was paid to drawings with low ratings, i.e. drawings with major changes – such drawings accounted for 25.9 per cent of all the reproductions. For those subjects who had received list 1 labellings, 74 per cent of these drawings resembled those labellings, e.g. the drawing of the first figure was actually of curtains in a window; for those subjects who had received list 2 labellings, 73 per cent of these low-rated drawings resembled the labellings given in list 2, e.g. the drawing of the first figure closely resembled a diamond in a rectangle. This demonstration experiment is often reported in textbooks of introductory psychology (e.g. Darley *et al.*, 1984).

It was also in the context of a discussion of the Gestalt notion that traces tend toward greater stability that MacColl (1939, pp. 142–143) reported another experiment on the recall of simple geometrical designs. Each of twelve designs was presented either with a complete outline or with a broken outline. Separate groups of subjects were tested for recall (drawing) of the designs after 15 minutes, 4 hours or 24 hours. There was no striking difference between any of the three groups in the percentage of originally closed versus broken designs that were reproduced. But 15 per cent of the broken-outline figures were reproduced as closed by the group tested after 15 minutes, 36 per cent after 4 hours and 48 per cent after 24 hours. There was thus a strong tendency for designs with gaps in them to be recalled as not having gaps, a tendency that increased within time. Whether this was because the subjects remembered only a verbal code for reproducing the figures (ignoring whether the figures were complete or broken in outline) or whether there was a genuine forgetting of the gaps cannot be decided.

Interactions between traces

Köhler's critique of associationism

We have seen that the literature on the time-error indicates that when a trace is set up it can alter the state of the organism in such a way that a repetition of the stimulus identical to the one that set up the trace is perceived in the context of the original trace. And we have seen how the literature arising from Wulf's work, while giving us no clear answer to the question of whether there is an automatic tendency for the trace to change in a particular direction because of structure-conditioned forces, nevertheless revealed that retrieval of a trace is predominantly determined by the manner in which the trace was encoded verbally. In the next set of studies to be examined we look at interactions between traces, particularly traces related to verbal material. Verbal material is easier to study than non-verbal material (memories of intensities, nonsense figures, etc.) because errors are clear-cut and assertions about forgetting do not depend on indirect inferences about a presumed 'fading' in the intensity-quality of a trace and do not depend on subjects' abilities to draw or on repeated reproductions.

The starting point for the later Gestalt work on how memories interact was probably Köhler's critique of associationism and behaviourism in his *Gestalt Psychology* (1929). It will be recalled from Chapter 1 that for the behaviourists, and also the associationists, the 'strength' of a habit was predominantly a function of how frequently it had been used. What applied to the memory for motor skills presumably also applied to nonsense syllables – the more frequently they were rehearsed, the better they would be retained. Furthermore, according to Köhler, the traditional explanation of why pairs of nonsense syllables were harder to learn than words in a paired-associates paradigm was that nonsense syllables were new to the learner, whereas word-pairs consisted of familiar words that had often been seen or spoken before: the greater ease with which words were learned as compared with syllables was thereby attributed to the law of frequency. Even if words have not been paired before, each word has a meaning which may have some pre-existing association with the other word, so that the process of learning has only to strengthen bonds which have existed beforehand. But Köhler felt that matters were not so simple as this. He wrote:

> Let somebody read a few times the following pairs of nouns: lake-sugar, boot-plate, girl-kangaroo, pencil-gasoline, palace-bicycle, railroad-elephant, book-toothpaste. Learning of this series will be considerably easier than that of the same number of nonsense syllables. But can one really say that between lake and sugar, palace and bicycle and so forth, there are strong pre-experimental associations which merely need some light refreshing, and thus make learning an easy task? It seems to me that we cannot, since thousands of times the same words have occurred in other much more regular connections. (pp. 156–157)

I took this same list of words and made a list of equal length of nonsense syllables, consisting of jef-nuk, lus-zim, ris-tun, fut-nar, mol-fif, jal-wem and mif-tas. I read the syllables aloud at a rate of 1 syllable per second, with 3 seconds between each pair, to a class of 19 undergraduates at Queen's University taking a course in the history of psychology. The first syllable of each pair was then read out (in an order different from that of the presentation) and the subjects attempted to write down the second syllable from memory, being given a few seconds to do so. The percentage of syllables correctly recalled was 19.54 per cent. I then read out Köhler's list of words in the same way: the percentage of words recalled was 84.96 per cent. Nonsense syllable responses were indeed enormously more difficult to recall in a paired-associate task than were word responses, after one presentation.

Köhler actually offered two explanations for the difficulty of learning the nonsense syllables. First, he emphasized that nonsense syllable learning presented an extreme case far removed from the ordinary contingencies of real-life learning. In 1929 he explained that word-pairs are easier than nonsense syllable pairs because word pairs form well-organized units that nonsense syllables do not:

> When I read those words I can imagine, as a series of strange pictures, how a lump of sugar dissolves in a lake, how a boot rests on a plate, how a girl feeds a kangaroo, and so forth. If this happens during the reading of the series, I experience in imagination a number of well-organized, though quite unusual, wholes. It may be that learning is here so easy because a material of this kind readily lends itself to organization . . . if I am not mistaken, the combination and associations which are even more easily associated in everyday life are simply instances of entirely spontaneous organizations. (p. 157)

Most of the students in my classroom experiment reported using associations of this kind in learning the words, for example, one person said she memorized 'pencil-gasoline' by imagining herself using a large pencil as a hose for filling the gas (petrol) tank in a car. Nonsense syllable pairs do not possess this built-in tendency to be organized in terms of meaning and memorized in the form of images (all of the students in my class raised their hand when I asked if they had used visual imagery for remembering the word-pairs).

Second, nonsense syllable pairs, probably because they do not form a series of separate image-type Gestalten, have a certain homogeneity; they look and sound much the same, so that when the subject is asked to recall a particular one, given the first member of the pair, the answer does not emerge easily from a memory of a jumbled set of consonants and letters. This led Köhler to instigate research on how far the homogeneous or heterogeneous nature of a *list* could determine subsequent recall or recognition of individual members of the list, research that was carried out in a famous but as yet untranslated series of experiments by Hedwig von Restorff (1933).

She was born in Berlin on 14 December 1906, specialized in Greek and Latin at her Oberlyzeum (senior high school) at Berlin, and entered the University of Berlin in 1926, where she studied experimental psychology along with philosophy and natural sciences, eventually obtaining her PhD with Köhler in 1933. Her research, which was published under her sole authorship in the *Psychologische Forschung* in 1933 and in a paper by Köhler and von Restorff in 1937, will be described below. Also in 1933, however, the Nazis came to power and von Restorff found herself a 'stellvertretende Assistentin' for the next two years – this term possibly means a research assistant on half-pay; Köhler had already left the Institute. In the winter of 1935 she decided to study medicine, and after taking the required courses at Berlin, was licensed to practice medicine in 1939. She also wrote a second thesis, in 1940, concerned with changes in the blood following the administration of sulphanilamide derivatives. This thesis was prefaced by a short autobiography. In 1942 she married another doctor, Helmut Trendelenburg, who unfortunately went missing in action in East Prussia three years later. After the war she moved to Freiburg in southern Germany and practised medicine; she died on 6 July 1962. I am indebted for the above information to her cousin Professor Dr W. von Restorff (personal communication).

Her results were so striking that when Köhler's *Gestalt Psychology* was reprinted in 1947, he added a footnote stating that:

> The outcome of these studies (those of von Restorff and others) is perfectly clear: series of nonsense syllables constitute a difficult material to learn, not so much because the items have no meaning as because in such monotonous series sub-groups do not spontaneously form. (p. 161)

There are thus two complementary reasons why word-pairs are so much easier to learn than nonsense syllable pairs: each word-pair can easily be the subject of a vivid image, even though separate words may never have been seen as a pair before. The *list* thus contains, say, six clear demarcated organized wholes with a retrieval cue (the first member of a pair) sufficing to elicit the second word within each whole; whereas in the case of nonsense syllables, even though efforts are made to form meaningful associations, the whole list consists of only fragmentary units and the lack of organization within the list means that a presentation of the first syllable of a pair is insufficient to evoke the memory of a *particular* second syllable: it may arouse a confusing set of competing syllables or part-syllables. It is clear that there are two separate issues here, the question of how a unit in a list stands out from other members of the list in memory, and the question of meaningful organization as an important aspect of learning. We shall deal with Gestalt contributions to an answering of these two questions in this order, but note that a simple behaviouristic account of the advantages for learning words over nonsense syllables in terms of the degree of prior experience with these materials seems *prima facie* an *incomplete* account of the cognitive processes of learning; at a very deep level, prior experience with words could explain why images are easily formed and why nonsense syllables as individual units have to be memorized in a way that individual words do not; but a *description* of what subjects do during memorizing seems incomplete. Furthermore, the Gestalt psychologists claimed that only material that possessed some form of integral structure, or well-organized wholeness, could be retained without extensive effort; this was the way the human brain had evolved.

The importance of the heterogeneity of items in list learning

In a sense, this issue had already been broached in the research of Ranschburg (1905) who had shown that lists consisting of pairs like

ber-tof   kid-sem   bür-tif   kad-söm . . .

were much harder to memorize, and retrieve later, than lists consisting of pairs like

jum-dir   bel-fam   sük-voz   pec-tög . . .

The pairs in the former list were more confusable, or expressing it another way, the pairs were homogeneous and similar to each other. However von Restorff (1933), in discussing Ranschburg's work, argued that in Ranschburg's experiment the subjects might have understood how the homogeneous lists were constructed. Ranschburg also had the same subjects relearn the same lists in later experimental sessions, confusing interpretations of the results. However, von Restorff noted that Ranschburg had found that differences between the recall of the homogeneous lists and the heterogeneous lists were more striking after a retention interval longer than one minute. She therefore developed a new series of experiments, which in turn led to extensive discussion of how interference in retrieval in general might be related to the degree to which individual memories were 'isolated' from each other. In describing the sequence of events, I shall first present von Restorff's evidence for the isolation effect, then show how she tried to use the isolation effect to explain interference in memory (retroaction and proactive inhibition), and indicate how her arguments in this respect were expanded by a colleague, Ilse Müller.

Von Restorff's experiments employed G.E. Müller's method of hits. In one of her first experiments for example, she used eight pairs of items, but the kinds of item varied. With five kinds of material – nonsense syllables, nonsense figures, two-digit numbers, coloured rectangles, and individual letters of the alphabet – she composed lists in which there were four pairs of one kind of material and four pairs consisting of one each of the four remaining kinds of material. For example, a list might consist (in jumbled order) of four pairs of nonsense syllables and one pair each of figures, numbers, colours and letters. Another list would have four pairs of figures and one pair each of syllables, numbers, colours and letters. A total of five lists, in each of which the material for the set of four is different, means that each kind of material is tested on a total of eight occasions; on four of those occasions, the material was isolated from the other materials in the list, and on four of those occasions the material was all drawn from a single list. Von Restorff used the words *Isolierung* (isolation) and *Häufung* (literally 'heaping'; we shall translate it as 'crowding') for these two kinds of occasions. She carried out many experiments involving the variation of list length, the use of various retention intervals, and serial presentation versus seeing the whole list at once, but the result was always the same: the percentage of correct responses (correct recall of the second member of the pair given the first) was always higher for 'isolated' conditions than for 'crowded' conditions. This was found whether the results were scored *across* lists (e.g. memory for all the syllables or all the figures, adding across the lists used in any experiment) or *within* lists (e.g. in the first kind of list mentioned above, the percentage recalled of the four nonsense syllables was less than the percentage recalled of the other four kinds of material, each presented once, taken together). The size of the effect varied somewhat with the kind of material, being most marked for two-digit numbers and least marked for letters of the alphabet, but was always in the same direction. For example, analyzing the hits *within* lists and adding across 22 subjects in five experiments that differed in details that need not be enumerated, isolated numbers yielded 83 per cent correct recall as contrasted with crowded numbers which yielded 26 per cent correct recall, and 70 per cent of the isolated letters were correctly recalled as contrasted with 59 per cent of the crowded letters.

Among other results obtained in von Restorff's first series of studies, she found that when only three kinds of material were used (syllables, figures, and numbers), so that each list had six crowded items of one kind of material and two isolated items each of a different material, the isolation effect was exaggerated. Measuring *across* lists, the percentages recalled were: isolated syllables 85 per cent, crowded syllables 27 per cent; isolated figures 90 per cent, crowded figures 18 per cent; isolated two-digit numbers 85 per cent, crowded two-digit numbers 31 per cent. When the extreme cases were studied of lists of 20 pairs presented serially for 15 seconds each with a 10 minute retention interval in which the subjects were free to do as they wished, each list containing either 19 syllable pairs plus 1 number pair, or 19 number pairs plus 1 syllable pair, the percentages of hits were: isolated syllables 92 per cent, crowded syllables 41 per cent; isolated numbers 100 per cent, crowded numbers 39 per cent.

Another series of studies in the first section of von Restorff's paper showed that recognition tests yielded noticeable, but far less striking, isolation effects than had the recall tests (tests of statistical significance were not reported).

Von Restorff's paper had two more sections. In the second, she showed that if an isolated item C is in a list in which each other item is as different from C as it is from the rest of the other items, e.g.

A B C D E F G H I J K

the isolation effect is less marked than it is if C is in a list in which each other item is different from C but similar to all the other items, e.g.

$K_1 \; K_2 \; C_3 \; K_3 \; K_4 \; K_5 \; K_5 \; K_6 \; K_7 \; K_8 \; K_9$

It will be recalled from Chapter 2 that in perception, grouping by similarity is most effective if the similar items are not only different from all the other items in the visual field, but these other items are also similar to each other. Von Restorff gave a similar example applying to nonsense figures; a simple figure embedded in a heterogeneous set of nonsense figures stands out less than if it is embedded in a homogeneous set. In Figure 3.6, taken from von Restorff's paper, the third figure from the left in the top row of figures is identical to the third figure from the left in the bottom row, but the third figure stands out far more in the top series than in the bottom because of the homogeneous nature of the top row.

She therefore composed lists in which an isolated syllable was set in an array of nine two-digit numbers or in an array of nine different kinds of material (e.g. syllable, colour, letter, word, photograph, mathematical symbol, button, punctuation mark, name of a chemical compound). Each list was exposed serially just

Figure 3.6 Figures used to illustrate von Restorff's argument that how 'isolated' a figure is in a list depends on the homogeneity of the other items in the list. In the top row, the third figure stands out from the remainder of the list more than it does in the bottom row. (Source: from H. von Restorff (1933), *Psychologische Forschung*, **18**, p. 314 (bottom row) and p. 315 (top row).)

once (1.5 seconds per item) and the isolated item was always in the second or third serial position. After exposing the list, 10 minutes was spent learning meaningful text, followed by recall of as many items of the list as possible (note that von Restorff here is using what we now call 'free recall' and not the method of hits), followed by a final recall of the interpolated text. Both numbers and syllables served as the material to be isolated. Combining the results for these two kinds of material, recall of the isolated items in a list like the top row of Figure 3.6 when all the other items were similar to each other reached 70 per cent, whereas when the same items were in lists where all the other items were different from each other (as in the bottom row of Figure 3.6), recall was only 40 per cent. In the first of these, where the non-isolated items were similar to each other, the mean recall of those items only reached 22 per cent. This effect could be reduced if the subjects saw the original list three times.

In an interesting side comment, von Restorff noted that primacy effects (better recall of initial than middle items) and recency effects (better recall of final than middle items) might arise because both items have a 'free space' on one side, tending to isolate the item. She also speculated that isolation effects might become exaggerated over time; the forces that led a 'figure' to stand out from a 'ground' in perception might have parallels in the trace field, where an isolated item is less subject to field forces than is a memory object that is part of a homogeneous field. However, von Restorff resisted making many speculations of this kind.

The third section is theoretically the most striking because it made connection with previous work by G.E. Müller and also with contemporary work by American psychologists. Von Restorff believed that the isolation effect was intimately associated with retroactive inhibition and also with 'proactive inhibition', which G.E. Müller had discussed in principle. In 1933 von Restorff called the latter, in German, 'forward-acting inhibition' (*vorwärtswirkende Hemmung*); in 1936 Whitely and Blankenship called it in English 'proactive inhibition'. The relationship between the isolation effect and retroactive inhibition can be seen in microcosm from a discovery she made: if a list consisting of two syllable pairs, two figure pairs and five number pairs (in jumbled order) was learned over a sequence of four presentations and was then followed *either* by the learning of a new list of six syllable pairs and three number pairs *or* by the learning of a new list of six figure pairs and three number pairs, subsequent recall of the first list showed forgetting, presumably caused by the learning of the second list. But the forgetting was of a specific kind: 54 per cent of the syllables from the first list were recalled when the second list consisted mainly of syllables, but 90 per cent were recalled when the second list consisted mainly of figures. Correspondingly, 43 per cent of the figures from the first list were recalled when the second list consisted mainly of figures, but 69 per cent were recalled when the second list contained mainly syllables. Other studies showed similar patterns of forgetting, which was of course considerably reduced if there was no second-list learning in the retention interval.

Von Restorff argued that this was clear evidence for retroactive inhibition (forgetting of specific *material* from the first list primarily caused by some kind of interference associated with the learning of similar material in the second list) and suggested that retroactive inhibition might represent a special case of the isolation effect. By adding the material from the second list (say, syllables), the memories of the syllables in the first list lost distinctiveness. Adding the learning of syllables in the second list was tantamount thus to an accumulation of syllables in memory and a subsequent reduction in the degree to which the syllables in the first list were isolated in memory. By re-analyzing some of her data from the first section of the paper, she also showed how proactive inhibition could also be interpreted as a special case of the isolation effect. Both with respect to retroactive inhibition and to proactive inhibition, isolation effects are argued to extend not only to items *within* lists but to items accumulated across successive lists. Neither proactive inhibition nor retroactive inhibition could be demonstrated so easily for recognition as for recall, a fact whose correspondence with the earlier finding that the isolation effect was less marked in recognition than in recall suggests a common basis for all three phenomena, the isolation effect, retroactive inhibition and proactive inhibition. Von Restorff concluded her paper by speculating that in order to recall something, more precise information is needed in memory than is required in order to recognize something; a given trace that has faded over time might be adequate for recognition but not for recall.

Von Restorff's work was complemented in a thesis carried out at the University of Greifswald by Ilse Müller (1938); she was advised by both Köhler and von Restorff. Her paper appeared in the last issue of *Psychologische Forschung* before the Second World War and in it she made four important additions to von Restorff's findings.

1. She carried out an experiment deliberately designed to demonstrate proactive inhibition using the same experimental material that von Restorff had used to demonstrate retroactive inhibition. For example, she had subjects learn four lists each containing either three two-digit numbers and six figures or three numbers and six syllables. Eight minutes later subjects were given three trials to learn a target list consisting of three figures, three syllables, and five numbers. Then followed 20 minutes of listening to a scientific lecture, after which the students had to recall the target list. Several experiments gave the same result; in one of them, using a large sample of 55 subjects, if syllables had dominated the lists learned before the target list, recall of the syllables for the target list was 64 per cent, while recall of the figures was 90 per cent; whereas, using a sample of 76 subjects, if figures had dominated the list learned before the target list, recall of the figures was 59 per cent while recall of the syllables was 86 per cent.

2. Von Restorff had assumed that the isolation effect could be observed for material presented over quite long periods of time and not just in the time it

took to present, or learn, a single list with an isolated item. In an ingenious experiment, Ilse Müller presented a sequence of eight five-item lists, each to be recalled after one presentation, spaced at 10-minute intervals filled with other activities. In the following diagram of the eight lists, A refers to a two-digit number, B to nonsense syllables and C to nonsense figures.

List	1	2	3	4	5	6	7	8
Items	A	A	A	A	A	A	A	A
	B	B	C	B	C	B	B	B
	A	A	A	A	A	A	A	A
	A	A	A	A	A	A	A	A
	A	A	A	A	A	A	A	A

At the end of the experimental session (which had taken about 1 hour 15 minutes), subjects were asked to recall as many items as they could from the *whole* session. In the above design, using 20 subjects, where the two C-figures were more isolated across the session than were the six B-syllables, the subject recalled 95 per cent of the C-figures and 45 per cent of the B-syllables. If the materials were changed so that the C-items were syllables and the B-items were figures, 78 per cent of the C-syllables were correctly recalled and 58 per cent of the B-figures. This experiment gives a foundation for believing that arguments based on the isolation effect can apply to presentations of material that last for more than a few minutes.

3. The von Restorff effect was extended to the case where subjects carried out a series of *tasks* of different kinds and were then, at a later interval, asked to recall the tasks. The tasks could be arithmetical (e.g. calculate the square of 3475) or verbal (name six rivers beginning with D). Ilse Müller showed that if verbal tasks had been relatively isolated among arithmetic tasks, they were better recalled (98 per cent of the verbal tasks as opposed to 70 per cent of the arithmetic tasks), but the effect was not found if arithmetic tasks were isolated (85 per cent recalled), while the verbal tasks were crowded (86 per cent recalled). However the experiment was repeated with schoolgirls aged 13 and 14 years old using drawing tasks (e.g. draw a house) and grammatical tasks (e.g. write down four verbs); 89 per cent of the isolated tasks were recalled, but only 59 per cent of the accumulated tasks. The effect however disappeared if arithmetic tasks were isolated (61 per cent recalled), while grammatical tasks were accumulated (60 per cent recalled). Thus, with both adults and young adolescents it was difficult to obtain the isolation effect when the isolated tasks were arithmetical in nature, indicating that the nature of the task itself is a variable influencing performance in this kind of experiment.

4. In an experiment on retroactive inhibition, Ilse Müller suggested that when retroactive inhibition is found, it need not only be due to a damaging effect of the interpolated material on the trace of the original material.

Table 3.1 Percentage recalled of original lists.

	(a) Immediate	(b) After 10 min.	(c) After 22 min. (prior to recall)	Percentage decline from (a) to (c)
When the interpolated list had 6 figures, 2 numbers:				
Recall of 2 figures from original list	69	61	25	63.77
Recall of 2 syllables from original list	86	82	64	25.58
When the interpolated list had 6 syllables, 2 numbers:				
Recall of 2 syllables from original list	48	20	13	79.02
Recall of 2 figures from original list	90	75	20	22.22

These data are extracted from I. Müller (1938), Tables 12 and 13, *Psychologische Forschung*, **22**, pp. 200 and 201 respectively. They show that items in the original list that were relatively isolated (did not have similar items in the interpolated list) were proportionally less disrupted by retroactive inhibition from the interpolated list just prior to recall than were items that were not so isolated.

She showed that putting the interpolated material just before the recall of the original material was particularly effective in increasing retroactive inhibition. The original list had two syllables, two figures and five two-digit numbers; the interpolated material was either six figures and three numbers or six syllables and three numbers. The material was interpolated either immediately after learning, after 10 minutes, or after 22 minutes (immediately before recall of the original list). The gist of the results may be summarized as follows: recall of the two syllables and the two figures in the original list was much poorer if the interpolated list occurred just prior to recall as opposed to when it occurred earlier in the retention interval. The effect held *both* for figures that followed interference from lists containing mainly figures and for syllables following the same kind of interference. However the deficit was proportionally greater for crowded items than it was for isolated items (see Table 3.1).

She also carried out a subsequent study that established that the interference from an interpolated list learned just prior to recall was due to its temporal location *relative* to recall; an interpolated task after a retention interval of 12 minutes only had its effect on recall if recall followed immediately and was not delayed by another 12 minutes.

Ilse Müller concluded from this finding that a theory of retroactive inhibition could not be based on the notion of interference with traces alone. She argued there was an interference with the action of retrieval of the original material (*Reproduktionsstörung*) caused by the effect of interpolated learning just prior to the retrieval of the original material. This is a two-factor theory of retroactive inhibition: one factor concerns interference by the interpolated learning with the trace of the original learning (if G.E. Müller was correct, this kind of interference would be maximal shortly after learning of the original material); the other factor concerns the setting up of new traces by the interpolated learning which interfere with the retrieval of the original trace (this kind of interference should be maximal shortly before recall of the original material). However Ilse Müller's theory has had little impact on the subsequent literature on retroactive inhibition. One reason might simply be that it was not available in English, although Köhler (1940, pp. 110–117) gave it prominent mention. Another is that later studies have indicated that the importance of the timing of the interpolated material is still not understood because of inconsistencies in the data, as already noted. Osgood (1953) reviewed this issue, and concluded that

> Although both the point at which interpolated material is inserted and the lengths of the retention interval are shown to be important variables, exactly how they function is not clear. Unspecifiable variations among experiments in terms of both material and procedures are again responsible. . . Other factors, such as the similarity of original and interpolated materials used in different experiments are also confounded with the temporal factor. Until such procedural differences are ironed out, little conclusive evidence can be expected. (p. 537)

Since Osgood wrote this, not much work has been carried out on this issue, in part because the cognitive revolution abandoned traditional verbal learning studies for studies of encoding processes, short-term memory and retrieval processes.

But a third reason why Ilse Müller's two-factor theory was forgotten was because Melton and von Lackum (1941) produced an alternative two-factor theory in which G.E. Müller's notion of trace-damage was ignored. One factor determining retroactive inhibition was response competition, in which two traces, both of which were still retained, interfered with each other's being retrieved. This factor is similar to Ilse Müller's 'disturbance of retrieval'. But the second factor was what Melton and von Lackum called 'unlearning' of the original list during the activities of learning the interpolated list. They were led to this conclusion by an analysis of errors which showed that intrusions of memories of the interpolated material into the recall of the original list accounted for only a small proportion of the errors in the recall of that list. It is of considerable interest to note, however, that in late twentieth century work, there has been some scepticism about the value of the concept of 'unlearning', and Mensink and Raaijmakers (1988) prefer to replace 'unlearning' with more associational concepts in their theory of retroactive inhibition (see p. 122 below).

Nevertheless this series of studies by von Restorff and Ilse Müller deserves to be remembered because it raised new questions of interpretation of data obtained not only by the Gestalt psychologists but also by the American functionalists. Von Restorff's notion that retroactive inhibition is due to the accumulation of traces similar to the traces of the target material, rendering it less isolated, has in fact received some support in the later literature on retroactive inhibition. Ceraso (1967) interpreted some literature of the early 1960s on retroactive inhibition not only in terms of unlearning and of confusion at retrieval between items from the two lists, but also in terms of a 'crowding' between those items. He acknowledged Koffka's writings on memory, but did not specifically mention von Restorff. Postman and Underwood (1973), in their review of the classic literature on interference between memories, point out that many errors in experiments on retroactive inhibition are made because of a failure of list differentiation at the time of retrieving individual items: the subject cannot remember whether an item that comes to mind during attempted recall of the original material is actually from the original list or from the interpolated list. This literature is reviewed in more detail on p. 118–123.

But not all cases of retrieval involve deciding whether a given item is a member of one list or another. If we let x represent the trace set up by a stimulus X, then according to Köhler (1940, p. 117) retrieval of x can sometimes fail because a re-presentation of X can interact with traces of events laid down between the setting up of x and the re-presentation of X, as in the time-error. On other occasions it can fail because x forms part of a natural group of traces $x\,y\,z$ ... but the group does not stand out from the mass of other traces surrounding it, just as a group of elements in a perceptual display can be camouflaged. This brings us to the question of how memories are *organized* or grouped.

Before discussing this, however, it is appropriate to note that the von Restorff effect was replicated in a large number of laboratories in subsequent years. A review of this research was provided by Wallace (1965). He noted in his review that, prior to von Restorff's study, other researchers had demonstrated the importance of the 'vividness' of the material in determining retrieval: Calkins (1894) improved recall by varying the size or colour of items in a paired-associate paradigm; Jersild (1929) increased the recall of sentences by preceding them or following them with a emphatic statement; van Buskirk (1932) enhanced free recall by presenting isolated items in different sizes or colours from the remaining items. Wallace suggested that isolation indeed enhances recall of individual items, but it is probably at the expense of other items in the list, because lists having isolated items were not more easily learned in general than were lists not containing any isolated items (Newman and Saltz, 1958). The more isolated an item is, the more easily it will be learned: as the proportion recalled of isolated item decreases, the more isolated items there are in a list (Pillsbury and Raush, 1943). The von Restorff effect is more likely to be obtained when learning is intentional as opposed to incidental (Postman and Phillips, 1954).

The Gestalt theory that isolated items are better retained because of better figure-quality was questioned by some interference theorists, who argued that the homogeneous items in the list are more likely to be forgotten because of greater proactive and retroactive inhibition based on the similarity of the homogeneous items to each other. Some support for this view came from a discovery by Saul and Osgood (1950), who, using two isolated items in a list of 20 items in a free recall learning paradigm, found that only the first item showed a significant isolation effect and argued that this was because the first item was subject to much less proactive inhibition than the second. In an attempt to evaluate this argument, Ericksen (1963) prepared lists of nine paired-associates; four pairs had trigrams as stimuli and numbers as responses, four pairs had numbers as stimuli and trigrams as responses, and one pair (the isolated pair) consisted of two trigrams. These nine items were presented in random order. The amount of retroactive and proactive inhibition from similar material affecting this last pair was ostensibly equated in this design, yet there were still more correct responses to that pair as opposed to the mean number of responses given to the eight other pairs. Wallace (1965) argued that simple interference theory was therefore to be augmented by a theory asserting that isolated items excite extra 'mediating responses' which reduce the degree to which they are interfered with by traces from other items: they excite extra 'attention'. In none of these studies was it mentioned that von Restorff and Ilse Müller considered retroactive and proactive inhibition to be by-products of the isolation effect rather than the other way round.

The importance of organization in learning

Throughout Koffka's analysis of memory and learning in his *Principles of Gestalt Psychology*, it is stressed that the most salient difference between Gestalt theory and traditional theories such as associationism and behaviourism was that the latter theories did not say enough about the way the learner organized the material for retention purposes. They were content to stress the role of practice and frequency on the establishment of habits, but ignored the role played by the human subject both in *spontaneously* organizing the material and in deliberately *encoding* the to-be-remembered material in such a way that it was better retrieved later. Koffka (1935a, p. 549) explicitly blamed the traditionalists for underestimating the importance of organization in Gestalt theory, because they believed that, since organization in perception was asserted by Gestalt theorists to involve innate processes these innate processes might be being dragged into the discussion of how we memorize. While the Gestalt psychologists did suggest that the mechanism of recognition followed innate laws similar to those involved in perceptual grouping (see below), they also stressed the role of experience in the behaviour of the active subject who clearly applies his or her prior knowledge during the processes of organizing and encoding to-be-remembered material for subsequent recall.

Organization was at the heart of the learning experience for the Gestalt psychologists. They wrote a little about the active processes of organizing during learning, but they more particularly stressed that some materials were easier to learn because the material itself possessed a structure which made it easy for the learner to organize without effort. Koffka (1935a, pp. 557–558) pointed out that raw association cannot explain why a line of meaningful prose such as

A thing of beauty is a joy forever

is easier to learn than is a sequence of nonsense syllables such as

pud sol dap rus mik nom

If associationism based solely on a law of contiguity were at work, the first word 'a' in the sentence, which has been associated with thousands of other words in the subject's lifetime, should arouse many competing associations making it *more* difficult to learn the sentence, when obviously this is not true. The first sentence is easier to learn partly because the words are familiar, but also because it arouses a meaningful and unified constellation of ideas, whereas the string of nonsense syllables has no meaning – as Koffka says, 'it is, to use a German term, entirely *sachfremd*, i.e., external, adventitious, contingent' (p. 558). The sentence forms an organized whole because of its meaning; the string of nonsense syllables remains a string. As we noted earlier, Köhler (1929) had pointed out that pairs of random words are more easy to unite into organized wholes than are pairs of nonsense syllables, partly through the medium of imagery. Pairs such as 'lake-sugar' and 'pencil-gasoline' can be easily encoded into well organized, if bizarre, images.

To prove that a learned series is essentially an *organized* series, Koffka referred to some experiments by Witasek (1918). He had asked subjects to learn four sequences of lists of nonsense syllables with a rhythmic emphasis on the first member of each pair. Two such sequences were

$A'_1\ A_2\ A'_3\ A_4\ A'_5\ A_6\ A'_7\ A_8\ A'_9\ A_{10}$

and

$B'_1\ B_2\ B'_3\ B_4\ B'_5\ B_6\ B'_7\ B_8\ B'_9\ B_{10}$

and similarly for lists $C_1 \ldots C_{10}$ and $D_1 \ldots D_{10}$. Then the subjects had to learn new lists in which individual items from the four lists already learned were reassembled. For example, one such new list involved the sequence

(new pair) $D'_3\ D_4\ A'_5\ A_6\ B'_7\ B_8\ C'_9\ C_{10}$

again with the emphasis on the first item of each pair. Since learning this new list involved the assemblage of old *pairs* from the lists learned earlier, learning was not difficult. But a different new list (with y representing new syllables) could consist of:

$$y'A_3\ A_4'\ B_5\ B_6'\ C_7\ C_8'\ D_9\ D_{10}'y$$

Here learning was very difficult because, even though the list consisted mainly of previously learned syllables, the *pairing* of the syllables was new. For example, the well learned pair $B_5'\ B_6$ was now split up so that B_5 was now unaccented (following A_4') and B_6' was now accented (leading to C_7, now unaccented). Since this experiment examined serial learning, not paired-associates learning, it clearly indicates that if a list has been learned with a certain organization (in this case, paired articulation with a rhythmic emphasis on each first item), that learning will not easily transfer to a new list that contains the same syllables but with new pairings. For Koffka, these experiments suggested that 'a *learned* series is an *organized* series and therefore the traces must be organized too' (p. 566). Koffka also reviewed some experiments by Lewin (1922) which suggested that when a stimulus A, that has previously been contiguous with another stimulus B, is presented it will not necessarily arouse B; it will only arouse B if the pair AB had been stored as a unit. Lewin stressed in this paper that the subject must form a deliberate intention to learn a particular pair – there is a 'vector' from the subject towards learning the pair.

Koffka went on to develop the notion that the 'organization' of material to be learned does depend frequently on the subject's intentions, and we shall return to this issue shortly. But after Koffka's book had been published in 1935, both Köhler and von Restorff (1937) and Katona (1940) elaborated further on organizational processes in memory.

Köhler and von Restorff (1937) made an explicit connection between the Gestalt laws of organization in perception and the role of organization in memory. They reviewed the literature on theories of recognition, concluding with Semon, although they do not mention him, that what determines the arousal of a trace x by a stimulus X is the similarity of the X to x. They believed it is highly unlikely that X acts indirectly to arouse x by first arousing a trace w which is associated with the trace x, directly or via intermediary associations. Instead they believed that the arousal X is instantaneous and not mediated by associations through specific 'pathways'. It is something like a resonance, although Köhler and von Restorff were at pains to stress that it is improbable that a stimulus like the letter A would arouse a trace corresponding to the letter A that had somehow been planted in the brain before birth. Traces were laid down (after birth) according to how the stimuli they represented were perceived and the laws of perception include those of Gestalt organization. Just as in a visual display two elements may be grouped together because of similarity, so in memory a present stimulus X may be grouped together with a trace x because of similarity; in the former case we have a spatial field with a spatial interval or between-field (*Zwischenfeld*) separating the two elements. In the latter case we have a temporal field with a temporal interval separating X from the moment of laying down x. Traces can be thought of as sediments laid down by experience, layer upon layer, with the vertical dimension representing time. Köhler and von Restorff even remarked, engagingly, that the insight that led to this analogy came to them one day and was itself an example of pairwise organization, based on their noticing of a similarity between the spatial and temporal between-fields. Von Restorff's original study had examined interactions between traces. Köhler and von Restorff's study would examine the interaction between a particular event (such as X) and its excitation of a trace (such as x). In such a study it was important to demonstrate that, just as the organization of pairs in a visual field is spontaneous, so the evocation of x by X is also spontaneous. Hence Köhler and von Restorff explicitly chose tasks in which the subjects did not expect to have their memory abilities tested. The authors wished to avoid the setting up of Lewin-type vectors which could lead subjects to organize perceptual stimuli in ways which might even seem counter to spontaneous Gestalt organizations.

In their experiments they focused on the fact that the contents of the spatial between-field determine whether two elements will be paired by similarity in perception; for example, two circles are more difficult to pair if they appear in an array of curved shapes as opposed to an array of figures composed of straight lines. It ought to be the same with respect to the temporal between-field: if a stimulus such as X is to arouse a recognition response based on a trace x, it should do so more easily if the temporal interval is filled with events dissimilar to x as opposed to similar. In their first experiment, they exposed a five-letter nonsense syllable such as BROSK for 3 seconds to two groups of subjects; BROSK was clearly readable, but the subjects were not led to expect to see it again. Then the 'unfavourable' group (20 subjects) were shown 7 similar nonsense syllables (e.g. GLUMT, FRESP) five times each in succession at exposures of 0.25 seconds. At these exposure durations, the syllables were very difficult to read; on only 5 per cent of trials were they written down correctly on the first exposure, though by the fifth exposure they were correctly written down 56 per cent of the time. Then BROSK was re-presented for 0.25 seconds. It was correctly identified on 30 per cent of the trials at the first exposure and on 92 per cent by the fifth exposure. Clearly BROSK was identified better than the other words, presumably because of a recognition act connected with the trace of BROSK that had been laid down 15 minutes earlier. Nowadays, some might say that the first exposure of BROSK had 'primed' the subject's nervous system so that identification of BROSK on its second exposure was facilitated. However the real point of the experiment was that in the other group of 20 subjects, the 'favourable' group, BROSK was correctly identified on 75 per cent of the trials on its first exposure. The difference between the two groups was that the 'favourable' group had seen, and drawn, a sequence of nonsense figures shown on a screen during the 15-minute interval following the first presentation (for 3 seconds) of BROSK.

This experiment seems to show that filling the retention interval with material similar to the X that had led to the trace x reduces the probability that x will be 'recognized' given a re-presentation of X. However it could also be claimed that the intervening syllables shown to the 'unfavourable' group damaged the trace of x more than did the nonsense figures presented to the 'favourable' group because the syllables were more similar to BROSK than were the nonsense figures. Retroactive inhibition due to trace damage (or possibly response competition) may have been greater in the former case. To get round this objection, Köhler and von Restorff devised an experiment which was essentially of the form:

	Original presentation	*Interpolated material*	*Test phase*
Group 1	$x \rightarrow y$	items moderately similar to x	An item very similar to x: will it lead to y?
Group 2	$x \rightarrow y$	items dissimilar to x	An item very similar to x: will it lead to y?

Here the task studied was memory for how to solve a problem. An arithmetic task which could be solved using a shortcut was presented:

$$21\,[(91/7) + 6] + 14$$

The expression in square brackets comes to 19, so the subject has to multiply 21 by 19; 21 is $(20 + 1)$ and 19 is $(20 - 1)$. From the rule that

$$(a + b)\,(a - b) = a^2 - b^2$$

we can evaluate

$$20^2 - 1^2 = 400 - 1 = 399$$

more easily in our heads than we can calculate 21×19 using conventional multiplication. Here the first term of the calculation, $21[(91/7) + 6]$, represents x and the shortcut represents y.

The 'unfavourable' group (34 subjects) were instructed in this trick by the experimenter for the example shown above; then they carried out a series of arithmetic tasks for 10–15 minutes, none of which could be solved using the shortcut; then they were given

$$(15 + 64 - 47) \times 28 + (-20 + 34)$$

The first expression of this equation is like x in format: the value of the number in the first bracket comes to 32, so the subjects have to multiply 32×28 and can apply the shortcut knowing that $32 = 30 + 2$ and $28 = 30 - 2$. But only

26 per cent of the subjects did so. On the other hand, of 37 subjects in the favourable group who were taught the shortcut, and who then solved puzzles with matchsticks for ten minutes, 73 per cent used the shortcut when given the arithmetic task that included an initial term like x. In an experiment reported much later in the paper (p. 102), Köhler and von Restorff also explored a condition where the tasks following the teaching of the shortcut were hetero-geneous, including naming cities, building from modelling clay, and a jigsaw puzzle. It turned out that 51 per cent of subjects used the shortcut when the appropriate task appeared.

A similar kind of experiment was carried out by a PhD student, Hellmut Bartel (1938), which gave similar results. Here the shortcut involved using a tool to aid in the construction of squares from assorted objects like nuts, bolts, and screws. The 'unfavourable' group made various shapes, such as triangles, in the temporal interval that did not need the shortcut while the 'favourable' group carried out arithmetic tasks.

It was argued that retroactive inhibition by trace-damage or response competition from the intervening calculations may have affected memory for expressions like x, but not of the shortcut y. The fact that y was used by the 'favourable' group and, to a lesser extent by the 'unfavourable' group, on the test item argues in support of the view that the between-field influenced its usage. But it still might be objected that, in the case of the 'unfavourable' group, the arithmetic tasks involved other strategies which might have led to retroactive inhibition, probably by unlearning of the shortcut. This objection could not be raised to the next experiment which essentially showed that recognition of x, given X in a *new* context, was more impaired in a group with an unfavourable between-field than it was in a group with a favourable between-field; but subsequent recognition of x, given X in the *same* context, was not. Had the trace been damaged by similar events intervening between original learning and retrieval, this latter result would not have been expected.

The design was as follows. As the *original* material, twelve complicated nonsense figures incorporating thick black lines were presented sequentially (examples of these materials in the experiment are shown in Figure 3.7(a)). The sixth item would subsequently be tested for recognition but the subjects were given no hint that any of the items were to be memorized or re-presented later.

Then the 'unfavourable' group saw nine less complicated smaller nonsense figures, each in a different colour (examples are shown in Figure 3.7(b)). The tenth figure was the sixth item from the original list but now in a much smaller size and in green. The 'favourable' group saw a visual display including nonsense words, arrangements of numbers, and other patterns, all quite complex; the tenth stimulus was, again, the sixth item from the original list, much smaller and in green. Both groups had to make verbal reports, of any kind they liked, about these ten items. Of the 20 subjects in the 'unfavourable' group, 15 per cent *spontaneously* reported recognizing the tenth item (at least one not being sure where he had seen it before); of the 20 subjects in the 'favourable' group, 75 per

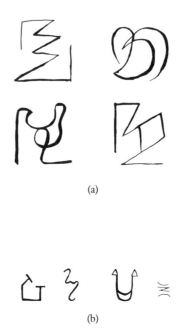

(a)

(b)

Figure 3.7 Twelve figures like those in (a) were presented, and one of these would subsequently be re-presented for recognition. In the retention interval, some subjects saw smaller coloured figures, like those in (b), and others saw verbal material. Interference with the recognition of a small coloured version of the target shape from (a) was greater when the figures of (b) filled the retention interval than when verbal material filled it. (Source: reprinted from W. Köhler and H. von Restorff (1937), *Psychologische Forschung*, **21**, pp. 87–88.)

cent *spontaneously* reported recognizing the tenth item. This, then, is another demonstration of the importance of the task filling the between-field in determining recognition. But, after this part of the experiment was completed, the original twelve black figures were re-presented with express instructions to subjects to report on whether or not they recognized each one; the percentages recognized of *all* the twelve items were 61 per cent for the 'unfavourable' group and 57 per cent for the 'favourable' group; as for the sixth item alone, it was recognized 35 per cent of the time by the 'unfavourable' group and 38 per cent of the time for the 'favourable' group. Clearly this result is difficult to explain on the grounds of trace-damage resulting from the intervening activity. Recognition of the original twelve figures, in the same *context* as that in which they had originally been seen was not affected differentially by the contents of the between-fields in *this* experiment. The contents of the between-fields affected recognition of a stimulus only when it was in a new context, the context of the between-field. Items in the between-field similar to the original items apparently caused *x* (the trace of the sixth item) to be aroused only rarely by *X* (the shape of the sixth item in a different colour). That this was not *only* due to recognition failure caused by a change in size or colour was shown by the fact that the sixth item was recognized by 75 per cent of the subjects in the favourable group even when it was of a different size and colour, but had been preceded by items in the between-field radically different from the black sixth figure in the original list.

However in a subsequent series of experiments, Köhler and von Restorff, instead of presenting the tenth figure as a much smaller, green version of the large black sixth original item, presented it in black, three-quarters of its original size. With the 'unfavourable' interpolated list, recognition of the small green figure had been 15 per cent; when it was black, recognition was raised to 35 per cent. With the 'favourable' interpolated group, recognition of the small green figure had been 75 per cent; when it was black it was 80 per cent. These results were found even though a disrupting task (drawing a house) had been interpolated between the original series of twelve figures and the interpolated series of ten stimuli. Clearly recognition of the small green figure was poorer than that of a larger black figure *both* because of the change in the colour and size of the figure itself (a relatively minor effect) and because of a change in the context and intent to recognize (a major effect).

For Köhler and von Restorff, the lesson to be drawn from this series of studies was that spontaneous recognition of an *X*-stimulus as having contents identical to those of an *x*-trace depended on the contents of the between-field, that is, it depended on the *context* in which *X* was presented. Recognition failure could occur because the context surrounding the original *x*-trace was not reinstated during presentation of the *X*-stimulus. Here it is important to distinguish between the spatial context and the temporal context. There is some modern research demonstrating how a reinstatement of the spatial context of *x* facilitates its being recognized when *X* is presented (e.g. Thomson *et al.*, 1982), but there is relatively little research as to the importance of the temporal context. This modern work will be discussed more extensively in Chapter 4. For the moment we note that in this research not merely do we have stated clearly the analogy between the Gestalt laws of grouping in perception and the laws determining whether a stimulus *X* will be 'grouped' with a trace *x*, we also have clear demonstrations of the pronounced effect of the temporal context on the occurrence of spontaneous recognition.

In Köhler and von Restorff's study, they deliberately tried to prevent subjects from using organizing strategies during their perception of the original material. However George Katona (1901–1981) was also interested in the use of deliberate strategies in memorizing, and his book *Organizing and Memorizing* (1940) represents one of the later contributions by Gestalt psychologists to the study of human memory.

Katona had worked with G.E. Müller before he emigrated to the United States in 1933, taught at the New School from 1938 to 1942, then taught both psychology and economics at the University of Michigan from 1946–1972. In

Chapter 1, we noted how Newell and Simon (1972) mentioned his book as having been almost 'lost during the distractions of the war'.

Katona's book dealt chiefly with two kinds of learning, learning by understanding and learning by memorizing. Learning by understanding involves the subject's learning a principle which will help to solve tasks of a certain kind, for example, matchsticks problems. Because this kind of learning is most important for tasks involving reasoning and problem-solving, we shall revisit this topic later in Chapter 5. But learning by memorizing is part and parcel of the learning by heart of lists of syllables and numbers and it was in this context that Katona brought out the importance of deliberate organization by the subject. First, he reviewed earlier work; as mentioned at the beginning of this chapter, it was G.E. Müller and Schumann (1893) who first studied the importance of rhythmizing during the memorization of nonsense syllables. But the best demonstration of the importance of rhythmic articulation had been those of Witasek (1918), as Koffka had emphasized. According to Katona (1940, p. 168), G.E. Müller, in various publications, had laid down four rules about grouping:

Rule 1. Between members of the same group there is a stronger association than between members of different groups.

Rule 2. Part of a group has the tendency to reproduce the entire group.

Rule 3. Groups have their own associations, which may be different from the associations of their members.

Rule 4. Grouping facilitates learning.

In Appendix 3 to his book, Katona reviewed earlier evidence supporting each of these views. For Rule 1, the evidence from G.E. Müller and Schumann's paper, and many others, indicated that if a list contains syllables

$a' \, b/c' \, d/e' \, f//g' \, h$

then if, say, c is presented by the experimenter, the subject can easily recall d; but if d is presented, the subject may not so easily recall e because the latter is in a different group. (The ease with which d will yield e as a response will in part depend on whether the instructions were to learn the list as a serial list or as a set of paired associates.) Evidence for Rule 2 came from studies by G.E. Müller concerning groups of three items that read as follows:

$abc'/def'/ghi' \ldots$

Then if c' or f' or i' is given, the preferred responses are a, d, and g respectively, or, even more likely, ab, de, and gh. Rule 3 is supported by the well-known fact that not only do groups have associations between their members of the group but also associations of their own, notably with respect to their serial position in a list. If a list of groups is learned, the first and last groups are generally easier to localize in the list, and if a list consisting of a series of groups has been learned in a forward direction, it is extremely difficult to recite backwards, particularly if the groups are large. Rule 4 was supported by evidence that subjects instructed to group will generally learn a list faster than subjects not so instructed. Yet Katona points out that some American studies of memorizing paid relatively little attention to grouping and that in his mathematical model of human learning, Hull (1935; see also Hull *et al.*, 1940) assumed that the associative bonds joining adjacent syllables in a list were all of equal strength.

Katona concluded his review by reference to experiments by Frings (1914), which had also been referred to by Köhler (1929, p. 173). If a pair *ab* has been learned, it is known that it is more difficult to learn than a new pair *ac* than a neutral pair (e.g. *dc*). But if we have learned a group (*ac*)*d*, it is *not* more difficult to learn a new group such as (*bc*)*e* than it is to learn a new group (*fg*)*e*. Here the syllable *c* forms part of a pair *ac* or *bc* and its role, so to speak, is subjugated to the influence of the first letter.

Katona then exemplified the importance of group membership by the following experiment. On the first day twelve pairs of nonsense syllables were learned by six subjects. The syllable pairs may be represented as

$$A_1 B_1, A_2 B_2, \ldots . A_{12} B_{12}$$

The next day the subjects learned twelve syllables but this time paired with two-digit numbers. The twelve syllables consisted of six new syllables and six 'old' B syllables

$$B_3, B_5, B_7, B_8, B_{10} \text{ and } B_{11}$$

Two days later they were presented with six more new syllables and six 'old' syllables

$$A_3, A_5, A_7, A_8, A_{10} \text{ and } A_{11}$$

But all they had to do was 'give any number between ten and ninety-nine' which came to mind when they saw these new syllables and the six A syllables. Out of 36 trials (six subjects times six A-syllables), only four yielded the number that had been learned two days earlier along with the corresponding B-syllable. That is, if a subject had learned (A_3 B_3) on the first day and (B_3 79) on the second day, they tended *not* to respond '79' when presented with A_3 on the final day of the experiment. (A_3 B_3) was one group, (B_3 79) another. No connection was made, although it was noted that many of the numbers given were numbers that had been seen two days earlier. However these were generally given to the 'wrong' syllables. Katona pointed out that if two pairs with a common element are learned in such a way that they *can* be put together as a group, then mediated associations can follow. For example, having learned the pairs

> Capital of New York State – Albany
> Albany – on the Hudson River

a subject *will* put the first and third terms together and cognize that the capital of New York State is on the Hudson River.

Katona described another experiment of his own. He showed that if subjects had to learn sequences of 24 numbers such as

> 2 9 3 3 3 6 4 0 4 3 4 7
>
> 5 8 1 2 1 5 1 9 2 2 2 6

the percentage of subjects who memorized the list in groups of three (293, 336, etc.) who recalled the list correctly after 30 minutes was 33 per cent, and after three weeks it was 0 per cent. But another group were told the numbers followed a principle, which they were urged to find before memorizing it. (The principle for the list of twelve numbers is: $29 + 4 = 33$; $33 + 3 = 36$; $36 + 4 = 40$; $40 + 3 = 43$, and so on; the same holds for the second twelve.) After 30 minutes, 38 per cent of the subjects recalled the list correctly, but, in contrast to the first group, 23 per cent recalled it after three weeks. Presenting the same list of numbers but disguised as economic figures (e.g. the first twelve were said to be 'US Government expenditures' of $2,933,364,043.47), yielded the poorest recall (20 per cent of subjects recalled it correctly after 30 minutes and 0 per cent after three weeks). This of course shows how 'retrieval' can be made into a kind of re-construction if a principle can be found in organizing the material. Katona therefore distinguished between learning by *understanding* and learning by *memorizing*; the latter was only used as a last resort when straightforward learning by understanding was not possible.

Between 1940 and 1970 classical interference theory, based on the idea that interfering associations (both proactive and retroactive) could account for forgetting in long-term memory, dominated research on verbal learning in the Anglo-American world. Relatively little work in this milieu was carried out on 'organization' as Katona and the Gestalt psychologists had described it. The beginning of the late twentieth century research on 'organization' was possibly the demonstration by Tulving (1962) that in learning a list of words that have to be recalled in any order (free recall learning), subjects settle into a pattern where, on successive learning trials, the words tend to be reported in a regular order. The order itself varies from subject to subject, so Tulving called this phenomenon 'subjective organization'. A revival of research on organization as the Gestalt psychologists understood it then began in earnest and this research will be reviewed in the following chapter.

This revival of the word 'organization' caused some misgivings among interference theorists and a particularly important article on the meanings of 'interference' and 'organization' was written by Postman (1971). He claimed that 'the concepts of association and organization appear to stand in apparent opposition to each other. These concepts have their origins in different theoretical traditions and are characteristically anchored to different experimental operations. The classical paradigm for the analysis of associative processes has been, as the very name implies, the paired-associate task . . . The primary vehicle for the examination of organizational processes has been the free recall experiment' (p. 290).

Postman showed that, after a subjective organization of a list of words has been achieved following a sequence of free recall learning trials, learning of a new list of paired-associates using the same words in new combinations was hindered as compared with the case where the list of paired-associates used completely new words. He therefore maintained that there was a continuity between association and organization; a rapprochement is possible according to which a so-called organized series is in fact a series in which particular associations are learned that are very much under the control of the subject as opposed to the experimenter. But once these associations are established they can cause interference with new learning just as much as can associations learned in a previous paired-associate task involving elements in common with the new learning. So at least one prominent exponent of interference theory sought to integrate organizational theory into that tradition.

Systems of traces, including Koffka's Ego-system

The work by von Restorff on isolation and crowding and the work of various investigators on organization in memory indicate, that, if the word 'trace' is to be used at all, it is rarely used to refer to a *single* trace. Whether or not a trace is activated will depend on its relationship to other traces; 'crowded' traces would form homogeneous systems from which it would be difficult to single out any particular trace for activation, and the existence of grouping would imply that if one trace in a group is activated, other traces in the same group will be activated immediately and spontaneously. The most extensive treatment of *systems* of traces is found in Koffka's four chapters on memory and learning in his *Principles of Gestalt Psychology*.

The first of these chapters was mainly a theoretical discussion of the nature of trace *theory*; for example, Perkins (1932) had argued that a memory theory could do without 'traces' provided that a given situation, if it re-occurred, gave rise to similar responses. Koffka condemned this view and also criticized theories of the trace that focused on single traces and did not recognize that traces interacted. The second chapter included discussion of most of the experiments mentioned in the present chapter, but finished with an analysis of theories of trace systems which is important because it allows certain phenomena of memory to be integrated into a broader Gestalt theory. In particular, Koffka argued that there was a large system of traces that could be given the name Ego-system and that this consisted in turn of many subsystems of traces.

Koffka had been driven to bring in the notion of an Ego by evidence that one's sense of one's own identity was more fragile than we would like to believe and by evidence from studies of eye movements that the direction of eye movements was not merely under the control of the environment (as when a sudden movement leads to an involuntary eye movement in the direction of the movement) but also under the control of the person:

> it happens that we feel our eyes riveted to a certain object, that we cannot avert them and that when, with great power of will, we have looked elsewhere, we found an almost irresistible compulsion to turn our eyes back to this fascinating object . . . in these cases, the eyes are not merely indifferent receptor organs which work for us without telling us of their work; in such cases the eyes are very definitely part of our Ego, and not only the eyes, our whole Ego is in such cases pulled in the direction of the attracting object. (p. 318)

I recently had the alarming experience of driving at night in a lane almost adjacent to *two* lanes of oncoming traffic. I felt, not only my eyes, but also my whole being attracted to stare at the sea of lights coming at me and was constrained, heart thumping, to switch to another lane further away from the oncoming traffic. That Koffka uses the word 'Ego' in this rather specific sense of feeling one's whole being as a unity is illustrated by his other example. In 1893 an Austrian teacher, E.G. Lammer, had single-handedly made a first ascent in the Alps, but on the way down had fallen through a collapsing snowbridge into a chasm, hitting the side walls of the crevasse several times and losing consciousness. His awakening he described as follows:

> . . . fog . . . darkness . . . fog . . . whirling . . . grey veil with a small lighter spot . . . fog . . . faint dawn . . . a soft humming . . . dull discomfort . . . fog . . . something has happened to somebody . . . gloomy fog, and always that lighter point . . . a shivering shudder . . . something clammy . . . fog . . . how was it? . . . an effort at thinking . . . ah, still fog; but besides that light point there outside, there emerges a second point inside: right, that is *I*! . . . fog, dull ringing sound, fog . . . a dream? . . . Yes, indeed, a wild, wild, wild dream! – It has dreamed – no, rather *I* have dreamed . . . (pp. 323–324).

The arousal of the Ego-system of traces in this case seems to have been secondary to an initial arousal of consciousness in which a spot of light was visible (this was real, caused by light coming from a hole in a snowbridge halfway down the crevasse which Lammer's falling body had opened).

Koffka's 'Ego-system' was not an irreducible entity; he believed that it contained a sub-system that could be given the name 'self', which was a set of traces representing one's own abstract concept of one's own personality: one's self-esteem or self-ideal are aspects of this mental concept of one's being. A similar state of affairs seems to be arising in contemporary psychoanalysis, where the word 'self' is being used to represent the mental image or concept one has of one's own being. This contrasts with Freud's use of the word 'Ego' which refers to a subset of traces representing solutions to the problems raised by the demands of the id and of the superego (on the changing uses of the words 'self' and 'Ego' in contemporary psychoanalysis, see Meissner, 1978, p. 728).

Koffka's Ego-system also included a subsystem concerned with the carrying out of actions, a system he called the 'executive'. However, actions would not be performed without some sort of intention or what Koffka called 'stress', Lewin called a 'tension' or 'vector', and Köhler (1938) later called 'requiredness'. Stresses or tensions can be between sense data, such as that set up when a subject sees a sensory display, where the tension is relieved by an organization of this display by the usual Gestalt rules, or involve simple movements as when the display has peripheral elements that attract attention causing an eye movement to be carried out by the executive (even accommodation, fixation and convergence on a display are the result of executive actions), or involve a complex sequence of movements, as when I intend to write a letter and follow through a sequence of actions till the letter is written. A particularly striking kind of stress is set up when something that I see, such as a snake, might initiate a fear-response and a desire for flight – here the stress is set up between the Ego and an external object, the snake, a stress that will disappear when the snake is removed from my vicinity.

We now turn to the implications of these ideas for Koffka's theory of memory. We note immediately that Koffka sought for some other term that might replace the term 'trace system' and he found it in the word 'schema'. The word 'schema' had been introduced by Sir Henry Head in his *Studies in Neurology* (1920) to refer to the fact that, over a lifetime, traces are set up by individual movements of parts of the body, but these traces combine to form a system or 'schema' which can be used by the subject to control his movements better and, concomitantly, interpret sensations from those body-parts. Once a postural schema has been established, it serves as a standard

> against which all subsequent changes of posture are measured before they enter consciousness . . . By means of perpetual alterations in position we are always building up a model of ourselves which constantly changes. (Head, 1920, Vol. II, p. 605)

For Koffka, the postural schema represented a closely integrated system of memory traces, but even a melody, according to him, is a miniature schema because each new note of the melody is integrated into the framework provided by the preceding notes, just as a new movement is integrated into the framework provided by the 'model of ourselves'. In particular, Koffka's Ego-system is a schema which is, to a degree determined by the organism and by experience, separate from all the traces set up by the environmental field. Within the Ego-system subsystems of traces will be held together by the fact that underlying them are common interests, attitudes and appetites.

Readers familiar with the word 'schema', as used by Sir Frederic Bartlett

(1932), will see a strong resemblance between Koffka's use of the word 'schema' and Bartlett's use, but they are applied to psychology as a whole somewhat differently by the two authors. Like Koffka, Bartlett took over Head's invented word and used it in a broad way to refer to constellations of integrated traces united by common interests, instincts, and appetites. But Bartlett was vaguer than was Koffka about how 'traces' related to 'schemata', showing a dislike of the use of the word 'trace' in general, and it was unclear whether he shared Koffka's conviction that a special schema should be conceptually separated from others as constituting an Ego-schema. Koffka therefore *applies* the word 'schema' in psychology in a precise manner and in Koffka's system there is even a place for discussions of personality differences and of the cognitive aspects of mental illness, topics that Bartlett barely touched on in his book on *Remembering*. However, Bartlett and Koffka certainly agreed that experiments on nonsense syllable learning were inadequate if the scientific study of memory were to advance. Bartlett's research on the repeated reproduction of pictures amply confirmed the notion that memory for visual stimuli depends in part on how they were encoded at the time of perception and his research on stories clearly illustrated that memory for word sequences is rarely verbatim. Instead a story is organized into a beginning, a middle and an end connected by a strong thread of meaning and this organized schema determines how stories will be recalled on future occasions, as well as the types of errors made.

Koffka believed that two series of experiments illustrated how memory traces could be kept activated if there were tensions in the Ego that demanded it. First, he emphasized some evidence by Aall (1913) showing that how well a learned list will be recalled at a later date depends in part on the subject's intentions at the time of learning. If the subject thinks he will be tested on the material the next day, he will memorize it in a way different from that associated with memorization for retrieval weeks later. Presumably some sort of tension (sporadic rehearsal?) will keep the memory alive for the longer period. If the tension is relieved (as in the case of subjects who expected a test the following day and were then told the test would not be given) the learned material was not further rehearsed, leading to poor recall when there was a surprise memory test weeks later. The other kind of experiment that Koffka believed supported the notion of Ego-involvement in the maintenance of traces concerned what has become known as the Zeigarnik effect. Bluma Zeigarnik was a student of Lewin's at Berlin, and her research was designed within the Lewinian framework according to which *all* memory phenomena were considered to be a product not merely of the availability of a stored trace or trace system but also of an 'energizing' force at the time of retrieval. All retrieval attempts represented states of tension relieved when the sought for item was found. These tensions, which do not have the same impact on the subject as genuine needs such as hunger, nevertheless had enough importance or salience for the subject to deserve the name 'quasi-needs' (Lewin, 1926).

In a long paper in the *Psychologische Forschung* for 1927 (summarized by Ellis,

1938), Zeigarnik described how she gave 18 to 22 small tasks to various groups of students, both adult and children. The tasks could be manual (making clay figures, constructing a box of cardboard, etc.) or verbal (mental arithmetic, word puzzles, etc.). Each task usually took 3 to 5 minutes to complete. However, the experimenter watched each subject closely for half the tasks and, at the time the subject appeared most engrossed in the task, the experimenter interrupted him or her. On half the experimental sessions, a particular set of tasks (A) was interrupted, and another set (B) was not interrupted; on the other half of the sessions, using different subjects, the B-set was interrupted and the A-set was not interrupted. No mention was made to the subjects whether the task could be completed later. At the end of all the tasks, the table was cleared of all the materials used in the work, and then the experimenter said, 'Please tell me what the tasks were upon which you worked during this experiment'. The finding from the first experiments, carried out with the experimenter working one-to-one with a sample of 32 subjects (students, teachers and children), was that interrupted tasks were recalled 90 per cent more often than were uninterrupted. In a second experiment using new tasks and 15 new subjects, interrupted tasks were recalled 100 per cent more often than noninterrupted. Using a group testing technique (18 tasks) with 47 adults, interrupted tasks were recalled 90 per cent better than were noninterrupted, and with teenagers with an average age of 14, interrupted tasks were recalled 110 per cent better than were uninterrupted. In this group test, the class was interrupted when it seemed that about half the class had completed a given task.

Unfortunately, Zeigarnik's results have not always been confirmed, as van Bergen (1968) has indicated in a rather scathing review of experiments on task interruption.

On the other hand, Koffka's notion that Ego-involvement may play a part in determining whether the Zeigarnik effect is obtained is supported by the following study. Dutta and Kanungo (1967) hypothesized that where instructions were Ego-oriented, subjects would better remember pleasant experiences associated with the tasks (i.e., completed tasks), whereas when the instructions were task-oriented, subjects would better remember unpleasant experiences (i.e., incomplete tasks). Sixty graduate students and research workers from Calcutta saw 20 puzzle pictures and had to name an object that was 'camouflaged' in the picture. They were told that their answers were either correct or wrong, but when they were wrong they were not given the correct answer. They also rated each task on a pleasantness-unpleasantness scale. The instructions for the Ego-oriented subjects stressed that their results would be compared with those of other subjects. The instructions for the task-oriented subjects implied that they were cooperating in a study designed to select good questions for a future intelligence test. Ego-oriented subjects remembered complete tasks better than incomplete, and task-oriented subjects remembered incomplete tasks better than complete, on tests both of recognition and recall. The probability of correct responses on the memory task was correlated with the intensity of feeling as measured by the pleasantness-unpleasantness scale. When there is a tension, therefore, items associated with the tension might carry feeling tones which serve as retrieval cues at the time of recall.

Interestingly, Sylvia H. MacColl of Duke University had already noticed in the 1930s that if Ego-involvement in Koffka's sense were determining how well tasks were recalled, tasks that had achieved stability within the Ego-system, that is, completed tasks, should be better recalled than incomplete tasks. In Lewin's system, on the other hand, which Zeigarnik explicitly set out to test, the incomplete tasks were associated with a 'tension' that made them accessible to recall at a later time. The discovery of this apparent conflict between the beliefs of Koffka and Lewin led MacColl (1939) to write a full-length dissertation comparing the two systems. Her discussion often involves very general concepts such as Lewin's 'Life Space' and Koffka's various 'fields', but it points out that Lewinian tensions may be useful concepts that are not properly integrated into Koffka's system, whereas Koffka's concept of trace stability is not part of Lewin's system. I suspect that this kind of theorizing may not have fitted well into the neo-behaviourist ambience of North America in 1940. The model of Hull *et al.* (1940) of serial learning, which seemed on the surface so much more testable, would probably have had more appeal to memory theorists of this time.

There is another body of literature in the 1950s that was influenced by Gestalt ideas and which it is appropriate to mention at this point because it was devoted to demonstrating that personal or 'Ego' needs and expectations influence 'cognition'. Under 'cognition' were subsumed tasks such as 'stimulus identification' and 'stimulus interpretation'. This literature has been reviewed by one of Köhler's students, Mary Henle (1955). It included evidence that purported to show that the identification of tachistoscopically presented words like 'succeed' was faster if the subject had recently had experiences of success (Postman and Brown, 1952). The identification of briefly exposed photographs of food became more efficient, the hungrier the subject was (Lazarus *et al.*, 1953) and the identification of need-related words was better when subjects were hungry or thirsty than when they had recently eaten or drunk (Wispé and Drambarean, 1953). Clearly trace activation is involved in these tasks and the Ego-state appears to have influenced what associations were activated by the ambiguously presented stimuli. Henle (1955) and Wallach (1949) both discussed the implications of these findings, and many others along the same line, for our understanding of cognition. Wallach insisted that a question that needed to be answered was how far Gestalt organizational processes had to act on the sensory processes aroused by a stimulus before that stimulus would activate memory traces; while Henle suggested that

> needs and attitudes may act by pointing or sensitizing, organizing and reorganizing, selecting, supplying context, arousing relevant memory traces, arousing expectations, discouraging the desire to understand, observing differences, disturbing the recognition process, altering the physiognomic aspects of experience, and animating the enlivening

aspects of experience. In addition, strength of motivation may influence performance on perceptual or other cognitive tasks without producing actual cognitive change. (Henle, 1955, pp. 183–185)

In this book we shall not pursue this literature further. It should be noted that although some of the persons contributing to that literature were oriented towards Gestalt psychology, others were not. For example, Postman and Brown's paper is couched in terms of neo-behaviourist learning theory rather than in terms of Gestalt psychology.

Chapter 4

How late twentieth century memory theory has elaborated on Gestalt memory theory

Short-term memory: interactions between traces

There is an important sense in which Köhler's work on the time-error was relatively isolated from the bulk of work, following the cognitive revolution, that has been carried out on short-term memory. In the time-error experiments, the stimuli to be remembered were non-verbal, noises of particular intensities, tones, visual stimuli of particular luminances, weights, etc. On the other hand, most modern research on short-term memory is concerned with alphanumeric or verbal material, that is, memory for digits, numbers, letters or words (hardly ever of nonsense syllables). Moreover most of the research using non-verbal material has tested memory for a stimulus after a second stimulus has been presented, rather than the appearance of the second stimulus, given the first (the time-error paradigm). But this modern research on non-verbal material clearly indicates interference by the second stimulus with the retrieval of the first.

Murray *et al.* (1975) studied recognition memory for distances on the skin that separated two 'touches' at particular points; they found that the probability of recognition decreased over 16 seconds and showed that if the retention interval was filled with more 'touch' experiences (e.g. the area between the two original sites touched was rubbed with a toothbrush) this caused more recognition failure than did a retention interval that contained no touch stimulation. Walk and Johns (1984) studied memory for odours over short retention intervals. The subjects sniffed at two vials containing odorous materials, then followed a retention interval of 26 seconds that was either 'empty' or that involved hearing words related to the odours (e.g. vanilla), words unrelated to the odours, or a new odour. The subject then had to pick out the 'old' odour from four alternatives. The authors discovered that recognition performance was lower (37.5 per cent accuracy) if the interval contained a new odour than it was if the retention interval contained no interference (55.6 per cent). Interestingly, recognition was much better (83.3 per cent) if the retention interval included a target-related word (e.g. 'vanilla') than if it contained an unrelated word (48.6 per cent). Finally, Broadbent and Broadbent (1981) showed how recognition for nonsense shapes decreased if other nonsense shapes were laid on top of the target items, a phenomenon they called 'overwriting'. These three studies agree in demonstrating 'modality specific interference', that is, a non-verbal stimulus is better recognized up to 30 seconds later if the retention interval is unfilled as contrasted with the case where more sensory material in the same modality is present. These are all modern authentications of Köhler and von Restorff's claim that 'crowding' a retention interval with stimuli similar to the target stimuli to be recognized causes interference with *recognition*.

Some persuasive evidence for modality-specific interference in short-term *recall* also comes from studies in which the material can be viewed as having two dimensions, a visual dimension and a verbal dimension. Imagine, for example, a matrix of 12 cells which contains letters in some cells but not in the others. The visual dimension concerns which *cells* are filled and which are not: the subject is likely to retrieve this information making use of a visual image. The verbal dimension concerns which *letters* are available in memory. The two dimensions can be shown to be separately vulnerable to modality-specific interference. For example, Meudell (1972) showed such a matrix tachistoscopally for one second. This was followed by a task which either involved verbal interference (counting backwards aloud), or interference involving the visual modality (visually tracking a moving spot on a screen). This activity filled retention intervals of 3 to 30 seconds. Then the subjects were asked to fill in an empty matrix from memory, putting the appropriate letters into the appropriate cells. Memory for which *cells* to fill in was worse following the visual tracking task than it was following the verbal task; memory for which *letters* to write was worse following the verbal task than it was following the visual tracking task. Again, Den Heyer and Barrett (1971) briefly exposed a 5×4 matrix including eight letters; verbally adding digits for 10 seconds following exposure of the matrix caused interference with the recall of the letters, whereas filling the same interval with a visual task involving the discrimination of dot patterns caused a disruption of memory for the location of the letters. And finally Murray and Newman (1973) showed that if a matrix of twelve cells contained three shapes (square, triangle, circle), memory for *where* the shapes went was interfered with more by a task involving the copying of arrows during the retention interval than it was by a task involving counting backwards aloud from a three-digit number, whereas the reverse was true for memory for what *shapes* went into what cells. These three studies indicate that memory for visual features and memory for verbal features can be selectively interfered with by the performance of tasks involving the same sensory dimension during the interval. Other work along the same lines includes the demonstration by Brooks (1967) that the performance of a task using visual imagination, such as mentally running one's 'eye' round the outline of a letter of the alphabet, is more disrupted by reading (a visual task) than by listening (an auditory task).

Equally important is the demonstration by these experiments that the contents of short-term memory can be conceived of as consisting of representations of sensory quality and intensity. However, although there have been many experiments since 1960 on memory for verbal material, only a few experiments have explored memory for non-verbal stimuli. Wickelgren (1966) carried out an experiment on short-term recognition for target tones of particular frequencies, observing how after-coming tones interfered with recognition of the target tones. He was led by this work to postulate the existence of traces whose strength depended on the duration of the target tone, but whose availability was a function partly of time and also of the duration of the tone interpolated during the retention interval. Later Wickelgren (1969) examined recognition memory for the frequency of tones (ranging from 400 to 490 Hz) with the insertion of an interfering tone (930 Hz) during the retention interval (1–180 milliseconds). He concluded that the internal representation of tone frequency had two components, a short-term trace and a long-term trace. Then Laming and Scheiwiller (1985) tried fitting not only Wickelgren's 1969 data, but also some nineteenth century data on tone recognition and on visual line length recognition, by various equations, concluding that no one equation was unequivocally the best for describing the fall in recognition accuracy as the retention interval increased. In an experiment on line length recognition carried out by themselves, they noted that one subject had a tendency to judge the comparison stimuli as 'longer', the greater the retention interval (up to 4 seconds). They noted that this finding was compatible with Köhler's theory of the time-error.

There is, of course, also a large body of literature concerned with alphanumeric material, in which it is demonstrated that subjects are influenced to some extent by the sensory modality of presentation. If the material is presented visually, the subjects generally re-code such stimuli as 348 or LVM into internal speech; this re-coding is more automatic and instantaneous if the subject hears the material as opposed to sees it. Penney (1989) has reviewed the literature on visual as opposed to auditory presentation of alphanumeric material for immediate retrieval and has shown that visual and auditory inputs can co-exist in 'separate streams' for a short while after presentation. But the auditory message tends to be better retrieved than the visual, partly because there is a longer lasting 'after-echo' following the hearing of a list and partly because there is less time taken encoding the auditory message into internal speech than is the case for the visual. The reliance by the subject on memory based on a phonological recoding of the stimulus has been demonstrated by the fact that errors in the retrieval of visually presented letters tend to consist of confusions between letters like B and V which share a common vowel sound; and by the fact that if the subject is prevented from phonologically recoding visually presented letters by having to say something else ('articulatory suppression'), retrieval is greatly inferior to that obtained where phonological re-coding is permitted (Murray, 1967, 1968). However, forgetting in short-term memory mainly seems to be based on interference from items in the same modality that enter memory after the target material has entered memory; Wickelgren and Norman (1966) showed how recognition of an item X fell as the number of items entering store after X increased, while Murray, Rowan and Smith (1988) showed how Wickelgren and Norman's formula could be applied both to cases where phonological encoding was permitted and to cases where it was not because articulatory suppression was being used.

Wulf (1922) clearly established that the retrieval of a target stimulus is greatly influenced by the way in which the stimulus was encoded at the time of presentation and Katona (1940) and others had shown that nonsense material tends to be grouped or organized so as to make it easier to retain. Modern research has gone a little further: it not only demonstrates that subjects will encode or re-organize nonsense material in a more meaningful manner, but also insists that the retrieval conditions have to be just right if the encoded or re-organized material is to be accurately retrieved. The retrieval conditions must match or reinstate the encoding conditions as well as possible. Koffka, of course, had said much the same thing, but in our own time Tulving (1983) has proposed the Encoding Specificity Principle, according to which a retrieval cue is most effective if it can easily revive the target memory in the form in which the latter was originally encoded. A by-product of this research has been the collection of evidence that target memories are also encoded in a general context, the place where the material was learned, the drug-state the subject might have been undergoing, the emotional mood of the subject, and so on. Researchers on state-dependent memory, particularly following Eich (1980), have endeavoured to show that both 'encoding' and 'context' are contributors to the formation of the trace representing a target stimulus, and that a proper reinstatement of the conditions of the original encoding and the original environmental or mood context at the time of retrieval can facilitate retrieval. This new work on encoding will be discussed in the next section and the new work on retrieval in the subsequent section.

Encoding and organizing to-be-remembered material

In reviewing modern evidence on the encoding and organization of to-be-remembered material, we shall begin with short-term memory and move on to long-term memory. As already indicated, there has been an enormous amount of research devoted to showing that, when alphanumeric material is presented visually, subjects will encode the material in overt or inner speech. We have already mentioned that articulatory suppression can severely reduce recall of visually presented verbal material and in his model of working memory Baddeley (1990) has suggested that the contents of consciousness immediately following a verbal input may include a visual representation, co-existing with a phonological representation that is kept 'alive' in consciousness by covert rehearsal using what he calls an 'articulatory loop'. Controlling everything is a central executive system, and the 'box' containing all this is called the 'working memory' system because it can be shown that mental calculations and similar tasks can be carried out at the same time as the articulatory loop is being used to rehearse recent information. The two tasks, the mental arithmetic and the rehearsing, do interfere with each other to an extent depending on the memory load in each task (Baddeley and Hitch, 1974). A considerable amount of evidence supporting the notion that working memory can maintain both a visual and an auditory memory load *concurrently* has been reviewed by Penney (1989). She has formulated what she calls the 'separate streams' hypothesis according to which a stream of visual information can be processed simultaneously with a stream of auditory information, although it is very difficult to perform two tasks both of which use visual inputs simultaneously, or auditory inputs simultaneously.

Apart from this evidence on speech-coding, there has also accumulated in recent years evidence that the memory span, assumed for years to be a relatively 'pure' measure of short-term memory, is, in fact, determined both by the efficiency with which the to-be-remembered list can be maintained in visual and/or phonological short-term memory *and* by the subject's skill at re-coding the material, using long-term memory, into a form that is more easily retained. We can give three examples.

G.A. Miller (1956), in a paper generally accredited with being one of the first contributions to the cognitive revolution, showed, for example, that learning, even in one trial, might consist of replacing single items, each demanding attention and rehearsal, by groups of items that can be attended to or rehearsed as a 'chunk'. This viewpoint has been elaborated considerably during the course of the cognitive revolution and now is at the heart of the theory of learning put forward by Newell (1990). The application of 'chunking' can be extended from single immediate memory tasks to all sorts of complicated learning, including the mastering of strategies in chess. In Miller's original paper, he described how a colleague, Sidney Smith, undertook to learn binary code. In this code there are only two digits, 0 and 1, and each decimal digit is given by a combination of zeroes and ones; for example, the number 1 is represented by 00, the number 2 by 01, the number 3 by 10, the number 4 by 11, and so forth. If the task is to recall a string of binary digits after one hearing, without any sort of training in translating binary sequences into decimal digits, the memory span is just under 10. But if the subject learns to replace every pair of binary digits by decimal digits, so that

```
01   00   11   10   00   is encoded as
 2    1    4    3    1
```

nearly 20 binary digits can be recalled after one presentation. This particular subject learned to replace triplets of digits by single numbers: the memory span came close to 30. The relative advantage of encoding by replacing groups of binary digits by decimal digits was not so marked in cases where quadruplets or quintuplets of binary digits were re-coded into decimal digits, but it is clear that the experiment furnishes convincing evidence for the importance of re-coding in memorization.

Another way of re-coding digits is to associate them with letters so that a string of digits can be translated into a string of letters that form a pronounceable unit. Slak (1970), for example, taught himself a code such that for each decimal digit there was a corresponding consonant and vowel, e.g. 6 would be associated with the letters D and A. So a sequence such as

2 6 5 6 7 0 1 9 3 (9 pronounceable units) could be re-coded as
b a f d i l t u n (3 pronounceable units)

Before learning the code, Slak's memory span for digits was 9.31; after learning the code, it became 14.33. A student whose memory span for digits before learning the code was 9.30 increased his span to 12.94 after learning the code. This trick of re-coding numbers into letters was used extensively in the eighteenth and nineteenth centuries to learn lists of historical dates and in the twentieth century it has been used by teachers of mnemonics in a way to be described below.

A third demonstration of how the memory span can be improved by re-coding was reported by Ericsson *et al.* (1980). They found a subject whose memory span before acquiring any re-coding strategy was about 10 digits, but he learned, after intensive practice, to improve his memory span to as many as 80 digits. This extraordinary feat was accomplished by taking groups of numbers and relating them to data of interest to the subject; for example, the sequence 3492 might be encoded as 3 minutes 49.2 seconds, the time associated with a running of a mile that took less than 4 minutes; 893 might be encoded as the age of an old man, 89.3 and 1944 might be encoded as a date near the end of the Second World War. It took hours of practice before the subject could carry out this kind of associative encoding fluently; it was only after 175 days of work that a memory span for digits of 80 was achieved.

These three reports clearly demonstrate that memory span can be improved by re-coding meaningless strings of digits into shorter units (digital or decimal), fewer units (digit to letter translation) or units that can be retrieved because of a thread of strong and no doubt visualizable associations (digit to 'association' translation).

The memory span, then, can be influenced by associative and semantic factors involving the use of long-term memory. We have to reconcile this with the evidence from the articulatory suppression literature that the memory span often depends on the use of a phonological code. It may be stated that if the material lacks meaning, i.e. is semantically disconnected and cannot be encoded in a meaningful image, then the limits of memory are mainly determined by the limits of speech. For example, Baddeley (1990, Chapter 4) has reviewed evidence showing that the amount retained of such material depends on how many separate speech-acts are involved in the phonological encoding of the material. The memory span for a sequence of long words (e.g. UNIVERSITY, TEMPERATURE ...) is lower than the span for a sequence of short words (e.g. DECK, LIST . . .) – the span is roughly equal to the number of words the subject can say in 2 seconds (Baddeley *et al.*, 1975). The memory span for digits increases with age from 4 to 10 years and there is a linear relationship between the span and the number of words the subject can read aloud per second (Hulme *et al.*, 1984). The memory span for digits is directly related to how many digits can be articulated in a given time. This varies from language to language and an inverse correlation can be shown between memory span and the mean numbers of syllables per digit in the language (Naveh-Benjamin and Ayres, 1986). All of this evidence indicates that when meaningless material is to be memorized, the limits are set by the rate of speaking.

But when the material contains meaning, there is less reliance on a phonological, visual or auditory code. As just indicated, the memory span for digits can be improved if the digits are re-coded as to make them meaningful. If the material already has meaning then the memory span is generally enhanced – for example, the memory span for a single sentence can be as long as 20 words, whereas the span for a string of unconnected words is about five.

The fact that the span for sentences is about twenty words and that memory span tasks may tap what Craik (1991) calls 'knowledge schemas' is of course coherent with Koffka's point that strings of meaningfully connected words are easier to memorize than strings of nonsense syllables because the former are well organized: they constitute a single package of meaning. Similarly, Köhler had stressed that word-pairs are easier to retain than are nonsense syllable pairs because they can form interesting images, which are also unique packages of meaning. The notion that serial learning was just a chain of stimulus-response associations was roundly attacked by Asch (1968b), who noted how individual items might be associated with particular ordinal positions and that end items might be more distinctive, as von Restorff had claimed. Asch, who had been with Köhler at Swarthmore, also pointed out that backward associations can be as strong as forward associations in paired-associate learning, and suggested that the pair was organized as a single mental representation. During the late 1960s and early 1970s, a large amount of research was carried out on imagery and organization as vehicles for the facilitation of the memorization of disconnected material. Some of this work may be briefly summarized. Many experiments not mentioned here will also be found in a book edited by Tulving and Donaldson entitled *Organization of Memory* (1972).

Köhler had assumed that images of interacting objects are better retained than word-pairs, that is, the use of a visual code might be better for long-term memory purposes than was a verbal code. Epstein *et al.* (1960) showed that if word-pairs such as BOTTLE-ROCK were presented, the cue BOTTLE was less likely to lead to the recall of ROCK than was the case when subjects were shown a picture of a bottle on a rock. In my lectures I describe the latter as a better Gestalt than is represented by the word-pair, and note that Paivio (1971, 1986) has elaborated on the view that visual imagery is particularly suited for retention because an image stores a lot of information in parallel. Later, Bower

(1970) presented lists of word-pairs to be memorized either by rote (no instruction to image), or to be memorized in terms of separate images, or to be memorized in terms of a fused image where the two items interact. For example, if the pair were BOTTLE-ROCK, the 'separate image' might have separate images of the bottle and the rock, whereas the 'interaction' image might have the bottle sitting on a rock. Recognition of the stimulus term (the first item in each pair) did not change as a function of these instructions, but the probability of recall of the response term (e.g. given BOTTLE, the subject must recall ROCK) was 0.30 for the rote learning group, 0.27 for the group using separate images and 0.53 for the group using fused images. In another study, Bower *et al.* (1969) showed that the serial learning of 38 high imagery nouns was better if subjects grouped each successive set of four words into an interactive image, and maintained that image over successive learning trials, than if they changed the images from trial to trial.

Memorization of a long set of words is also facilitated if the words are grouped into a hierarchical schema all or part of which may be stored in visual image form, although associations by meaning will also play a part. Bower *et al.* (1969) asked subjects to learn a list of 112 words for free recall (i.e. they did not have to recall the order of the words). On the first trial they recalled an average of 20.6 words, and by the fourth trial could recall an average of 70.1 words. But when the words were arranged into four hierarchical schemas such as the one shown in Figure 4.1, 73 of the words were recalled on the first trial and all 112 by the fourth trial. Broadbent *et al.* (1978) were able to show that the advantage for the hierarchical scheme probably lay in the fact that retrieval of one item in a column easily led to retrieval of the next item in the column; that it was item–item associations that determined successful recall was suggested by the fact that words arranged in columns in matrices, without any form of tree structure, were as well recalled later as the same words in a tree structure hierarchy. Sometimes it was even better, probably because with a tree structure one could forget about some branches more readily than others.

The Gestalt psychologists, particularly Koffka and Katona, had also emphasized grouping as a device for organizing sequential material. Bower and Winzenz (1969) elaborated on this by showing how grouping is an inherent part of list learning insofar as, when a list is being learned over several trials, it is vital that the grouping available on the first trial be maintained over the subsequent trials. A list of 12 digits could be grouped in more than one way, for instance

17 683 9452 7 56
176 839 45 275 6

In Bower and Winzenz's experiment, subjects saw a series of lists of 12 digits each. The lists may be named A, B, C and so on. In the above example, the same list is grouped in two different ways. A typical sequence of *lists* was

A B C B D B E B . . .

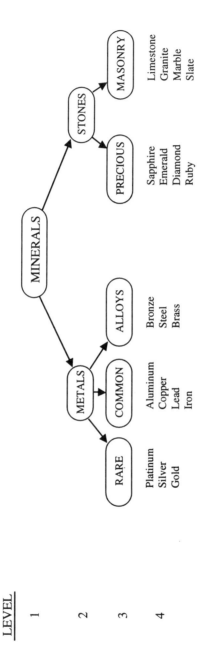

Figure 4.1 Example of a hierarchical scheme for arranging the names of minerals. (Source: reprinted from G.H. Bower *et al.* (1969), *Journal of Verbal Learning and Verbal Behavior*, **8**, p. 324.)

Here the B-list is repeated every second trial. Although each list is longer than the memory span, Hebb (1961) had discovered that the recall of lists that are repeated shows an improvement as the sequence progresses: this 'Hebb effect' has been taken as evidence for long-term storage. Bower and Winzenz discovered that if the B-lists all had the same grouping, there was a typical Hebb effect; over four repetitions of the B-lists, errors decreased. But if each of the B-lists was shown with a different grouping the Hebb effect was almost absent. Errors showed a very small decline over repetitions of the B-list. Hence, just as Koffka had stressed, grouping seems to be an intrinsic part of learning. It gives a structure or distinctiveness to individual elements in the list.

When subjects are faced with a sequence of unconnected items to memorize, they will usually impose a grouping of their own upon recall. For example, in short-term recall a graphic plot of how many items are recalled at each serial portion of the list is a sort of map of how they were grouped at input. Murray (1966), using forced-order recall in which subjects had to recall a list of 8 consonants in the order in which they had been presented, found that recall fell from the first to the last item reported, but there was an unexpected rise in recall of the fifth item. This suggested that, at the time of encoding, the subjects had grouped the eight items into two groups of four, with an emphasis on the fifth item, which would be the first item of the second group. Listening to subjects actually memorizing 8-letter lists that they had to say aloud at presentation showed that most subjects adopted a 4/4 grouping, but others used a 3/3/2 grouping. Given the opportunity to write down the items in any sequence, but with the instruction that the recalled items had to be allotted to their correct serial position, subjects often recalled the last group first then went back to fill in the items recalled from the earlier serial positions.

When the order of a supraspan list of words (say 20 words) does not have to be retained, but as many words are to be recalled as possible, subjects will also write down the last three or four items first (presumably from the articulatory loop or visual or auditory sensory storage) and then go back to recall as many of the early and middle items as they can. However if the list is long enough to require several trials before all the words can be correctly reported from memory, it will be found that, if we ignore the words reported from short-term memory, recall of the other words shows a subjective organization. As mentioned in Chapter 3, Tulving (1962) studied free recall of this type. On each trial the words were presented in a different random order but an analysis of the written records showed that each subject had a preferred order for recalling the words, an order that gradually crystallized over successive recalls, with, of course, new recalled words being added on each trial.

Experts have formed their own schemes for subjectively organizing material to be learned. In his chapter on organizing and learning in his book *Human Memory*, Baddeley (1990) discusses evidence from Stevens (1988) and Ericsson and Polson (1988) concerned with how waiters remembered complicated meal orders. Waiters rarely used just words, but linked orders with locations of customers or clustered the order so as to fit the layout of the restaurant kitchens; and bartenders tended to think of drinks in connection with glasses of particular shapes and colours. Ericsson and Polson studied one waiter in particular who could take up to 20 complete dinner orders without taking notes. He categorized salad dressings in terms of initial letters (e.g. B for 'blue cheese', T for 'thousand island', etc.), and remembered how steaks should be cooked ('well done' down to 'rare') in terms of a visuo-spatial scale with 'well done' at the top and 'rare' at the bottom. After completing some experiments in which it was shown that the waiter could still recall dinner orders even when the order of presentation was changed, Ericsson and Polson found that if the memory schema ('category structure') the waiter used for categorizing each individual item were eliminated, the waiter's memory for dinner orders was reduced. Ericsson and Polson postulated that exceptional skill at memory was based on retrieval structures stored in long-term memory (LTM) – 'at the time of presentation, information is not only encoded and stored in LTM, it is also associated with an organized set of retrieval cues. At the time of recall, these stable retrieval cues need only to be brought to attention, and the stored information can then be recalled by means of the retrieval cues alone' (Ericsson and Polson 1988, p. 305). Baddeley (1990, p. 185) also noted how Aborigines in the Australian desert remembered routes through the desert not only by means of visual memory based on natural landmarks but also by way of songs that contained references to those landmarks in the order that they would appear on a long journey. In his collection of papers concerning 'natural' memory, Neisser (1982) noted how professional story-tellers in various cultures remember the gist of a story and then tell it with slight variations each time.

But Neisser also noted how some individuals have extraordinary retention of particular kinds of material. I was most struck by the chapter on musical memory in which it was shown that certain individuals, such as the composer Saint-Saëns and the conductor Toscanini, were able to retain the details of musical scores so well that they did not need to supplement their retention of the literal details of the music by some kind of reduction or re-organization. This is an important point because the Gestalt psychologists always stressed that the reason we organize memory materials into groupings, images, and so on, is that these are the *natural* ways for the brain to process information; the contents of memory are to be articulated into natural groupings in the same way as are the data of perception. This natural grouping is held to occur at the time of perception, whose aim is to render the environment 'clear'. Clarity can be gained by reducing the amount of information to be processed but at the cost of ignoring details. Perhaps people with exceptional visuospatial or musical memory perform less of a reduction at the time of presentation. They are aware of more details and more details therefore get stored. Since one way to reduce the amount of information being processed is to attend to a subset of details and perhaps think about them in words, it could be that exceptional visuospatial or musical memory is associated with a *lack* of any kind of phonological processing at the time the material is first seen or heard.

Apart from imagery and grouping, the addition of meaningfulness to meaningless data will serve as a core for organizing it. Serial recall by students of a string of ten unconnected words after one hearing is about 13 per cent accurate, but if they are instructed to form the words into a connected narrative as they hear them, recall can reach 93 per cent accuracy (Bower and Clark, 1969). The learning of nonsense syllables is greatly facilitated if subjects make up 'natural language mediators' that allow them to be linked with everyday language. For example, DUP-TEZ might be re-coded as 'deputize', CEZ MUN as 'says man', or, more indirectly, BIH-XIR might be re-coded as '2 11' (2 because of bi- , 11 from the Roman numeral XI). Montague *et al.* (1966) showed that if subjects generated natural language mediators from nonsense syllable pairs, and 24 hours later were given a surprise recall task, subjects who had been given 30 seconds to generate each mediator recalled 74.7 per cent of the mediators associated with high meaningful syllable pairs and 50.5 per cent of those associated with low meaningful syllable pairs. Subjects given only 15 seconds to generate the mediators yielded lower recall of the mediators, indicating that the more time a subject has to produce a new encoding of a syllable-pair, the more likely it is to be retained. Finally, it might seem obvious that the memorability of word-pairs in a paired-associates task should increase with the degree of prior association of the words in question; one would expect CAT-DOG to be an association that was easy to retain and CAT-MAP to be less easy to retain. Early work on this subject relied on word-pairs drawn from word association tests and failed to demonstrate any strong effect of the 'associative strength' of the word-pair, but Murray (1982) claimed that these early results were due to ceiling effects – all words generated to a target word in word association tasks are relatively highly associated with that word. When more sensitive measures, using ratings, were made of the associative strengths of selected word-pairs, both immediate recall of the response-term (given the stimulus term) and the ease of learning of the associations were found to vary directly with rated associative strength when very long lists of pairs formed the target material.

This last result is important in view of Köhler's claim that the frequency of experience with word-pairs is probably not the main variable determining memorability. Instead he believed that imagibility and distinctiveness were the main determinants of how well associations could be learned. Rated associative strength is no doubt partly a measure of the degree of prior experience with a pair but is also no doubt related to the degree of 'belongingness' of the pair. The following pairs of stimuli have probably never been seen paired together by the reader:

  & @
  ? $

yet they are immediately associated as symbols on a keyboard and would probably be easily learned in a paired-associates task. Nevertheless, frequency of experience with the stimuli is a variable that certainly can influence performance on memory tasks. The ease of identification of tachistoscopally presented letter sequences increases with the predictability of those letter sequences; a sequence such as WALLYLOF that looks like near-English is more accurately identified than a sequence such as YRLZUPOC (Mewhort *et al.*, 1969). If subjects are asked to translate words from English to French, and the similarity of the English and French words is controlled, the translation is on average faster and more accurate the more common the English word (Murray, 1986). If subjects are asked to retrieve as many words as they can in two minutes whose first (or second . . . or fifth) letter is A (or B . . . or Z), common words are nearly always produced before rare words. It was shown also that the results of this experiment could be analyzed in such a way as to indicate that in the long-term memory lexicon of words possessed by a subject, the likelihood of retrieval of a word given a graphemic cue (e.g. name a word whose third letter is T) is determined by the mean word frequency of the words with that graphemic characteristic (Murray, 1975).

In these three tasks – tachistoscopic word identification, translation of isolated words, word generation given a graphemic cue – it is clear that word frequency, perhaps itself correlated with the degree of prior experience a subject will have had with the word in question, does determine performance, as the behaviourists claimed. But it can also be claimed that each of these tasks is artificial and does not demand any retrieval of the words' *meanings*. The production of a sentence or of a written document demands the use of knowledge-schemata that, so to speak, override the importance of word frequency. The word WATER may be produced as the English equivalent of the French word EAU, or as a word whose third letter is T, but it is doubtful that it would have appeared in this chapter on memory without the present context. Context, rather than word-frequency, determines the retrieval of words in most everyday situations. The speech of persons who lack the literacy to find the *mot juste* for any contingency is sprinkled with commonly-used, repetitive expletives. The low-level role played by habit strength in the Gestalt accounts of human memory emerged from their concern to deal with memories organized into schemata where retrieval *was* determined by meaning, be it related to a bizarre image, to a prior structure that determined the context of a list to be memorized, or to a grand agglomeration of traces representing a body of knowledge such as psychology.

More generally, mnemonic schemes that have been invented from Greek times onwards make use of images that serve to remind the memorizer of the more 'boring' material that he is supposed to retain. A shopping-list can be remembered by assigning each item in the list to a 'place' in an imagined building or geographical locale; by mentally moving from place to place in the image, one is reminded of each successive item in the shopping-list. If the item on the shopping-list is assigned a striking association with its particular place, the method is even more effective. Modern mnemonic schemes also involve associations between numbers and images; for example, the number 1 can be associated with the letter t or even the word 'tea' and then the first item of a list can be linked to 'tea', again with a striking image. Recalling the list involves going through the numbers from one onwards and retrieving the list item from the striking image associated with each number. The history of mnemonics was reviewed by Paivio (1971).

This section has reviewed contemporary evidence for organizational processes that determine the encoding of material for storage in long-term memory. There is a useful review of much of this work and of other research by Henle (1985), who showed in some detail how the Gestalt psychologists anticipated it. In particular, she stressed how the modern emphasis on the importance of context in determining retrieval was shared by the Gestalt psychologists. We must stress again, however, that although the modern research on organization reviewed above has a *correspondence* with earlier Gestalt work, it was probably not *influenced* by it very much.

The retrieval process

There have traditionally been two modes of retrieval that have been intensely studied, recognition and recall. For the Gestalt psychologists, recognition took place by a mechanism akin to resonance that depended on the similarity of the stimulus currently being perceived (the probe) to the stimulus associated with the stored trace (the target). However the Gestalt psychologists speculated that the 'grouping' of probe trace and target trace was akin to the grouping of similar objects in the visual field, and since the latter depended on the spatial between-field, the grouping of probe trace and target trace ought to depend on the temporal between-field. Moreover the Gestalt psychologists stressed that a stimulus was rarely perceived as an isolated entity: every stimulus was seen in relation to its context. We may for example note that reaction time to the onset of a light depends on the contrast the light presents to the background. Many other examples can be given from the literature on perception of the importance of the context in determining the judgments made about single stimuli and some of these examples will be given in Chapter 6. But if the context is important in perception, it must also be important in memory; a stimulus must leave a trace, but so must its context, and therefore traces are always 'embedded' so to speak in the spatiotemporal context in which they were set up.

Experimentation since 1960 has amply confirmed the importance of context in determining recognition, but in addition it has added a third kind of retrieval process, that associated with 'implicit memory'. As I understand it, if one can present evidence that a particular memory is available to a subject, but not by the obvious methods of recognition or recall, then one has demonstrated the existence of implicit memory. Since recognition and recall involve conscious processes, then demonstrating that the subject has retained information of which he is not consciously aware indicates that the subject 'knows something he did not know he knew'.

But Koffka himself (1935a, p. 591) distinguished between explicit and implicit recognition – he quoted Maccurdy (1928) who wrote that 'If I meet one of my students in London, I recognize him; if I see this same man in my lecture room in Cambridge, I do not recognize him, although I know he is there' (p. 113). In the first case, recognition of the subject was explicit; in the second case, the 'knowledge' is implicit even though no conscious recognition act occurs. Koffka was not too happy with this example because he felt that Maccurdy, if asked, could probably have said he did 'know' the student in the class, and Koffka did not continue to use the word 'implicit', but he went on to discuss the work of Claparède (1911), who showed that patients with Korsakoff's psychosis cannot consciously recognize persons or recall their names, but act towards them as if they did 'know' or retain some information. For example, one patient was introduced to Claparède, who was holding a pin that pricked the patient's hand when she shook his hand. Later the patient showed no evidence of remembering who Claparède was, yet flinched when re-introduced to him as if she remembered something of the pain. Maccurdy himself supplemented Claparède's evidence with the following experiment:

> I would give the patient my full name and address. Within a few minutes this was totally 'forgotten'. Later on, I would present the patient with a list of ten Christian names, another of the surnames, another of street numbers, and another of street names. From this he would be asked to guess which one was mine. To my surprise, the guesses were nearly as accurate as would be the conscious memory for such data of normal subjects. But the response remained to the subject a mere guess, it was associated with no feeling of me-ness; on no occasion did the patient think that he had the slightest reason for picking one name rather than the another from the list. (p. 121)

This evidence for what we now call 'implicit memory' was taken by Koffka to be evidence that access to a trace can take place even when there is no conscious sensation of 'this-is-familiar-to-*me*' – it was evidence coherent with Koffka's belief in an Ego-schema.

In fact modern theories of recognition lay a great deal of stress on familiarity – a probe that is recognized as having occurred at an earlier time is 'familiar', and several mathematical models have been put forward in which the likelihood of a probe's being considered to be familiar is hypothesized to be based on a computation by the brain. For example, the degree of familiarity has been suggested to increase with the number of features that match up in the trace of the probe and the trace of the target (Ratcliff, 1978). Another model of familiarity is based on the assumption that the target trace can be represented as a list or vector of features, and so can the probe trace; the degree of similarity between two vectors can be mapped by the 'dot product' of the vectors. A decision has to be carried out, based on this dot product, as to whether a 'yes' judgement should be given to the probe, this decision being based on the assumptions of signal detection theory (Murdock, 1982). But whatever the mechanism of recognition, Koffka specified that a recognition response should always be judged in terms of recognition in a context. I may rephrase this by saying that a 'yes' recognition response is always given to a probe if it is recognized *as* something or is familiar *as* something. Maccurdy's patient failed to recognize Maccurdy's name *as* the name of the experimenter, although he appears to have recognized it as something. In a recognition test in which the experimenter presents a list of three-digit numbers:

349 871 675 287   675
Targets   Probe

the probe 675 has to be recognized *as* having occurred in the preceding list. It does not have to be recognized *as* a number between 100 and 1000 or *as* a set of symbols one has seen sometime in one's lifetime. For Koffka, recognition tasks in general required the subject to recognize the probe *as* something related to their *own* experience.

But Koffka (1935a, p. 601) stressed that in order for a probe representing stimulus X to resonate with a trace x of X, X had to be viewed as part of a complex, just as every perceptual stimulus is part of a context. Thus it is possible that if there is a stimulus complex A B C D E F it will *not* necessarily happen that part of the complex, such as B C D, will serve as an adequate recognition cue for A B C D E F. If this is true, it implies that correct recognition of a probe will only occur if the context surrounding the probe is highly similar to the context surrounding the original stimulus. There is a fair amount of modern evidence to support this. For example, Light and Carter-Sobell (1970) showed subjects 54 sentences such as 'the boy stole the strawberry jam'. This was the only sentence in which the word 'jam' had occurred. They were shown 100 adjective-noun pairs and were asked to circle any words they recognized from the previous set of sentences. Included in the list of pairs were 'strawberry jam', 'raspberry jam' and 'traffic jam'. The word 'jam' was circled far more often when it was paired with 'strawberry' than when it was paired with 'traffic', while pairings with 'raspberry' yielded intermediate numbers of circlings. Watkins *et al.* (1976) showed subjects pairs of faces. If one face of a pair was then presented alone, the correct recognition level was 73 per cent, but if it was re-presented along with a face that was different from the one it has been associated with in the target list, its recognition level fell to 68 per cent. However, Baddeley (1990, p. 287) suggests that a distinction should be made between a context that interacts with a trace, as in strawberry JAM and one that does not, as in a simple random concatenation of words such as RUN JAM or a concatenation of two faces. The importance of the reinstatement of context will be greater in the former case than in the latter.

It is an amusing game to find instances of such failures of 'recognition *as*' in one's own experience. For example, for years I have been reading and writing about Korsakoff's psychosis (Murray and Hitchcock, 1973) and for even more years I have been listening to the music of the composer Rimsky-Korsakoff, but it was not until after about 20 years that I noticed that the word 'Korsakoff' occurs in both names. The reason was that 'Korsakoff's psychosis' was stored *as* a memory disorder within the context of my general knowledge-schema of memory theory and 'Rimsky Korsakoff' was stored *as* a composer in the context of my general knowledge-schema about music. I had never recognized the single word 'Korsakoff' as having occurred in both schemata. Another example of exactly the same kind of failure of an element from my psychological schema to be recognized as a component of my musical schema concerns the word 'Eusebius'. Eusebius was a fourth century historian of Christianity whom I have mentioned in my writing (Murray, 1988, p. 46) and for years I have been playing a piano piece by Schumann, from his suite *Carnival*, called 'Eusebius'. Here 'Eusebius' represents Schumann's serious side (he actually used the name of the historian) in contrast to his more romantic side (represented in Schumann's fantasy world by a character called 'Florestan'). For perhaps 15 years I never noticed that the word 'Eusebius', when I saw it on the sheet music I was playing, was the same as the name of the historian. Recognition of a probe X as part of a previous experience therefore demands some reinstatement of the context associated with that previous experience.

It should be noted that contexts themselves should be discriminable. When Köhler and von Restorff (1937) showed that a probe was more likely to be recognized if the interval between the target and the probe were filled with material that was clearly different from each of these, they showed that the temporal as well as the spatial context can be a determinant of recognition: when the material filling the interval is similar to both target and probe, neither target nor probe benefit from clearly discriminable temporal contexts.

As mentioned, a general 'encoding specificity principle' that will account for context-dependent recognition and recall has been put forward by Tulving (1983). It states that the best retrieval cue for any stored item will be a cue that was encoded along with that item at the time of original representation of the item. Evocation of the item, when the cue is presented, is carried out by an innate mechanism of 'synergistic ecphory', a term derived from Semon's theory (see pp. 53). Koffka (1935a, pp. 597–598) also put forward a principle for retrieval, although he explicitly states that he did not discuss the relationship with Semon's principle because he did not wish to break the course of his discussion. Instead of saying a 'retrieval cue is presented', Koffka says a 'process is aroused' which, for simplicity's sake, may be assumed to be a perceptual process caused by sensory stimulation. This process is aroused at a point in time represented by the 'tip of a trace column' – if traces are thought of as layers of sediment, the column will be at its highest at the present moment. The present process can communicate with any one of the innumerable trace systems, but Koffka maintained that the traces that would be aroused would be those most likely to contribute to the *stability* of the present process – 'those traces will communicate with the process which will give it the particular stability it needs'. Often this will be a *recent* trace (Koffka points to the law of organization by proximity, here, temporal proximity), or a *similar* trace (Koffka points to the work of Höffding and Semon on 'association by similarity'). The difference between Tulving's account and Koffka's, as far as I can see, is mainly that Koffka views the retrieval cue itself as something active, rather than passive: what is recalled or recognized, given the cue, will have some value for the survival of the cue itself in memory. Koffka acknowledged that this theory runs the risk of being teleological and attempted to escape from this charge by saying that greater stability was rendered to a process by virtue of the fact that the process-in-context made contact with a similar trace in a similar context, a mechanical event whose result was an improvement in the organization of a trace system. Koffka particularly referred to motor skills as showing adaptations to similar contexts with new aspects; a person from the southern United States transplanted to the north in winter would adapt his street-crossing habits, learned in the south, to the similar context of the north (street-crossing) but taking account of the new problems posed by ice and snow.

Implicit memory, as it is now called, was stressed by Koffka as suggesting that some 'retrieval' or excitations of traces could occur without the subject being aware of it. For Koffka, such evidence indicated the importance of an Ego-schema, whereas modern writers on implicit memory tend to think of it as another kind of trace activation in which a cue sufficient to allow the experimenter to conclude that a trace has been activated is insufficient to arouse a conscious identification, recognition, or recall response. For example, sufferers from amnesia due to brain damage frequently show an inability to recognize a word such as TABLET as having occurred in a previously seen list, but will nevertheless write TABLET when given the first two letters TA .... and instructed to write any word that comes to mind (the stem-completion task). The difference between the two tasks probably hinges on the fact that recognition of, say TABLET, as having come from an experimenter-defined list might require that the word in question was stored in an elaborative conceptual context whereas the completion of the stem TA .... might be possible on the basis of a trace of TABLET that had not been given conceptual context – as Mandler (1991) phrases it,

> both cued recall and recognition implicate both elaboration and activation, while simple [stem] completion involves only activation, and should have a less pronounced relationship with recognition. (p. 217)

Koffka would probably say that under 'elaboration' we should include processes of integration of the target material into the Ego-schema; material that is retained, but not so integrated, might be the subject of 'implicit' retrieval but not of deliberate recall or recognition.

Subsystems of traces

Koffka thought of many traces as having been integrated into a large schema to which he gave the name 'Ego'. Within the Ego are many subsystems of the kind referred to by contemporary psychologists, such as Craik (1991), as 'knowledge-schemata'. If a given element is activated within the context of one knowledge schema, it will not necessarily lead to the activation of an identical element that is stored in a different knowledge-schema. This may be thought of as indicating that, just as BCD may fail to arouse a recognition response if BCD is stored within the organized framework A B C D E F, so may an element of a large subsystem (e.g. 'Korsakoff' in a psychology subsystem) fail to arouse a recognition response, if the element is also stored in a separate subsystem (e.g. 'Korsakoff' in a music subsystem). There have been anecdotal reports of subsystems within an individual that seem to be separated on the basis of their emotional contents. In cases of multiple personality such as is reported in the case of *The Three Faces of Eve* (Thigpen and Cleckley, 1957), one 'personality' may co-exist with another and events that arouse recognition or recall responses in one system seem to leave traces integrated into that system only and not into another. There are cases of fugue where the subject 'wanders off' from a particular unpleasant situation, and there are reports that what is carried out during the fugue state is difficult to recall when the subject is out of the fugue state, and vice versa (Schacter *et al.*, 1982). Psychogenic amnesia cases also involve Freudian repression of individual wishes and memories that could disturb the patient, as in the case of Anna O. (Breuer and Freud, 1885). For example, this patient found it difficult under certain circumstances to drink water and she herself traced this to an unpleasant memory of watching her governess's dog drink out of a glass. Or there can be amnesia for whole systems (as when Eve White, the 'good Eve', had no recollection of Eve Black, the 'bad Eve').

There may even be cases of 'cryptamnesia' where details of what one has read lie unretrieved for years but then surface through some mode involving unconscious motor activity. In the case of a Mrs Curran, a medium who wrote a book using automatic writing, a book that she claimed came from a spirit named 'Patience Worth', it was shown that the book, which used archaic English, was probably based on memories from a novel published 13 years earlier (West, 1962, pp. 89–91). There is an interesting modern case reported by Nisbet (1975) where a group of people indulging in 'table-turning', where a table moves to spell out messages, obtained messages from a so-called spirit concerning a certain individual at a certain address who had died on a certain day. This information turned out to be correct, but none of the sitters had known previously about this person; however, Nisbet discovered that all this information was available in a newspaper article which somebody at the table may have read and 'forgotten' about. It is possible that retrieval of this information by that person was triggered by a coincidence. All the sittings were held in Nisbet's house in London and on the way to the room in which the sittings were held there was a photograph of a different 'Nisbet House' in Scotland, but in the same newspaper that included the obituary of the dead person, there had been an article concerning a third 'Nisbet House' in London. Did the 'Nisbet House' in the newspaper cause some sitter(s) to pay more attention to information in the newspaper than normal? Did they register information about the obituary as a result? Was the picture of 'Nisbet House' on the wall of the author's home a retrieval cue for the (implicit) recovery of the details of the obituary? There are other cases like this in the literature on parapsychology, as Schacter (1987) has noted.

Another kind of subsystem that might have an autonomous existence is a system of paranoid delusions. It is important to note that such systems should not be dismissed as 'unintegrated' or 'diffuse' because many persons diagnosed as 'schizophrenic' present delusions of grandeur or of persecution. There are also cases when persons who do not merit the diagnosis of schizophrenia suffer from delusional systems yet do not show the emotional and intellectual disorders characteristic of schizophrenia. For this reason, the influential psychiatrists Bleuler (1916) and Kraepelin (1909–13) both suggested that 'paranoia' be a separate diagnostic category from paranoid schizophrenia, stressing that the disease was psychological rather than physiological in origin, and the *Diagnostic and Statistical Manual-3-R* of the American Psychological Association currently distinguishes between 'paranoid schizophrenia' and 'delusional disorder', a term now preferred to 'paranoia', which has acquired undesirable overtones in popular parlance. The American Clifford W. Beers (1876–1943) underwent an episode of delusional disorder in 1900, and described his experiences in his book *A Mind that Found Itself* (1908). He had attempted to commit suicide and on recovering in a mental hospital imagined there was a vast plot by the police and almost everybody else, including the staff at the hospital and members of his family, to persecute him and punish him. He had many 'delusions of self-reference', imagining that newspapers were reporting about him, that a crowd in a street was demonstrating against him, that even the clink of ice in a glass was a device invented by detectives to spy on him. In the middle of this mental torment, he imagined that his brother was a detective *disguised* as his brother. But Beers carried out a test; he sent a letter to his brother and asked him to bring it with him on his next visit. When his brother did so, Beers reported that, almost instantaneously, his madness lifted. The proof that his brother was really his brother acted to unknot the whole delusional system from the rest of Beers's memories and from that point on he was no longer delusional although, naturally enough, he then showed signs of reactive depression. On release from the hospital, he wrote his book mainly with the goal of trying to improve conditions in American mental hospitals. But William James read the book and was intrigued by the evidence that a subsystem of memories (containing the delusions) could exist in such isolation from the main system of memories and encouraged Beers in his philanthropic work by giving him a large donation of money. Beers went on to become the founder of the International Society for Mental Hygiene. There is some evidence that the delusional system did not disappear but only lay dormant (as we would expect, if the system was a system of memory-traces); there was a recurrence of delusional fears of persecution in

Beers's old age, precipitated by the death of a sibling just as Beers's first suicide attempt had been (Dain, 1980).

Another example of a subsystem might be a 'religious' subsystem that can co-exist with a 'non-religious' subsystem in somebody who has been converted to a religion. In his book *Varieties of Religious Experience* (1902), William James describes conversions as representing sudden solutions to problems that have been worrying the individual before the conversion; these included emotional problems such as guilt, sloth or alcoholism, or metaphysical problems such as whether there is a God who takes a personal interest in us. At the time of the conversion lots of loose ends seem to snap into place; a single theory (e.g. the Christian doctrine of redemption) unifies desperate elements and the stage is set for a massive subsystem of memories to be induced in which religious figures play key parts. Just as delusional systems can be 'snapped out of' at an instant, as in Beers's case, religious systems can be inaugurated at an instant. So can paranoid systems. The autobiography of John Perceval (1803–1876), describing his paranoid experiences, indicates that his delusional system suddenly 'snapped in' (my expression) at a particular instant (see Bateson, 1974, p. 44). I have not found a comparable passage indicating an instantaneous 'loss' of religious belief, a sudden and effective 'loss of faith'.

The above subsystems – drawn from cases of dissociation of 'personalities', cases of cryptamnesia, cases of paranoid episodes, cases of religious conversions and, of course, the schemata for separate provinces of knowledge – indicate that the whole massive system of traces is, at least in some persons, not always held together as well as the notion of a single all-encompassing Ego-schema would suggest.

Modern memory theory also divides memory into various subsystems; the best known such classification is that of Tulving (1983) who divided memory into procedural (essentially involving memory for movements, including glandular, emotional and muscular responses in classical conditioning situations), episodic (involving memory for events that are 'tagged' in time; these include memory for personal experiences and memory for the materials presented in psychological experiments) and semantic (involving general knowledge, knowledge of languages, and other kinds of information where it is not particularly important *when* one learned the material). Tulving and Schacter (1990) added a fourth category, the 'perceptual representation system' (PRS) of which humans are little aware but which represents a kind of sensory memory of the environment. It operates at a pre-semantic level and can be demonstrated in experiments on priming; interestingly, drawings of impossible objects cannot be primed, leading Tulving and Schacter to comment that PRS 'has evolved to perform only ecologically valid computations' (p. 303); this comment would have delighted Koffka and the other Gestalt psychologists who had argued that the brain had evolved Gestalt processes as an adaptation for increasing the 'clarity' with which the natural world was perceived.

If we put this scheme together with Baddeley's scheme for working memory, we obtain the flowchart shown in Figure 4.2 which is modelled on a similar flowchart shown in Parkin (1987, p. 28). It is possible that this scheme could be amended further; for example, Donald (1991) suggests that, prior to the evolution of language, proto-humans not only had procedural memory and the ability to use visual memory (PRS?) but also to imitate the gestures of others, a talent ultimately leading to the art of dance, and requiring not only a memory of one's own movements (procedural memory) but also the ability mentally to represent the movements of others. Donald calls this ability 'mimetic memory' and he claims that prelinguistic memory associated with cognitive representations of visual stimuli and of patterns of movement were the precursors of language in the evolution of *homo sapiens*. However I have listed only Tulving's categories in the flowchart shown in Figure 4.2. The breakdown of working memory in this chart is more precise than anything found in Gestalt psychology, and so is the breakdown of long-term memory.

There are two tricky questions that arise when we compare this picture of memory with that presented in the writings of Koffka. Does episodic memory correspond exactly to Koffka's Ego-schema? And what is the relationship between Koffka's 'executive' and Baddeley's 'central executive'? On the first question, I think Koffka's 'Ego' was certainly meant to comprise episodic memory but his remarks on implicit memory, suggesting that amnesic patients fail to recognize stimuli because the patients fail to relate the stimuli to their own 'me-ness', is consistent with Tulving's distinction between PRS (revealed in implicit memory tasks) and episodic memory. There seems mainly to be a different emphasis in Koffka's model: Tulving emphasized time-tagging in his account of episodic memory, whereas Koffka stressed 'relation to me' in his account of the Ego-schema. By the same token, Koffka might have thought of an organized knowledge-schema, not so much as a branch of a separate kind of memory called 'semantic memory', but as a branch or subsystem within the Ego-schema. Dissociations of emotionally-toned memories from the block of the Ego-schema would be thought of as 're-organizations'. As for paranoid schemata, according to the Gestalt psychologist Heinrich Schulte (1924) we rarely think of 'me' as a separate entity in society but more often think 'we' – we always relate our own schemata of ourselves to other people, parents, relatives, spouses, partners, and social groups to which we belong. Paranoia can arise from 'we-crippledness'; any situation in which a person feels cut off from the persons or group immediately surrounding them leads to feelings of aloneness which are difficult to explain. In order to re-establish a sense of equilibrium, a cognitive scheme is invented in which the person's isolation can be explained in rational terms. One typical such invention is the development of a delusion of persecution or even of grandeur: 'I am different therefore I must be somebody special.' The development of a surrogate equilibrium is what Schulte calls a

> purely subjective reorganization in which actually non-existent relations are being posited, meanings reinterpreted, etc. The fabrication of this surrogate equilibrium proceeds as follows: (α) The chasm (caused by we-crippledness) is of such great

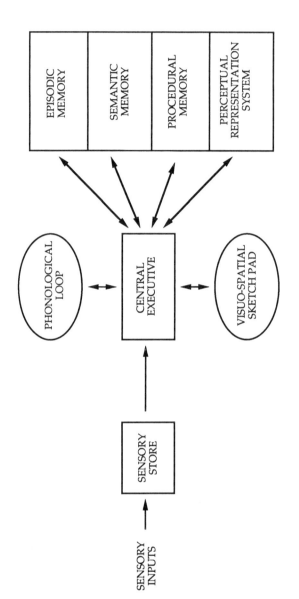

Figure 4.2 A flowchart representing modern views on the structure of human memory. The chart combines Baddeley's analysis of working memory with Tulving's analysis of long-term memory. (Source: reprinted with modifications from A.J. Parkin (1987), *Memory and Amnesia*, Blackwell, p. 28.)

significance, and influences the person's everyday behaviour so completely, that no ordinary 'explanation' for it will suffice. The only satisfactory resolution of the chasm-problem is some kind of union which *does not contain this chasm*. (β) The indifference and preoccupation of others is now seen in a new light ... he interprets the actions [of others] as directed towards, i.e. against him, and in place of the desired but unattainable 'we' there is now at least this union of antagonists. Self-reliance has thus accomplished a surrogate togetherness. (δ) The most important characteristic of this surrogate equilibrium is its abolition of the chasm, for now the behaviour of the others is intrinsically related to [the patient's] we-crippledness. (Ellis, 1938, p. 364)

This extract has been quoted at length because it confirms my impression that the Gestalt psychologists thought of the Ego-schema, *including* mental concepts concerned with social relations between the individual and others, as a primary schema which could, under stress, be fractionated to yield subsystems such as paranoid subsystems that had their own organization (or, rather, re-organization). The knowledge-schemata of Tulving's 'semantic memory' would, I suspect, also be thought of as subsystems of Koffka's Ego-system, but knowledge-schemata might be organized somewhat differently from schemata representing one's personal life.

On the second question, Baddeley's 'central executive' seems to be the *controller* of working memory, a sort of homunculus that decides what to rehearse in the phonological loop or what to image in the visuospatial sketch pad. The contents of these two systems are drawn either from perceptual inputs or from long-term memory. A great deal of retrieval of memories must occur at a preconscious level before the memories surface to the 'eye' of the central executive or are expressed in its output in speech or writing. Koffka's Ego-system on the other hand is a vast set of memories, of which the most recent are most powerful in consciousness, and the Ego is continuously working to build up stable life-improving habits and reduce instability. The actual result of these efforts to adapt to the environment are actions or silent thought: actions (e.g. movements, utterances, writings) are expressed through the 'executive'. In Koffka's system, the executive is, as it were, the device through which the Ego carries out its commands; it performs menial duties as compared with Baddeley's 'central executive'. It is Koffka's Ego, not Koffka's 'executive', that is therefore somewhat analogous to Baddeley's 'central executive'; both have homunculus-like qualities. Koffka's 'executive' does not have a counterpart in Figure 4.2, but in a precursor of Baddeley's flowchart, that of Broadbent (1958), there is a 'system for varying output till input is secured' connected with the system of motor and glandular effectors. Presumably, Koffka's executive operates at this level.

A number of serious questions are raised by the previous paragraph, notably the question of whether a model of human cognition requires a homunculus. This matter will be discussed in more detail in Chapter 6. For the moment we rest content to note that the introduction by the Gestalt psychologists of the notions of systems of traces (schemata) has received extensive elaboration in the contemporary literature on systems and subsystems of memory.

Some correspondences between the research of Köhler and von Restorff and late twentieth century research

Köhler (1923) had argued that memories fuse with each other; the trace of a new input can be fused into memory traces representing its spatiotemporal context, and a second input can leave a trace that is integrated with the fused memories of the first-input-and-its-context. In this section, we shall first discuss late twentieth century models of memory which attempt to be precise about these 'fusings' of traces into 'composite memories'. The discussion here will become a little mathematical, because precision is maximally achieved in any model if the objects under discussion can be measured and thereby be represented as variables in mathematical propositions. The problem here is how to measure a 'trace'; below we focus on one approach. Then we turn to von Restorff's 1933 paper and discuss (1) how her conjecture that retroactive and proactive inhibition are by-products of a 'crowding' of traces has received later support; (2) how her conjecture that primacy and recency effects result from different degrees of 'distinctiveness' in different parts of a list is being confirmed; and (3) how her general argument that the isolation of a stimulus X determines the retrievability of the resulting trace x is receiving support from late twentieth century research on the 'distinctiveness' of stimuli.

Composite memories

In several mathematical models of memory (TODAM, Murdock, 1982; MINERVA2, Hintzman, 1984; CHARM, Eich, 1982, Metcalfe, 1990) individual 'memories' are envisioned as being combined into composites. For example, in Murdock's model, an individual memory is represented as a list or 'vector' of features (elements). Memorizing a sequence of items is equivalent to setting up a new memory vector $\mathbf{M}$ in which the separate items **ABCDEFG** (and certain associations between these items) are represented in a particular kind of combination. To be more precise, at the start of memorizing, only **A** will be in the memory vector $\mathbf{M}$. When **B** is added, the new memory vector $\mathbf{M}_2$ will consist of **A** (reduced to a proportion α of itself by forgetting) plus **B** (weighted by γ to reflect the amount of attention paid to it) plus **A*B** (weighted by ω to reflect the degree of prior association between **A** and **B**). The notation **A*B** refers to a mathematical operation called 'convolution' carried out on the two vectors **A** and **B**. That is, we can write

$$\mathbf{M}_2 = \gamma\mathbf{B} + \omega(\mathbf{B}^*\mathbf{A}) + \alpha\mathbf{A}$$

When a third item **C** is added, the new memory vector $\mathbf{M}_3$ will be

$$\mathbf{M}_3 = \gamma\mathbf{C} + \omega(\mathbf{C}^*\mathbf{B}) + \alpha(\gamma\mathbf{B} + \omega(\mathbf{B}^*\mathbf{A})) + \alpha^2\mathbf{A}$$

This mode of representation of a memory vector shows how individual item information as well as individual order information is preserved within what is now a large vector with many elements. Recognition of a single item, say **C**, is achieved by an operation whereby the vector representing **C** is compared with the memory vector by taking the 'dot product' of the two – the higher the number, the more similar the two vectors are. The dot product will give the cognitive system an indication as to how similar the probe **C** and the **C**-as-embedded-in-the-memory-vector are; the subject will still have to decide whether the degree of similarity is such he can give a 'yes' response signifying that **C** was in the list, a decision modelled by signal detection theory in Murdock's model.

Our purpose in giving this sketch was only to emphasize that as new traces are added to previously existing systems, they are absorbed in a way which is reminiscent of the Gestalt notion of 'assimilation'. As in the cases of encoding and the delineation of types of trace systems, modern researchers are trying to be rigorous about what is otherwise a vague notion in Gestalt terminology: they are trying to make quantitative predictions based on precise assumptions about how traces combine. The general class of models to which Murdock's TODAM (Theory of Distributed Association Memory) belongs is one that assumes that traces should not be thought of as static 'nodes' in a network, but rather as of patterns of activation into which new patterns are continually absorbed, and as a consequence of being combined with other information, these new patterns are somewhat harder to excite in isolation because they are now part of a larger pattern.

Another model like this is Metcalfe's CHARM (Composite Holographic Associative Recall Model), which shares with TODAM the characteristic that *recall* is brought about when we have a memory vector which is a combination of various items, and a retrieval cue representing one of those items is effective in eliciting the retrieval of the remainder of the vector. This can happen when, if we have a combination vector, **F*G**, and we present the item vector **F**, **F** is subjected to a mathematical operation called 'correlation' with **F*G**. The result will be a vector **G′** which is similar but not identical to **G**; the subject must decide whether **G′** is sufficiently similar to **G** to be given as a recall to the retrieval cue **F**. Metcalfe's model, however, is more explicitly related to holography, a form of three-dimensional photography in which illumination of a part of a photographed scene can bring up the rest of the scene instantaneously, and the notion is clearly akin to the resonance model of Koffka and the concept of synergistic ecphory in Semon's theory.

It was Metcalfe (1991) who pointed out that these 'blendings' in memory are reminiscent of the blended 'composite' photographs invented by Sir Francis Galton (1822–1911). Galton made composite photographs by photographing, say, n faces, each time using the same piece of film. Each face was exposed for $1/n$ of the total exposure time and the faces were aligned, usually along the line of the eyes and the mouth, so that the final composite photograph was not blurry and confused but would be clearly seen as a face. Composite photographs like this were taken of members of a family or members of a University class, or even members of a clinically-defined group. The composite photographs themselves often looked youthful and attractive but Metcalfe's point was that human memories, as they blend in long-term memory, might also show 'composite' characteristics. In particular she referred to work carried out in the 1970s by Elizabeth Loftus (1979) on eyewitness testimony. If subjects saw a film, say, of a car accident, and a stop sign had been present in the film, then later the subjects' answers to questions about the accident indicated that the subjects had been subtly misled by the form of the question. For example, if it was suggested to subjects that the sign had been a yield sign, the subjects would change their reports in a way suggesting that the 'yield sign' of the interrogation period had been 'blended in' or 'integrated' into their memory (schema) of the film. Metcalfe (1990) was able to model this 'blending' by applying the CHARM model to simulated representations of Loftus's experiments. For recall, as mentioned above, a cue is correlated with the trace vector and the result is that all the events originally associated with the cue are retrieved, in a *superimposed* manner. As Metcalfe (1991) writes:

> Thus suppose that the cue 'corner' is associated with both a stop sign and a yield sign. When corner is correlated with the composite trace both stop sign and yield sign will be retrieved superimposed . . . Insofar as the model is a trace compositing or 'blending' model, the claim that memories are blended together gains some credence. (pp. 416–417)

Metcalfe pointed out that some of Bartlett's (1932) data on memory for drawings show that recall of a set of five faces viewed a week or two earlier indicated that features seem to 'drift' from one face to another – if person 4 had a moustache and person 5 had a pipe, recall of person 5 might give him a pipe and a moustache, particularly if he was recalled as representing a personality type (e.g. a military type).

It was the contention of the Gestalt psychologists that any new input is 'assimilated' into a previous trace-schema. This conclusion came from studies of the time-error, but the above research on the assimilation of new information into a framework of old memories, leading to possible errors of retrieval, extends the notion of 'assimilation' from situations involving short-term memory to situations involving long-term memory. It should be noted that the actual 'blending' in a composite memory might arise from grouping by similarity; I have a 'composite' memory of past Christmases in which memories, say, of Christmas 1990 blend with those for 1987 by virtue of their similarity (e.g. I lived in the same house during both Christmases).

Crowding as an explanation for retroactive inhibition

For many years after 1933, von Restorff's suggestion that retroactive and proactive inhibition should be seen as artifacts of the 'crowding' of similar memory traces was relatively ignored. Research on these topics was dominated by the approach of Melton and von Lackum (1941), whose two-factor theory of retroactive inhibition had been widely adopted. It will be recalled that the two factors were (a) interference at retrieval between two responses from the original list and responses from the interpolated list, combined with (b) some forgetting of the original list because it was 'unlearned' while the subject was concentrating on acquiring the interpolated list. In a related paper, Melton and Irwin (1940) had argued that proactive inhibition might be less 'potent' as a source of interference than was retroactive inhibition, because no unlearning of the original list was involved in a design where the original list had been either preceded or not preceded by another list. However, Underwood (1957) was able to show that proactive inhibition could be very powerful: he demonstrated, by an analysis of many experiments carried out by himself or others, that the more lists had preceded a particular list, the poorer the retrieval of that target list 24 hours later. This in itself ought to have suggested that proactive inhibition could be underestimated, but it was Barnes and Underwood (1959) who indicated that yet another factor (besides response interference and unlearning of the original list) could determine interference effects. Suppose we are studying paired-associates, and in the original list the subject must learn BEM–LAWN and in the interpolated list, BEM–AISLE. Barnes and Underwood found that subjects did not necessarily forget LAWN or AISLE as responses to BEM, but became confused as to whether, say, LAWN came from the original list or the interpolated list. So a third factor, called 'list differentiation' entered the picture, and it is obvious that this may bear some relationship to von Restorff's notion that the items from the interpolated list are causing a 'crowding' of responses associated with the stimulus BEM. A failure of list differentiation could be a sign of 'crowding'.

But better evidence that 'crowding' was indeed occurring, causing a loss of distinctiveness of the responses from *both* lists, was provided by Ceraso (1967). John Ceraso had worked as a research assistant with Köhler and Asch at Swarthmore. In a review of several experiments, Ceraso argued that there is a common pattern in retroactive inhibition experiments that needs explaining. Immediately after having learned an original list followed directly by an interpolated list, the interpolated list may be recalled with about 90 per cent accuracy. If memory for the original list is tested at the same time, it might be recalled with 60 per cent accuracy even though it was originally well learned. The drop is typical evidence for retroactive inhibition induced by having learned the interpolated list. But now if the subjects are retested 24 hours later, recall of the interpolated list drops to about 70 per cent (from 90 per cent), whereas recall of the original list remains unchanged at about 60 per cent. Why should the recall of the original list not also drop by the same proportion as recall of the interpolated list, given that all that has happened is the passing of a day's time? Ceraso concluded that the drop in recall of the *interpolated* list reflected what he called the 'crowding' of items in memory from the two lists. With respect to the *original* list, he said that the forgetting in the immediate test was due to its having been unlearned while the interpolated list was being memorized. But over the course of the day's interval, those 'unlearned' items spontaneously recovered, a process that had been demonstrated by Pavlov as occurring normally when conditioned responses had been temporarily extinguished, and which had been demonstrated by Underwood (1948) to also apply to list-learning by humans. The process of crowding should affect both lists equally over the day's interval, and indeed responses from the interpolated list were forgotten but the responses from the original list, which should also have been forgotten due to crowding, were subject to some spontaneous recovery. Spontaneous recovery was counteracting the forgetting due to crowding of the responses from the original list.

Ceraso went on to explore crowding more directly. He had one group of subjects learn an original list A, followed by 10 trials on a interpolated list B. Since both lists were learned about equally, it was expected that the crowding of A-responses by B-responses would be maximal. Another group of subjects learned list A, followed by one trial on a list B, one on a list C and so on for 10 trials, each trial using a different list. Since none of these responses would be learned very well, it was expected that the memory of the original A-responses would be relatively uncrowded. As a measure of memory for the A-responses, Ceraso calculated how much *interference* was due to the interpolated memorizing; on immediate recall, the maximally crowded A-list had 40 per cent interference, after 24 hours the interference had dropped slightly to 37 per cent. But the minimally crowded A-responses, which on immediate test suffered from 34 per cent interference by the interpolated list, after 24 hours showed a 24 per cent interference, a substantial reduction in interference. The minimally crowded items had more chance to spontaneously recover, according to Ceraso.

However, Ceraso challenged Koffka's explanation for crowding in terms of a 'physiological' interaction between traces. He claimed that

> Koffka believed that for each memory a 'memory trace' exists physically in the brain, and that when one recalls, say, an elephant, it is because the brain's memory trace for 'elephant' has somehow been stimulated. It was Koffka's opinion that if too many items of the same kind are learned at the same time, the memory traces will interact and become distorted. (p. 6)

But Ceraso claimed that since retroactive inhibition can often be demonstrated for recall but not necessarily for *recognition*, then the traces of the similar responses cannot ultimately destroy each other. He showed, for example, that if one learns an original list of paired-associates including, say, BEM–LAWN, followed by an interpolated list including, say, BEM–AISLE, subjects can quite accurately allot LAWN and AISLE to BEM when given all the words and syllables on cards and told to match each syllable-card with its two appropriate response-cards. Although there was marked interference with memories of the original list on an immediate test, this interference was greatly *diminished* after 24 hours. The association BEM–LAWN was not apparently destroyed by the association BEM–AISLE, otherwise it could not have 'recovered' 24 hours later. On the other hand, in the usual recall task the subject was given BEM and had to recall both LAWN and AISLE. It was found that recall of original list responses (e.g. BEM–LAWN) suffered retroactive inhibition to about the same extent both on an immediate test and a test a day later, while recall for the interpolated responses (e.g. BEM–AISLE) was much worse 24 hours later than immediately. The results for recall therefore confirm earlier results, but the results for the matching task (which is in part a recognition task) indicate that the traces representing the associates BEM–LAWN and BEM–AISLE, while hard to retrieve, had not mutually destroyed each other otherwise spontaneous recovery of BEM–LAWN could not have occurred.

Ceraso, then, offered an account parallel to that of von Restorff, namely, that retroactive inhibition could be due to crowding. Moreover, he modified it to integrate it with currently available evidence on unlearning and spontaneous recovery. I am not sure, however, that Koffka would have agreed with Ceraso's claim that trace-interaction necessarily involves trace *distortion*; and certainly Köhler and von Restorff (1937), in recounting their experiment showing a failure to recognize a target item because of the presence of items similar to the target in the interval between the target and the probe, argued that the traces of those similar items did not lead to the *destruction* of the trace of the target. As I read both Koffka and Köhler, trace 'crowding' does not imply trace 'destruction', but it certainly hinders the *distinguishing* of the trace during a retrieval act.

More generally, Ceraso and Tendler (1968) stressed that

> immediately after learning the two lists of a typical interference-experiment, these lists are distinct entities, whereas over time the distinctiveness is lost and the two lists merge into one long list, making recall more difficult. A similar notion, list differentiation, has been used previously by Underwood. Underwood, however, stressed the effect of differentiation on the subject's ability to assign an item to the list in which it had been learned, while here its effect on item-retrieval is argued. (p. 48)

Following publication of Ceraso's 1967 article, there was a concerted effort to evaluate Melton and von Lackum's two-factor theory of retroactive inhibition as being due to response interference and to the unlearning of list 1 items. Postman and Underwood (1973) appeared to endorse the two-factor theory, with the addendum that a number of papers on the actual process of 'unlearning' had indicated that subjects tended to think of the whole of list 1 as a 'response set', so that the 'unlearning' could be characterized as a case of 'response set suppression'. Moreover, evidence from experiments in which subjects recalled responses from both lists (e.g. recalling both LAWN and AISLE, given BEM) indicated that a failure of list differentiation did occur. But no reference in this paper was made to Ceraso's introduction of the concept of 'crowding' as a close relative of list differentiation, nor was his theory as outlined above even mentioned.

The next major advance occurred when Mensink and Raaijmakers (1988) offered a mathematical model that predicted such phenomena as the decrease in original list responses as a function of the number of trials on the interpolated materials (when testing occurred immediately after the latter); the spontaneous recovery of original list responses after an interval had elapsed since the interpolated learning; the pattern of intrusions of responses from the interpolated learning into recall of original list items, representing failures of list differentiation; and the fact that recognition of the original list items was less affected by interpolated learning than was recall. It will be noted that each of one of these issues had been incorporated into Ceraso's 1967 model based on the notion that original list items and interpolated list items were 'crowded' together in memory, but there is no mention of Ceraso's work by Mensink and Raaijmakers.

However, their model is instructive because it can fairly easily be viewed as sharing a feature in common with Gestalt psychology. In their theory, which is based on the SAM model, items in the original list leave associations in memory (e.g. BEM–LAWN) whose strength is a function of the amount of time they were studied in the *context* of that list, the *context* of that time period and, possibly, the *context* of the place where learning occurred. Similarly, associations from the interpolated lists (e.g. BEM–AISLE) are learned in a particular context. The probability of retrieval of either BEM–LAWN or BEM–AISLE is a function of the extent to which both the item cues (e.g. BEM) and the context cues overlap between the context at the time of storage and the context at the time of retrieval. Mensink and Raaijmakers developed a contextual fluctuation model according to which the contextual association strength fluctuated with the amount of attention given to learning each item. While the original list was being learned, BEM–LAWN was being strengthened, and some contextual elements would be stored along the memory of BEM–LAWN (called the 'image' of BEM–LAWN in the SAM model). Then during interpolated learning not only would BEM–AISLE be stored but so would contextual elements unique to that association. At any moment after both lists had been learned, some contextual elements would be active and others inactive. Using precise mathematical postulates as to the roles of time spent studying, time spent searching, and the rate at which active elements become inactive over time and vice versa, Mensink and Raaijmakers made numerical estimates as to the course of learning and forgetting of the two lists in the typical A–B, A–C retroactive inhibition paradigm. They also extended their predictions to cover Osgood's 1949 model of transfer and retroactive inhibition, to proactive inhibition, and to retrieval latencies with respect to the recovery of associations from both lists.

Yet perhaps their most interesting discovery was that their model predicted relative independence of the associations in the two lists. In early writings on the unlearning of original list associations during the acquisition of the interpolated list, the suggestion had been made that the 'strength' of the original list associations was reduced. The same notion of trace destruction had been popular at the time Köhler and Koffka were writing, though they had attacked it. Work by Greeno *et al.* (1978) had indicated that if 'unlearning' did occur, it did not actually reduce the strength of the association of original list responses like BEM–LAWN; in the SAM model, associating a second response like AISLE to BEM did not affect the strength of the association of LAWN to BEM. However, contextual cues (e.g. recalling items in the interpolated list) did alter the retrievability of LAWN, given BEM. This new evidence supported Ceraso's contention that interpolated learning affected only the probability of recalling the original list and did not affect the strength of the associations in the original list (his proof had involved showing that a task involving the matching of associations like LAWN to BEM was relatively unaffected by interpolated learning). Postman and Underwood (1973) had argued that the postulate that responses became associated to the same stimulus in independent fashion does not necessarily contradict the assumption that unlearning reduces the strength of the associations in the original list. Mensink and Raaijmakers did not join this debate but focused on the evidence favouring the view that if an association A–B has been established, learning A–C will not in any permanent way displace or reduce the strength of A–B.

In this model, list differentiation is essentially subsumed under the notion that contextual cues at the moment of retrieval play a major role. If contextual cues are not unique because they might be associated with either list, there will be intrusions in recall. Even if I asserted this was a Gestalt view because Koffka stressed the importance of context reinstatement at recall, and, more hesitantly, because von Restorff had stressed that interference at retrieval resulted when particular memories were not sufficiently isolated from similar memories (BEM–LAWN and BEM–AISLE are insufficiently 'isolated' from each other because they have the common element BEM), I doubt that Mensink and Raaijmakers would be persuaded to abandon a historical conception according to which SAM is a modern variant of classical associationism. But what SAM does is bring rigour into scientific explanations in which context cues matter as much as item-specific cues, and this, I am sure, would have pleased both Koffka and von Restorff. Their plea was for a psychology that included list-contexts, and the contents of temporal between-fields, as determinants of the retrieval of simple elements in lists. Late twentieth century psychology is lending quantitative rigour to the qualitative generalizations of the Gestalt psychologists and the result may be that the barriers between the Gestalt and associationistic traditions steadily collapse.

Primacy and recency effects

Von Restorff (1933) explicitly asserted that when, in ordered recall, the first and last items of a list were better recalled, this was an illustration of the isolation effect. In a list such as

L V M K T N C S

all the letters are flanked by two others except L and S, which are each flanked on one side by a letter and on the other side by a space. L and S were therefore more 'isolated'. Recall of the L that was superior to that of the other letters (except, possibly, S) would illustrate what is now called a primacy effect; superior recall of the S would be an example of a recency effect. Whether primacy or recency effects predominate is well known to be a function of the nature of the retrieval task. If we have immediate ordered recall starting from the beginning of the list, there is a strong primacy effect and a modest recency effect that is more marked following auditory presentation than it is following visual presentation (see e.g. Murray, 1966; Cantor and Engle, 1989). If the task is that of probed recognition, there is a very strong recency effect and a modest primacy effect (see e.g. Murray *et al.*, 1988). Clearly, the kind of retrieval task determines the relative dominance of primacy versus recency, but in almost all retrieval tasks the effects are present.

More importantly perhaps, they are present not only in tasks when the material has been clearly encoded phonologically, as in the above studies, but also when the memory material is a more purely sensory form. Frick (1988a) has studied more purely auditory short-term storage and considers primacy and recency effects as 'boundary effects'. Boundary effects can also be induced by putting a pause in the middle of a list: the effect is to group the items and primacy and recency effects can be detected for the items at the beginning and the end respectively of each group (Ryan, 1969a, b). Frick (1988a) reviews various possible explanations for these boundary effects, including the importance of order of report, selective attention, proactive inhibition for later items in the group, chunking, and a reduction in the probability of order errors in reporting first or last items as opposed to middle items. He finds all these explanations wanting and claims that the true explanation lies in the nature of a 'parsed and categorizing' process that must be carried out on the purely sensory material before it can be reported. For Frick, pure auditory storage is to some extent pre-conscious: in order for the material to be made available to consciousness it has to be 'parsed and categorized'. For example, a sequence of words like

chin time path reef

must be broken up into units in order for the units to be categorized as common words. If we had only

chintimepathreef

and parsed at random from a certain sound, say 'th', the categorizer or decoder would not know if 'th' started a word, was the middle of a word or ended a word. Providing pauses aids the parsing process so that categorization can proceed unhampered. As a corollary principle, items at the boundary of an as yet unparsed representation are held to be more easily identified than items in the interior of a representation. The process of 'recovery' of information in auditory short-term storage (by which Frick means the process of decoding the unparsed uncategorized information in a manner acceptable to the subject's conscious wish to retain the material) is greatly facilitated if pauses are used to delimit 'groups' of items, and Frick explicitly states that these groups arise between pauses because of the Gestalt principles of grouping. The primacy and recency effects arise because 'an item next to the boundary of a presentation is easier to identify during recovery, because one of its edges is already defined' (p. 234).

Frick's argument was extended to the case of purely visual short-term memory storage (Frick, 1988b), which again he considered to be pre-conscious, unparsed and uncategorized. Research on this kind of storage is difficult because subjects will attempt to phonologically encode visually presented matrices of letters or other verbal material. But following a careful analysis of data presented by Wolford and Hollingsworth (1974), Harcum and Skrzypek (1965) and himself, Frick showed that when spaces were inserted into visually presented lists, the space induced primacy and recency effects for the items flanking the space. As with auditory short-term storage, Frick rejected other explanations (including interference from lateral items) in favour of the view that items next to spaces were easier to identify during the parsing and categorization stages.

It should be noted that these arguments refer to the *process* of translating information from a purely sensory form into a phonological (or, perhaps, conscious image) form. But by the time the information from the whole list is available in properly encoded form, the advantages for the first and last items will have been preserved.

For some situations, it has generally been agreed that once the information has been put into phonological store, primacy effects can be enhanced by intralist rehearsal and recency effects can be enhanced because they are 'fresh' in the memory. In the case of free recall of, say, 20 words, the last items are usually recalled first while they are still in working memory, while the first items can be shown to benefit more than other items from intralist rehearsal (Rundus, 1971). But primacy and recency effects can also be found for long sequences of items learned by heart for serial recall, or even in the free recall of the Presidents of the United States. Crowder and Neath (1991) remark that

> Attitudes commonly accepted for serial position effects in free recall include extra rehearsal for the primacy items and a recency buffer in STM for the last few. These attitudes are of questionable value for the early part of the series [Presidents] (Madison might possibly be 'rehearsed' more than Buchanan) but so silly as to be beneath discussion for the last few. (p. 119)

Instead Crowder and Neath favour the view, called by Murdock (1960) the 'serial position distinctiveness hypothesis', that primacy and recency result because the boundary items are more distinctive. Neath and Crowder (1990) considered that the recall of a particular item is proportional to its 'temporal discriminability' – this could be defined as the ratio of its spacing from the previous item to its delay before the recall episode. As an analogy, the subject at the time of recall was considered to look backwards towards the list, which could be compared to gazing

> back towards a series of telephone poles, each representing the temporal occurrence of a memory item, the whole series viewed from near or far depending on whether the retention interval had been short or long, respectively. (Crowder and Neath, 1991, p. 116)

As an example they showed that *free* recall of five word-pairs showed a strong recency and a small primacy effect when these items were spaced temporally as follows

1 1 1   1   1

When they were spaced as follows

1   1   1   1 1

recency was still greater than primacy, but the degree of recency was reduced and the degree of primacy was enhanced. This result was put down to a greater temporal discriminability of the late items in the first case and greater temporal discriminability of the early items in the second case, particularly as viewed from a perspective that looked back at this list. Subjects may indeed adopt different perspectives for looking at the telephone poles; there can be a forward perspective or a backward perspective. Free recall, as in the above experiment, probably involved a backward perspective, but in other experimental situations, a forward perspective may be preferred, and this is usually how items are rehearsed. In fact, Forrin and Cunningham (1973) showed that if a list of five digits were presented for probed recognition and the probe was presented immediately, the reaction times to correctly say 'yes' if the probe was an old item (hits) showed a strong recency effect (the most recent items gave the shortest reaction times). But if two seconds elapsed before the probe, which is just about enough time to rehearse the list phonologically, reaction times for hits were almost equal for all five items. There seems to have been a shift from a backward perspective to a forward perspective.

In the study of the retrieval of five word-pairs, the backward perspective shown in free recall can be shifted to a forward perspective by forcing the subject to give forward serial recall; if the items are presented very rapidly, leaving little time for rehearsal to disguise the effect of temporal discriminability, there was a stronger primacy effect for all conditions. But recall of the third and fourth items of a list like

1 1 1   1   1

was now better than recall of the third and fourth items in a list like

1   1   1   1 1

This had not been the case in free recall and the shift appears to have been due to a shift in perspective for viewing the list.

Following on from this, Neath (1993) went on to show that there is another way in which serial position can be manipulated so that either recency or primacy effects dominate the retrieval pattern. Using the short-term recognition of snowflake patterns as the retrieval task, Neath replicated some research of Wright *et al.* (1985), who had shown, using both human and animal subjects, that recognition given immediately after the presentation of a series of visual pictures (i.e. nonverbal stimuli) shows strong recency effects, whereas recognition after a delay showed a strong primacy effect, with recency less than was the case for immediate recognition. Neath found that the same pattern of results held both when probe delay was a between-subjects variable and when it was a within-subjects variable. He then calculated a score of 'distinctiveness' for each of the four snowflake patterns in each list, with the distinctiveness being a function of the probe delay; the shorter the delay, the more distinctive the last item in the target sequence, the longer the delay the less distinctive this was with respect to the other members of the list. The calculation of distinctiveness followed a line of mathematical argument pioneered by Murdock (1960) and Johnson (1991). More will be said about it in the next section. The main finding that Neath obtained was that the shift from a dominant recency effect to a dominant primacy effect as probe delay increased could be well modelled by assuming that retrieval was a function of stimulus distinctiveness. Neath also showed that the distinctiveness model could yield predictions which well matched the data in a verification task described by Gernsbacher *et al.* (1989). They presented sentences such as 'Tina gathered the kindling as Lisa set up the tent' and then asked simple questions about the sentences. The reaction time to answer questions about 'Lisa' was faster than that to answer questions about 'Tina' when the question was asked immediately after the sentence, but if the question was delayed by 2 seconds, answers about 'Tina' were given faster than answers about 'Lisa'. The same argument holds true as time passes, the more recent of two items becomes less distinctive with respect to the earlier item, by the sort of telescoping process outlined by Neath and Crowder. At the beginning of the article, Neath (1993) noted that Koffka (1935a) had stressed stimulus isolation as an important factor determining retrieval, and that von Restorff (1933) had manipulated physical variables as a means of varying stimulus distinctiveness. But he also noted that Aristotle may have been the first to stress distinctiveness as a determinant of memorability.

More generally, Lewandowsky and Murdock (1989) have shown that TODAM can be used to model primacy and recency effects both in free recall and serial recall. The model incorporated an earlier notion (Murdock, 1960) that performance is relatively better at the endpoints of a series than in the interior of the series because the endpoints were more distinctive particularly from a temporal point of view. Glenberg and Swanson (1986) have elaborated on the temporal distinctiveness theory of recency and Glenberg (1987) suggested that, as the retention interval increases, temporal discriminability becomes 'blurred'. Thus there would be a greater subjective discrimination between memories of Christmas 1990 and Christmas 1987 than there would be between memories of Christmas 1980 and Christmas 1977. But it is surely a matter of words as to whether we choose to say with Murdock, Glenberg, Crowder, Neath and other contemporary writers that the endpoints of a list are 'temporally distinctive' or whether we choose to say with Köhler and von Restorff that the items at endpoints are more isolated than are the items at midpoints because the former are bounded on one side by a pause or a space whereas the latter are crowded together. The modern research reviewed above has, however, given a more sophisticated account of *relative* levels of distinctiveness than is available in the Gestalt literature. But this modern research is also based on the question of the 'distinctiveness' of items at different serial positions in a list, as will now be discussed.

'Distinctiveness' as a variable determining retrieval in general

In the previous section it was noted that primacy and recency effects might hinge on the temporal or spatial distinctiveness of the endpoints of a list. However, the view also exists that memorability in general depends on distinctiveness. In the Roman treatise of unknown authorship entitled *Rhetorica ad Herennium*, the writer remarks that events that are 'exceptionally base, dishonourable, extraordinary, great, unbelievable or laughable' are the best remembered. There is some experimental evidence to support some of these contentions: exceptionally 'base' things would include traumatic experiences, and Christianson and Loftus (1987) found that the gist of videotapes showing traumatic scenes (e.g. of a boy shot in the face) were better recalled than was the gist of videotapes not containing traumatic scenes; however more peripheral details were forgotten in the videotape that included unpleasant scenes. 'Unbelievable' events would include bizarre events – McDaniel and Einstein (1986) asked subjects to form images of nouns in sentences which were either conventional (e.g. 'the dog chased the bicycle down the street') or bizarre (e.g. 'the dog rode the bicycle down the street'); free recall was better for the bizarre sentences, with some loss of recall of conventional sentences in the same list. 'Laughable' events would include humorous examples in a lecture in introductory psychology – Kaplan and Pascoe (1977) presented humorous examples in such a lecture to one group, and only serious examples in an otherwise similar lecture to another group. Both groups recalled material from both types of lectures equally in a test of immediate recall, but after 6 weeks the group that had the humorous examples recalled those examples better than did the other group. Each of these experiments raises a problem. The traumatic events may have been recalled well because they aroused a defensive autonomic response, the bizarre events may have only been remembered because they surprised the subject (a claim made by Hirshman *et al.*, 1989), the humorous examples may also have caused increased arousal of the sympathetic nervous system. Is memory enhancement that results from a concomitant physiological response merely another example of distinctiveness, or does the physiological response somehow strengthen the trace? This is not known.

Yet there are many other instances where distinctiveness, defined much as von Restorff defined isolation, clearly enhances recall (and sometimes recognition). Schmidt (1991) has presented a thorough and comprehensive analysis of evidence from memory experiments that, not only must distinctiveness be defined as distinctiveness *in a context*, but also that distinctiveness in a context enhances memory. For example, recall of a list containing only bizarre items was about the same as recall of a list containing only conventional items. But if one group of subjects read *two* lists prior to an unexpected recall test, one bizarre and one conventional, recall of the first list was better than was found in a second group of subjects for whom both lists contained conventional items (McDaniel and Einstein, 1986). Both recall and recognition of an animal name in a list of people's names and countries was better than when that name was included in a list of other animal names (Schmidt, 1985). Schmidt (1991) refers to the latter condition as involving 'embedding', a near-synonym for 'crowding'. If paragraphs of printed text included unpredictable words, these words were better recalled than were words that could have been predicted from the preceding context (O'Brien and Myers, 1985). Following a list consisting entirely of weakly-related word-pairs (e.g. PATCH–LETTUCE), free recall did not yield significantly better recall than was found for a list of strongly related word-pairs (CABBAGE–LETTUCE), but when weakly related pairs and strongly related pairs were intermixed, free recall of the weakly related pairs was superior provided they were not in a clear majority (Hirshman, 1988). Many other examples stressing that distinctiveness must be defined in a *context* are given in Schmidt's 1991 paper, and other instances where distinctiveness has been invoked to explain why some words are better retrieved than others include the classic evidence for the value of depth processing (i.e. semantic elaboration) for subsequent recall or recognition (Craik and Tulving, 1975) and the finding that words that are actively generated by the subject from a cue (e.g. doing a fragment completion task) are often better retrieved than are identical words perceived passively (Slamecka and Graf, 1978).

Schmidt reviewed sixteen different types of experiment which ostensibly demonstrated the importance of distinctiveness in determining retrieval performance. The materials used in the experiments were:

Emotional distinctiveness:
    pictures of nudes inserted in a series of magazine pictures

videotapes or stories involving events
enhanced memory for events surrounding major news stories (flashbulb memories)
lectures or sentences involving humour

Distinctiveness in which one or a few elements do not fit the conceptual framework associated with the other elements (primary distinctiveness):

perceptual distinctiveness (e.g. an item printed in red among a series printed in black)
categorical distinctiveness (e.g. an animal name in a list of countries)
high-priority events (e.g. being instructed to pay special attention to particular items)
encoding-task distinctiveness
consistency effect (e.g. an object that is out-of-place in a familiar scene)

Distinctiveness in which one or a few events do not fit preconceptions based on long-term memory (secondary distinctiveness):

orthographic distinctiveness (e.g. a word spelled unusually such as LLAMA)
unusual faces
bizarre imagery
the word-generation effect

Some cases where well-known memory phenomena may possibly be attributed to distinctiveness:

depth of processing
better memory for concrete as opposed to abstract words
evidence that long-term memory for words is in part a function of whether the words were seen, heard or vocalized

Schmidt gives appropriate references in all these cases, and enumerates a number of other experiments whose results probably depend on distinctiveness, including the well-known fact that rare words are often recognized better than are common words from lists that include both kinds of word (Gregg, 1976). However, after this extensive review, Schmidt concluded that:

a compelling theory of distinctiveness has not been developed. In the absence of a compelling theory, a common definition, or a cogent structure of empirical phenomena, the concept of distinctiveness in memory is of little heuristic value. (p. 534)

But Schmidt reviewed some earlier theories and himself came to the conclusion that the essence of 'distinctiveness' was 'incongruity': an item that was 'distinct' from others around it seemed 'incongruent' in the sense of 'not fitting in' or 'deserving a different kind of response from others'.

Despite its apparent vagueness, however, there have been some rather successful attempts to measure distinctiveness. Murdock (1960), in a study which is now receiving more attention than it did when it appeared, showed that if we have a set of increasing loudnesses, and measure how different each one is from each of the others, the softest and the loudest stimuli have the greatest distinctiveness as measured by the sum of all the differences between them and the others. Johnson (1991), following a suggestion in Murdock's paper, measured the distinctiveness of separate items in a list of nonsense syllables: the fewer remote associations with other items a given item possessed, the more distinctive it was taken to be. This assertion simplifies the matter overmuch because Johnson also related distinctiveness to an 'adaptation level' determined by the total set of items; but the upshot was that Johnson was able to predict the pattern of data obtained in serial learning tasks very well, including the prediction of the fact that the hardest items to learn in a list are about five-eighths of the way through the list. And we have already mentioned the successful account given by Neath (1993) of the different serial position curves following various delays of the probe in recognition tasks.

Since Gestalt theory stresses that the mind evaluates stimuli within the framework of surrounding stimuli, we may be on the edge of an application of Gestalt theory to learning theory which would have heartened Köhler and von Restorff, and at the same time pleased neobehaviourists like Hull and Hovland because of its mathematical rigour. It must be remembered, however, that Murdock himself, the inventor of this method for measuring distinctiveness, went on to devise the TODAM model, which is very specific about how items combine into memory vectors, and that TODAM can also be used to predict serial learning data very well (Lewandowsky and Murdock, 1989). Moreover, he has elaborated the model into a TODAM2 version that says more about how memory vectors can be combined into 'chunks' in the process of learning (Murdock, 1993). I personally find it is easy to think of a 'chunk' as a linking together of discrete units to form a new 'Gestalt' in which the parts are subordinate to the whole, a matter that will surface again in the context of problem-solving in the next chapter.

Chapter 5

Gestalt ideas about thinking and problem-solving

Gestalt contributions to our understanding of problem-solving

In Chapter 2 we introduced the reader to some of the main contributions of Gestalt psychology to our understanding of productive thinking. In his initial study carried out in World War I of problem-solving by apes, Köhler, in the *Mentality of Apes*, had introduced three important notions:

1. Solutions are often attained in a moment of insight when the elements or objects available to the subject are used in a new way: a short stick can be used to pull in a long stick which in turn can be used to knock down the banana hanging from the cage ceiling. It was critical that the ape be able to survey all elements of the problem and it helped if the ape had already had experience in one or more of the stages in the sequence. For example, apes would sometimes think of a stick as something to be climbed up to grasp the bananas, rather than as an object with which to strike the bananas. Only when the stick could be conceived of as a striking tool could it be used in the sequence mentioned above.
2. Solutions often failed to be attained if the ape persisted in old habits or ways of perceiving objects.
3. There were good errors and bad errors: good errors were often stepping stones to solutions, as when climbing up a box precariously perched on its edge gave way to using the box as an object to stand on (or leap from) to grasp the banana.

The notion that insight could be attained by a new look at the problem situation was stressed by Wertheimer (1925) in his seminal article entitled 'On inference processes in productive thinking'. This article took as its starting point the logical syllogism such as

All men are mortal.
Socrates is a man.
Therefore, Socrates is mortal.

The conclusion follows logically from the definition of 'all' but Wertheimer pointed out that sometimes new scientific knowledge might be arrived at from syllogisms of this pattern. For example, in investigating the unknown composition of a liquid, I might observe that, if I heat the liquid and note that first a yellowish gas is discharged, then a bluish gas, then a greyish gas, and at the end the yellowish gas is on top, I might infer the following syllogism:

The first gas to be discharged is yellowish.
The yellowish gas comes to the top.
Therefore, the first gas to be discharged comes to the top.

The interesting inference is that the component of the liquid that has the lowest boiling point also has the lowest specific gravity, because it rises to the top.

In this example we feel a certain 'click' which allows us to look at the bare facts of a syllogism and see the total in a new light. But most problems are not simple syllogisms of the above pattern whose conclusion can be easily arrived at by deduction. Indeed some conclusions from syllogisms are difficult to infer. Newell (1990, p. 378) points out that it is not so easy to arrive at the appropriate conclusion from the two premises:

Some B are not A.
All B are C.
Therefore, ?

The answer is 'Some C are not A'. Over the years between publication of the initial paper of Newell *et al.* (1958) on inference making and Newell's book of 1990, these authors and their colleagues have persuasively shown that the mental processes humans undergo when trying to prove that such a syllogism is logically valid can be modelled by a computer program. In the early stages of this research endeavour, Newell *et al.* (1958) described a program called the Logic Theorist which attempted to *prove* the validity of specific syllogistic chains of reasoning like those above. The proofs included various rules of inference. In later work, Newell (1990), using a program called Syl-Soar/S88 developed by himself and his colleagues, went further and attempted to model the *mental* processes associated with humans' attempts to infer conclusions or prove logical theorems. This work was strongly influenced by the theory of Johnson-Laird (1983) that in solving problems we all set up a 'mental model' or 'mental representation' of the task. Since the work of Newell and Simon dominates modern research on thinking, we mention the above facts to show that Wertheimer and other authors started from a similar issue, that of syllogistic reasoning.

When a 'click' does occur following a sequence of reasoning, the effect can often be that the elements in the situation are seen in a new light. Wertheimer quoted the case of two friends, Peter and Paul, who regularly attend their club's annual meeting, at which a statement of accounts is given, but who do not attend other meetings of the executive committee. One day Peter finds a letter stating that a decision about the accounts was reached at a recent meeting at which he had been absent and at which the accounts had been discussed, in contradiction to the usual procedure, moreover, the decision had been made on a motion of Paul. This decision is distasteful to Peter, and suddenly the concept of 'Paul' is seen in a new light. It was Wertheimer's strong contention that many problems involving reasoning demand that the elements in the problem be '*re*-formed, *re*-grouped, *re*-centred' (Ellis, 1938, p. 278) in a specific way and that the re-conceptualization of Paul by Peter, following a sequence of events like the above, is psychologically the same kind of re-conceptualization as takes place when, in a moment of insight, the elements of a problem are seen in a new light. Over the years these various 're-' words crystallized into the single word 're-structuring' – for Wertheimer successful solutions to problems involved a re-structuring of the elements. He taught a seminar on productive thinking at the New School for Social Research between 1936 and 1941, and the detailed protocols of these lectures made by Luchins and Luchins (1970) indicate that Wertheimer was firmly persuaded of the need for a psychology of thought to centre on re-structuring and on obstacles to re-structuring. Being fixated on a previous function associated with a problem-element or on a previously successful strategy was one of the obstacles to re-structuring, and Luchins (1939) wrote a PhD thesis on such fixations in problem-solving.

The notion that a fixation on a previous strategy can blind one to a solution for which the strategy is not the optimal one was first explored experimentally, apparently by Müller and Schumann (1898) in a study on psychophysics. As related by Luchins and Luchins (1970, Vol. III, p. 39):

> Wertheimer described the classical weight judgment of Müller and Schumann (1898). In this study, the subject's task was to lift two weights and to state which was the heavier one. The subject first compared the standard weight, 676 grams, with the other weights, the heaviest of which was 876 grams. He then compared the standard weight thirty times with a weight of 2,476 grams. After this, he compared the standard weight once with each of the following weights: 926, 876, and 826 grams. In the last three comparisons, the hand that held the variable weight flew up into the air in an exaggerated fashion and the subject reported (erroneously) that each of the variable weights was lighter than the standard weight. In comparing the standard weight with a weight of 2,476 grams, Müller and Schumann said, the subject had developed a motor adjustment which he carried over to the last three comparisons. They called this an *Einstellung*, a set which immediately predisposed one to one kind of mental or motor activity.

This concept of *Einstellung* was extended to problem-solving and explored extensively in Luchins' thesis (1939) and reported in Luchins (1942). Wertheimer was involved at all stages of the research, which investigated a variety of tasks, but whose common format was:

1. Show that strategy X works for problems $X_1, X_2, X_3 \ldots$
2. Then present problem Y which has a superficial resemblance to $X_1, X_2, X_3 \ldots$ but which can be solved in an easier way than by using strategy X.

Result: subjects do not notice the easier solution but 'blindly' apply strategy *X*.

Some tasks investigated by Luchins include the following:

Line judgements

1. In a task in which subject *S* had to judge which of two lines was shorter, and heard the judgement of the previous subject, who was always 'correct', subjects came to adopt the strategy of imitating the judgement of the previous subject. In fact the two lines were always equal.
2. Then the two lines were made visibly unequal. The previous subject started giving wrong answers, and so did subject *S*. It was only after a few trials that subject *S* looked at the lines, saw the correct answer, and did not rely on the previous subject's answer.

Hidden words

1. The subjects are shown a 5×5 array of letters and have to find a hidden word. For example, in

AMIKM		LGHSW
NOLOS	and	SEDOF
KPUYT		EZMPG
RSEMI		KAPOR
ELNBR		NYZPN

the hidden word starts in the rightmost letter of the top row and runs down diagonally leftwards towards the first letter of the bottom row. In the first of the above arrays, the hidden word is MOUSE, in the second, it is WOMAN. After a few trials, the subject settles in to a strategy of always processing these letters first.
2. Then he or she is shown

GRAVE
POIVR
VCEPT
NZGLM
JORTU

Usually they do not notice that the top line spells the word GRAVE because they begin processing the right-to-left diagonal letters first, which, in this case, gives the nonsense sequence EVEZJ.

Water-jar problem

1. Imagine you have 3 empty jars of water, *A* holding 4 quarts (when it is filled), *B* holding 12 quarts, and *C* holding 5 quarts. How would you get a jar (any) holding 3 quarts (it need not necessarily be full)? The answer is to fill *B* (which holds 12 quarts), empty some of *B* into *A* (which holds 4 quarts),

leaving 8 quarts in *B*, then empty some of *B* into *C* (which holds 5 quarts), leaving exactly 3 quarts in *B*.

   If the numbers are changed so that *A* holds 3 quarts, *B* holds 12 quarts and *C* holds 4, and the task is to obtain a jar holding exactly 5 quarts, the above strategy can be successfully repeated: fill *B*, then fill *A* till it's full, then *C* till it's full, and there will be 5 quarts remaining in *B*.

   A series of such tasks is carried out, in all of which the same strategy – fill *B*, pour some *B* to fill *A*, then some *B* to fill *C*, leaving the required amount in *B* – can be successfully deployed.

2. Then the following values are given: *A* holds 2 quarts, *B* holds 12 quarts, and *C* holds 8 quarts. The task is to have a jar with exactly 2 quarts. It *can* be done by the above strategy – fill *B*, pour some *B* to fill *A* (2 quarts), then some *B* to fill *C* (8 quarts), leaving 2 quarts in *B* – but the simplest way is to simply fill *A*, which holds exactly 2 quarts. But subjects miss seeing this because they were blindly following the strategy that had been successful in previous trials.

Luchins (1942) and Luchins and Luchins (1970, Vol. III) describe an enormous amount of research on instructional and other variables influencing the extent to which the *Einstellung* effect is demonstrated. They focused in particular on the water-jar problem.

The *Einstellung* effect is related to the notion of 'functional fixedness', where subjects are blinded by their experience of a function of an object (e.g. a pair of pliers as a gripping device) to its possible use in another function (e.g. as a weight). An extensive series of studies by Maier (1930, 1931, 1945), who started his research at Berlin before moving to the University of Michigan, exemplified beautifully the way in which subjects could fail to solve a problem involving new uses of common objects unless they were given strong hints that allowed them to see the objects in a new light. For example, two cords were suspended from the ceiling and had to be tied together at the bottom, but they were too far apart for the subject to grasp both at the same time. The subjects were given a pair of pliers; no subject figured out how to solve the task, but when the experimenter 'accidentally' bumped into one of the cords, setting it swaying, several subjects realized that they could set one cord swinging like a pendulum, using the pliers as a weight, and, while holding onto the other cord, seize it as it swung towards them; they could then tie the two cords together (Maier, 1931). Maier stressed that problem-solving demanded a 'direction' and that a theory of problem-solving could not be based simply on 'experience' if it were to account for genuinely new solutions to problems.

Wertheimer eventually published his book *Productive Thinking* in 1945. In it he described how he took some problems illustrating the importance of re-structuring which he had discussed in the 1920 paper and gave them to school children to solve. At the same time, he encouraged verbal reports of the children's thought processes. Verbal reports of thought processes had, of course, been analyzed by the members of the Würzburg school, and also by Otto Selz

(1881–1944), a contemporary of Wertheimer, who taught at Bonn and Mann-heim. Selz wrote two long books on thinking (Selz, 1913, 1922), which we shall discuss in more detail shortly but his work is not referred to in *Productive Thinking*, possibly because his work had been criticized by Koffka (see p. 156 below). Verbal reports had been condemned both by Wundt and by the behaviourists on the grounds that attempts to analyze what one had done in the course of a sequence of thoughts were necessarily retrospective and therefore prone to error and introspection of this kind was dismissed out of hand by the behaviourists not only because it might be erroneous but also because it did not provide quantitative data. Köhler, in his *Gestalt Psychology* of 1929, had also criticized introspection but in the context of perceptual anomalies, such as illusions and size constancy, resulting from subjects' evaluating the visual field in terms of prior experience. Köhler wished to claim that these phenomena occurred as a result of direct brain-processing of the elements of the field and were therefore not open to introspection. However, in the study of thinking processes and problem-solving, he seems to have had no objection to the collection of verbal reports as a means of obtaining information about thought processes. Wertheimer used the method extensively and so did Karl Duncker, whose monograph on thinking (1935) is the most extensive Gestalt document on thought (see pp. 140–147).

Moreover verbal reports continued to be the main avenue by which thought processes were studied in the work of Newell and Simon. Their book, entitled *Human Problem Solving* (1972), is full of first person protocols describing the subjects' thought processes as they solved problems in logic, chess and cryptarithmetic. In the last kind of problem, subjects are asked what digits can validly replace letters in such 'sums' as

    DONALD
+   GERALD
    ROBERT

Given that D = 5, you know that T must equal 0, but figuring out the rest is quite difficult. Ericsson and Simon (1980) wrote an extensive article entitled 'Verbal reports as data', later expanded into a book (Ericsson and Simon, 1984), in which they claimed that simply *reporting* what is thought at a given time does not interfere with problem-solving itself to the extent that performance is significantly lowered as compared with the case where subjects are silent. If, however, subjects are forced to verbalize information that they would not normally attend to, this can interfere with the problem-solving process. Moreover, when subjects are asked not to *recall* their thought processes but to make retrospective inferences about the determinants of the thought processes, such activity can lead to inaccuracies. The important point is that the collection of verbal data should focus on what the subject says is occupying his short-term memory. Such analyses, according to Ericsson and Simon, may validly be used as data helping us to understand thought processes, and, in particular, they help us to understand how solving a problem often involves a series of solutions of sub-problems (or attaining sub-goals).

Wertheimer, then, was analyzing verbal reports at the same time as Duncker, and describing his results in his New School seminars, but the condensation of his findings into the book *Productive Thinking* was delayed until after his death. He had finished the manuscript in 1943, died the same year, and Asch, Köhler and Maier saw the book through its final publication stages in 1945. Among the problems Wertheimer gave to school children to solve were some that he had mentioned in the 1920 article and some new ones:

1. The following anecdote was reported in the article:

> It is reported of Karl Gauss that one day the teacher asked his class who could first give the total $1 + 2 + 3 + 4 + 5 + 6 + 7 + 8$. Almost at once Karl's hand was raised. When the teacher asked how he had done it, Karl answered 'If I had to add 1 and 2 and 3, it would have taken a long time; but 1 and 8 are 9, and 7 and 2 are 9, and 3 and 6 are 9, and 4 and 5 are 9 – 4 9's, the answer is 36'. (Wertheimer, 1925, in Ellis, 1938, p. 280)

Wertheimer devoted a whole chapter to this problem in *Productive Thinking*, stressing that Gauss's answer represented a re-structuring of the problem. He argued that the more school children had been drilled to add numbers in succession, the less likely they would be to perform a re-structuring of the kind demonstrated by the six-year-old Gauss. Wertheimer presented the same task to children and students: sometimes people did discover the Gauss re-grouping, or achieved an equally valid re-grouping by trying to find a pattern in the whole series. For example, one twelve-year-old said:

> Oh, I have an idea! I simply take this number in the centre and multiple it by the number of terms in the series - which is, of course, equal to the end number. (Wertheimer, 1945, p. 93)

Wertheimer then remarked:

> It was clearly a discovery for him. Asked to show what he meant, he took the middle number [of the sum $1 + 2 + 3 + 4 + 5 + 6 + 7$], 4, and multiplied it by 7. Given a series ending with 8, he took the middle value between 4 and 5, viz. $4\frac{1}{2}$.

The correct solution to the latter problem, 36, is indeed yielded by $4\frac{1}{2} \times 8$.

Gauss's solution can be expressed as a formula: if there are n consecutive numbers to be added, find the number of pairs $(n/2)$ and multiply by $(n + 1)$; the boy's solution involves finding the middle term, which is $[(n + 1)/2]$, and multiplying it by n. But the formulae are equivalent:

$$(n + 1)(n/2) = [(n+1)/2]n$$

The formulae differ only in structure, corresponding to the differences in re-structuring of the problem as expressed by the six-year-old Gauss and by Wertheimer's 12-year-old. In describing the way in which most subjects are 'blind' to such re-structurings, Wertheimer noted Luchins's work on the *Einstellung* effect which at the time had just got underway.

The sum of a series of consecutive numbers is difficult to re-structure because of the strength or Gestalt character of the series itself, which has been overlearned by most subjects. Wertheimer showed how you could present other series in which the re-structuring as more apparent, e.g.,

$$99.8 + 99.9 + 100 + 100.1 + 100.2 =$$

In a series such as this, subjects look for a structure other than the number series because their attention is drawn to the middle item.

2. Wertheimer took various other problems from geometry, such as (a) finding the area of a parallelogram, (b) proving that if two straight lines intersect, opposite angles are equal, and (c) finding the sum of the interior angles of a polygon. In each of these cases he showed how a 'new look' at the problem could greatly simplify the problem. In this last case he described how he gradually developed a theory for finding the sum of the interior angles of a polygon based on an analysis of the sum of the *exterior* angles (see Wertheimer, 1945, pp. 148–159). This realization that the problem could be simplified by looking at the exterior angles came as an 'intuition' or insight after about 4 days of carrying out his routine work following his introduction to the problem.

3. One of the most fascinating chapters in *Productive Thinking* describes how Albert Einstein (1879–1955) told Wertheimer of Einstein's thought processes during the development of the theory of relativity. Einstein and Wertheimer were close friends who frequently played chamber music together. The development of the theory hinged on a particular moment of insight following a long period of puzzlement about certain phenomena to do with the speed of light: the insight was to realize that the word 'simultaneous' can be ambiguous. If two bolts of lightning strike 'simultaneously' at the same place, there is no ambiguity, but when two events occur 'simultaneously' in different places, there is a problem. Imagine the lightning flashes hitting the ground a mile apart. Put two mirrors at 90 degrees to each other exactly halfway between the two flashes, so that the flash from one hits one mirror and the flash from the other hits the other mirror. To a man at rest watching the two mirrors, the flashes would appear simultaneous. But Einstein asked

> what happens if, in the time during which the light rays approach my mirrors, I move with them, away from one source of light out toward the other. Obviously, if the two events appeared simultaneous to a man at rest, they would not then appear so to me, who am moving with my mirrors. His statement and mine must differ. We

see then that our statements about simultaneity *involve essentially reference to the movement of the observer.* (p. 176)

It was this insight, that the definition of simultaneity will be relative to the observer's movement, that was the foundation stone of the general theory of relativity, with its axioms, that made Einstein famous. For Wertheimer, however, Einstein's discovery came about in a manner *opposite* to that usually associated with the development of deductions from axioms: the axioms were not first invented and then the new 'structure' of physics developed deductively, instead the 're-structuring' came first:

> Surely Einstein's thought did not put ready-made axioms or mathematical formulae together. The axioms were not the beginning but the outcome of what was going on. Before they came into the picture as formulated propositions, the situation as to the velocity of light and related topics had for a long time been structurally questionable to him, had in certain respects become inadequate, was in a state of transition. The axioms were only a matter of later formulation – after the real thing, the main discovery, had happened. (p. 183)

Einstein's retrospective analysis of his thought processes stressed that he did not think much in words but always had a sense of 'direction'; there was a sense of puzzlement (over the data to do with the speed of light), a sense of incompletion, that was eventually resolved with the insight about simultaneity and much later formulated in the axioms that appeared in his printed papers.

It has often been contended that Köhler and Wertheimer pointed to phenomena such as insight and re-structuring but never actually offered a theory of problem-solving that would be a rival to associationist or behaviourist theories that depended on such notions as prior experience and trial-and-error learning. However Karl Duncker, who was taught at Berlin by Köhler and Wertheimer, wrote a book in German in 1935 which became difficult to obtain until translated into English by L.S. Lees in 1945. In this book not only were verbal reports of problem-solving processes analyzed, but a more formal theory of re-structuring was also included.

Duncke, who had been born in Leipzig on 2 February 1903, studied both in Germany and in the United States; then he moved back to Germany where, after obtaining his PhD at the University of Berlin in 1929, he worked as a research assistant for Köhler. But after losing his position in 1935, after the Nazis had come to power just about the time he was finishing his book, he went first to England to work with Bartlett at Cambridge then followed Köhler to Swarthmore in the United States. Depressed by the outbreak of war, he took his own life on 23 February 1940, at the age of 37.

As a preamble to his book, Duncker noted that Maier's assertion that problem-solving occurred when parts of previous experiences were combined in a new pattern under the influence of a definite 'direction' could be simplified by avoiding the term 'direction'. Instead the solution of the problem contained several phases of which the earliest was the 'reformulation of the problem as it initiates the solution-process concerned' (Duncker, 1945, p. 16). In any problem, each step towards a solution may be viewed as having a process-character with respect to what follows and a solution-character with respect to what preceded it. The problem sets up in the subject a goal (the problem is to be 'solved') and from it there proceeds a series of attempts at a solution (a series of 'sub-goals') until the final solution is attained by way of these 'mediatory phases'.

As an example, Duncker presented students with the following problem:

> Given a human being with an inoperable stomach tumour, and rays which destroy organic tissue at sufficient intensity, by what procedure can one free him of the tumour by these rays and at the same time avoid destroying the healthy tissue which surrounds it? (p. 1)

Duncker presented a typical verbal report – it had 13 'steps', most of which represented an idea that was rejected by the experimenter and by the subject. Figure 5.1 shows these steps re-assembled into a schema in which different forms of possible solutions are classified under three main headings – the solution at the extreme right is the one preferred by Duncker. In the protocol at the twelfth step, Duncker wrote

> 12. (Student's reply:) I see no more than two possibilities: either to protect the body or to make the rays harmless.
> (Experimenter: How could one decrease the intensity of the rays en route? . . .)
> 13. (Reply:) Somehow divert it . . . diffuse rays . . . disperse . . . stop! Send a broad and weak bundle of rays through a lens in such a way that the tumour lies at the local [focal?] point and thus receives intensive radiation. (p. 3)

The total time in finding this solution was about half an hour. Osgood (1953) pointed out that

> Since the rays in question cannot be deflected by ordinary lenses, the 'best' solution is the crossing of several weak bundles of rays at the tumour so that the intensity necessary for destruction is reached only there. (p. 627)

Duncker also presented subjects with the problem of designing a pendulum that would swing regularly despite changes in temperature that could change the length of the pendulum. The actual solution is shown in Figure 5.2; a structure is attached to the pendulum arm, a structure made of two metals of differing coefficients of expansion such that expansion of the structure in one direction is compensated for by an equally great expansion in the opposite direction. In the usual way subjects went through a variety of steps, but each step involved a reformulation of the problem and thereby set up a sub-goal, that of accepting or rejecting each new 'solution' as it entered the subject's mind. When a possible solution is rejected, that causes a transition to a different phase in the solution, one which may be an improvement on the previous phase because the subject can learn from his or her mistakes.

The next step in Duncker's argument was to classify various solutions. Often a

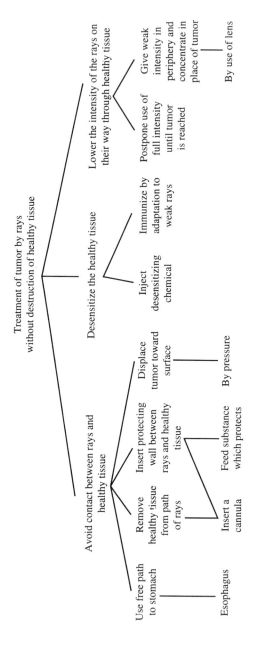

Figure 5.1 Duncker's representation of the various attempts to solve the tumour problem as a hierarchical tree; the favoured solution is at the extreme right. (Source: reprinted from K. Duncker (1945), *Psychological Monographs*, **58**, whole no. 270, p. 5.)

Figure 5.2 The solution to Duncker's pendulum problem. A structure is added to the pendulum *c* that is made of two metals. The bars *a* and *a'*, when heated, can expand only downwards, and are made of one metal. The bars *b* and *b'*, being fastened below, can expand only upwards; they are made of a different metal from *a* and *a'*, one that has a greater coefficient of expansion than the metal composing *a*, *a'* and *c*. The bars *b* and *b'* are meant to raise the strip of metal to which *c* is fastened by exactly as much as *a*, *a'* and *c* expand downwards on being heated. Thus, on being heated, *c* will never change its length and the pendulum will continue to swing normally. (Source: reprinted from K. Duncker (1945), *Psychological Monographs*, **58**, whole no. 270, p. 7.)

solution would arise by a 'resonance-effect' based on previous experience. For example,

> For certain experiments in the psychology of perception, someone needs yellow illumination. There is no colour filter available. What to do? It occurs to him how, the other day, a blue folder reflected the light of a lamp as blue-tinted, 'led to' a colouring. Aha! The reflection from yellow paper . . . (p. 19)

There are solutions based on aids, as when Maier 'accidentally' brushed the hanging cord and gave the subjects the idea of swinging it. Sometimes something intended as an aid can in fact cause a fixation which prevents the solution of the problem – in presenting the radiation problem, Duncker had sometimes accompanied it with a sketch (Figure 5.3). Of 11 subjects who received the sketch along with the question, only 9 per cent gave a correct solution; of 11 who did not see the sketch, 36 per cent gave a correct solution. There are also solutions based on '*par force*' (by force), a French term introduced by Duncker; with the pendulum problem, one subject imagined that in hot conditions the pendulum would expand (and bend) if the end-parts were held firmly in position – this crude unsuccessful solution led however by a process of association to

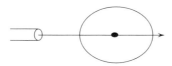

Figure 5.3 The sketch with which Duncker's instructions about the tumour problem were sometimes accompanied. It seemed to hinder progress with the problem rather than help it. (Source: reprinted from K. Duncker (1945), *Psychological Monographs*, **58**, whole no. 270, p. 2.)

other more correct forms of solutions in which expansion could be countered by expansion in the opposite direction. In all of these different types of solutions, however, some 're-structuration' of the original problem takes place.

Like Wertheimer, Duncker also presented protocols for solutions to various problems in mathematics, including one which has become quite famous: Why are all six-place numbers of the type 276,276, 591,591, 112,112, divisible by 13? Here is a protocol from a 14-minute session in which the subject arrived at the correct solution:

1. Are the triplets themselves divisible by 13?
2. Is there perhaps some sort of rule here about the sum of the digits, as there is with divisibility by 9?
3. The thing must follow from a hidden common principle of structure – the first triplet is 10 times the second, 591,591 is 591 multiplied by 11, no: by 101 (Experimenter: So?) No: by 1001. Is 1001 divisible by 13? (p. 31)

Since $1001 = 13 \times 77$, and $591,591 = 591 \times 1001$, any six-digit number of this type is divisible by 13; the trick in proving it is to realize that 591,591 and similar numbers are divisible by 1001, a realization that will come more quickly to some people than others. Duncker did experiments showing how an aid such as '1001 is divisible by 13' led to 5 out of 10 subjects arriving at the solution, while an aid such as 'Different numbers can have in common a divisor which is in turn divisible' led to no correct solutions from 10 subjects. Without any aids, only 8 per cent of 26 subjects succeeded in solving the problem. A similar analysis was undertaken of some geometrical problems.

Duncker attempted to put re-structuration within the context of a general analysis of different kinds of ways in which we perceive. In the eighteenth century, Kant had distinguished between different kinds of propositions: there were analytic propositions in which the content added little to knowledge and was for practical purposes tautological, such as, 'A brother is a male sibling'. And there were synthetic propositions in which new information was imparted and required verification in order for their truth value to be known, for example, 'Napoleon lost the Battle of Waterloo'. Duncker attempted a similar analysis but it was not so much of propositions in respect of truth value as it was of sensory evidence with respect to whether one can learn something new over and above the evidence. Analytic evidence was self-contained or, as Duncker called it, 'constitutively co-contained'; for example, evidence that a straight line is determined by two points or evidence that a house has a grey roof. 'Non-constitutive co-containedness' was a characteristic of evidence from which new inferences could be made; for example, if you know that $a > b > c$, you can infer that $a > c$. With non-constitutive co-contained evidence, individual parts are brought into relationships which can change depending on the context in which the part is viewed. For example, I can draw a straight line L (as in Figure 5.4) and drop three perpendiculars α, β, γ from the line, with α being shorter than β and β shorter than γ. But if I now add a square below L, with the square's upper

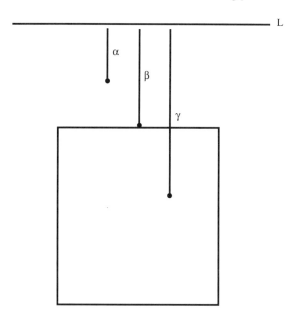

Figure 5.4 Duncker's illustration of how the addition of a new element to a display causes a re-structuring of the interpretation of the display. Without the square, lines α, β and γ are mere perpendiculars dropped from *L*; adding the square causes α, β and γ to be related to the square. (Source: reprinted from K. Duncker (1945), *Psychological Monographs*, **58**, whole no. 270, p. 53.)

side parallel to L, the end points of α, β, and γ determine that α, β, and γ will be seen in a new relationship; they do not relate merely to L, but also to the square, with α being outside the square, β being on the square and γ being inside the square. As Duncker remarked of each end-point: 'In terms of Gestalt theory: it has altered its concrete "function" by the fact that it has entered a new organization' (p. 53).

It was Duncker's contention that a problem represents a particular situation in which the solution must (a) be 'intelligible' with respect to the problem as set (Duncker had earlier analyzed the meaning of 'intelligible' with respect to evidence) and (b) be determined by a synthetic judgement resulting from the problem as set. When synthetic evidence did not readily come to mind, the subject embarked on a sequence of phases of 'search' in which synthetic evidence that was available given the problem was used to set a sub-goal which in turn would yield new synthetic evidence leading to a second sub-goal and so on till the problem was solved. In looking for synthetic evidence, the subject could easily fail to see appropriate evidence because of past habits of viewing the evidence. This could be particularly well demonstrated in problems in which drawings or physical objects were part of the problem because these drawings or objects could literally be 'viewed' in different ways. In the second half of his monograph, Duncker reported several experiments on problem-solving utilizing geometrical problems involving drawings or construction problems in which physical objects had to be put together in a particular way.

For example, Duncker set several construction problems to students in which each was presented with a hint as to how an object should be used, or without such a hint. Here is Duncker's statement of the 'box problem', slightly reworded:

> On the door, at the height of the eyes, three small candles are to be put side by side [the subjects were told this was for the purpose of 'visual experiments']. On the table lie, among many other objects, a few tacks and the crucial objects, three little pasteboard boxes (about the size of an ordinary matchbox, differing somewhat in form and colour and put in different places).
> *Solution*: With a tack apiece, the three boxes are fastened to the door, each to serve as a platform for the candles.
> [With a hint] The three boxes were empty.
> [Without a hint] The three boxes were filled with experimental material: in one there were several thin little candles, tacks in another and matches in the third. (p. 86)

In the first case, the empty boxes were more likely to be seen as 'platforms' whereas in the second, the full boxes were more likely to be seen as 'containers' and the subject would not *view* them as 'platforms'. There were five problems of this kind; in the above problem, a box had to be viewed as a 'platform' rather than as a container; in the other problems, a gimlet had to be used as a thing from which to hang a card rather than as a boring device; a pair of pliers had to be used as a support for a board rather than as a gripping device; a weight had to be used as a hammer rather than as a pendulum weight; and a paper-clip had to be unbent and used as a hook rather than as an affixing device. When a hint was given as to the novel use of the tool in question, 85 per cent of the total number of problems set to subjects were solved; when there was no hint, and presumably functional fixedness was present, 58.2 per cent of the problems were solved. The number of subjects allotted to each problem, with separate subjects in the 'hint' and 'no hint' groups for each problem, varied between 7 and 15.

Duncker went on to show the role of functional fixedness in preventing subjects from solving mathematical problems (particularly geometrical problems). He pointed out that functional fixedness can be overcome if the parts in question are made more salient; if all the objects given to the subject in the box problem are not green, while the three boxes are all painted green, and the hint is given that the 'solution object is green. Look for something green', then the boxes will be immediately used in the manner proper to the solution of the problem. Parts of elements of a problem that are associated with increased Prägnanz (Duncker's term) will more readily be utilized in a re-centring or re-structuring process. Hence it follows that functional fixedness prevents the emergence of the new centring of the object. Duncker's monograph finished with a discussion of why it is that some persons fail to re-structure problems, particularly geometrical problems – Duncker believed that it was not so much due to some sort of 'inelasticity of the thought material' as to the fact that the subject viewed the geometrical problem as having a particular perceptual structure that blinded him to a view more conducive to a solution.

This research by Maier and Duncker was carried out and reported in the early 1930s, while Wertheimer's research did not appear in print until 1945. For this reason, Koffka's analysis of thinking in his *Principles of Gestalt Psychology* (1935a) incorporated some findings of Maier and Duncker, but made only casual reference to Wertheimer; for evidence on re-structuration and functional fixedness, Koffka quoted mainly Maier's work. But Koffka's analysis of thinking differed in an important way from that of the three other authors because Koffka conceived of 'thinking' as essentially memory retrieval. Even a re-structuring involves the use of memory, but what is retrieved is more 'remote' and less directly associated with the problem as set than is the case with a problem that can be solved directly using a memory resonance (e.g. Duncker's solution of the 'yellow light' problem). Moreover, memory is clearly involved in cases of functional fixedness. For this reason, Koffka (somewhat surprisingly, given the interest generally evoked in the 1930s by the research on re-structuration) relegated his discussion of thinking to the last half of his fourth chapter on memory.

For Koffka, the solution of a problem involved two steps: the achievement of a communication with the proper trace systems and the proper effect of this communication upon the process of problem-solving. The second might not always follow from the first; Koffka quotes the following example. Here is a joke told by A to B:

A: What did Noah say when he heard the rain patter on the roof?
B: I don't know.
A: 'Ark!

But if B perceives this reply *only* as a version of 'hark' and retells the joke to C as:

A: What did Noah say when he heard the rain patter on the roof?
C: I don't know.
A: Listen!

then the second stage was missing; B's trace system corresponding to 'hark-listen' was aroused, but that corresponding to Noah's ark had not been communicated with, and the 'proper effect' of the solution of the problem (the punning answer) was not attained by B. In fact, Koffka made a great deal of the contribution of Harrower (1932) to our understanding of memory processes by way of a series of experiments using jokes as the material. Harrower showed, for example, that unfinished jokes are better recalled at a later interval than finished jokes (a variant of the Zeigarnik effect); and she demonstrated that if subjects have to complete jokes and two possible answers are equally good, they are biased in their selection of an answer by the answer to a previous (complete) joke that they had just heard. For example,

> Prisoner in Court: But, your worship, I wasn't going 50 miles per hour nor 40, nor 30 . . .
>
> Judge (Positive answer, continuing the prisoner's sequence): Well, you'll be going backwards soon, OR
>
> Judge (Negative answer, reversing the prisoner's sequence): No, I suppose you were going 60 miles per hour.

Eight subjects who had just heard a series of jokes with the last being a similar joke with a *positive* punch line completed the above joke with a positive answer; seven subjects who had just heard the joke with a *negative* punch line completed the above joke with a negative answer. It is appropriate to think of Harrower's finding as demonstrating the role of prior experience in solving open-ended problems; the findings on functional fixedness demonstrated the importance of prior experience in closed-ended problems. That an answer to a problem can be camouflaged by being embedded in a different context was demonstrated by an experiment in which Harrower asked subjects to complete jokes; potential answers shown after the joke were also presented either before or after the jokes were shown, but the potential answers were either embedded in a text of connected prose, or presented among a set of disconnected sentences. Only in the latter case were subjects helped to find the appropriate answer. When the potential answers were embedded in connected prose, there was also a failure of automatic access, as Tulving (1983) called it: the punch line failed to be recognized *as* a solution to the joke.

Yet, even though he believed memory to lie at the heart of a psychology of problem-solving, Koffka insisted that the analysis of problem-solving shows us that we are not mere reflex machines: new behaviours can be elicited by a problem, and he insisted that, in many instances, we needed to bring in the concept of an Ego trace system to explain new behaviour. In the *Principles* (pp. 626–627), he gave a striking case reported by the psychologist, G.J. von Allesch, a colleague of Wertheimer and Köhler at Berlin. It will be best to quote Koffka's anecdote in full:

> During the war [von Allesch] was on a patrol in the Alps. He had to make a descent from a rocky crag by means of a chimney whose upper mouth gaped about ten metres under and four to the side of his position. Having climbed down on a rope, he found himself hanging in the air and several metres to the left of the chimney, with no more rope for a further descent which would have landed him on a ledge by which he had hoped to reach the chimney. He determined to reach the opening by swinging on the rope. In doing this, the rope slipped from his feet, and his hands were not able to support his weight. The situation was extremely critical. No emotions arose, instead suddenly the clearly formulated thought, 'This is the end'. The next moment the author

realized (and this point is absolutely certain in his observation) that he had taken hold of the rope with his teeth. Thereupon followed another formulated thought, 'That cannot last long either'. In the next moment his feet waving in the air had caught hold of a projecting piece of a slab [and thus he succeeded in saving himself and reaching the chimney]. (pp. 626–627)

In a life-threatening problem situation, von Allesch had spontaneously, *without* formulating the thought, carried out a movement that was entirely new in his experience (grabbing a rope with his teeth). Koffka concluded:

The solution was *not* produced by an act of thought, but at a time when the rational part of the organism had concluded that no solution was possible – 'This is the end'. The stress between Ego and surrounding field succeeded in finding *that* movement which alone could relieve it. (p. 627)

It was Koffka's opinion that this case represented an extreme (and impressive) example of what normally happens in problem-solving: a new perspective on a situation can arise even when there is no conscious formulation of the perspective. Such a new perspective represents insight. Koffka, in his earlier book *The Growth of the Mind*, had insisted that insight cannot occur as the result of processes travelling along predetermined pathways: it presupposes processes of organization and re-organization. He gave an example of how an algebraic problem can be solved by a re-organization of the question. His analysis is too lengthy to give here but it is along the lines of Wertheimer's analysis of the problem of summing a series of successive numbers.

In further discussing the role of the Ego, Koffka admitted that many problems could be solved without involving the 'Ego-forces' other than a determination to do well – examples are mathematical problems or joke completions. In Köhler's stick problems, the ape has to 'extend its arm' by using a stick and there are therefore forces between the Ego and the environment that will influence the finding of a solution – the easier a stick is to find, or to grasp perceptually, the more readily the problem will be solved.

However, Koffka's most challenging remarks concern the relation between perception and thought. In a re-structuring event in a series of thoughts concerned with solving a problem, the elements of the problem can be brought together in a new relation much as the elements in a picture can be seen in a different organization. Moreover, any solution to a problem involves finding a part which 'fits' into the whole, as the boxes in Duncker's problem 'fit' their new role as supports for candles. Koffka noted that

Since all problem solutions can be said to consist in finding the *fitting* part which will relieve the existing stress, a law of fittingness would be the most universal law to explain thinking, and with it the arousal of new processes. Such a law would be a generalization of the laws of good continuation and closure. (p. 638)

However Koffka was also aware that a large logical leap was involved in trying to assimilate the laws of thinking with the laws of perception. Earlier in the same chapter he had noted:

> The perceptual problem keeps us closer to the actual physiological events than the thought problems where physiological hypotheses are speculative to a much greater degree even than in the field of perception. On the other hand, the 'purer' thought processes are, the more they will reveal the efficacy of properties which are apt to be observed in perception because of the contingent stimulus distribution.
>
> At the present time problems in perception and in thinking will, therefore, probably have to be investigated at 'different levels'. Answers which must satisfy our curiosity on the level of thought will have to be much more concrete on the level of perception. (p. 632)

More will be said on this issue soon, but we may close this summary of Koffka's views on thinking by observing that he believed that Thorndike's Law of Effect, which stressed the importance of reward and punishment in determining learning, was an instantiation of a general rule that if an act was rewarded, say, the reward itself caused the memory of the preceding act to be viewed in a new organization: the act is viewed in relation to the possibility of attaining a pleasant state. How successful reward will be in determining a repetition of the act will depend on whether the act is seen by the human or animal subject as part of the total 'act-reward' situation. Koffka referred to an experiment by McDougall and McDougall (1927); a rat had to solve the problem of opening a Latch 1 which was locked by another Latch 2. It concentrated all of its efforts on opening Latch 1 but once, accidentally, unlocked Latch 2 by a random movement of its hind paw and thereby released Latch 1. But afterwards it continued to work at Latch 1 and never apparently made the connection between the unlocking of Latch 2 and the unlocking of Latch 1. The rewarded act had not been part of the total 'unlock Latch 1' goal that the rat apparently strove to attain. This cognitive description of the effect of reward on an animal's performance was, of course, unacceptable to the behaviourists, but not to Tolman, who, as noted in Chapter 1, analyzed rat behaviour in terms of associations called 'sign-gestalts' that the rat made between the elements of an environment such as a maze and the achievement of a satisfying state such as being rewarded with freedom or food in that environment.

This almost completes our discussion of Gestalt views on problem-solving as they were expressed in the heyday of the movement. It only remains to be added that Maier continued to work on problem-solving until the 1970s, elaborating and refining his views in several papers. For example, Maier (1945) first showed subjects how to make a construction in which two boards were clamped together to make a longer structure, two of these structures acted as supports for a third board wedged to the ceiling which bridged them, and two such bridges were set far enough apart so that cords hanging from them could not be simultaneously grasped by a subject standing between the bridge (see Figure 5.5(a)). With hints, the subject learned within about 10 minutes the trick of setting one cord in

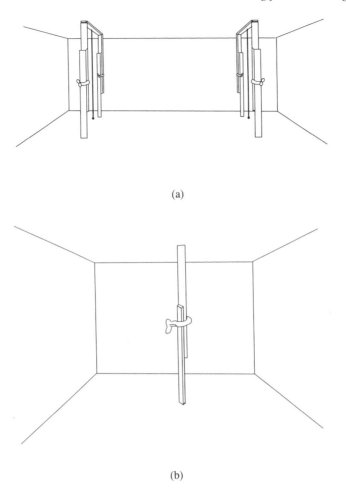

(a)

(b)

Figure 5.5 (a) The preliminary demonstration in Maier's 1945 experiment: how cords can be hung from the ceiling using boards and clamps; (b) The problem: construct a hatrack from two boards and a clamp. (Source: reprinted from *Problem Solving and Creativity in Individuals and Groups*, by N.R.F. Maier, pp. 145 and 146. Copyright © 1970 by Wadsworth Publishing Co., Inc. Reprinted by permission of Brooks/Cole Publishing Co., Pacific Grove, CA.)

motion weighted so that it behaved like a pendulum and catching it while holding the other string. This was the problem that Maier (1931) had previously investigated.

But in the 1945 paper, this exercise simply served as preliminary practice, for the real aim of the experiment was to find whether subjects could make a hatrack using only two boards and a clamp. The question was whether the subjects would figure out how to clamp the two boards together, wedge them between the floor and the ceiling and use the clamp screw as the hook for a hat (as in Figure 5.5(b)). There were three groups of subjects: one had the bridge structures of Figure 5.5(a)a in full view while working on the hatrack, one worked on the hatrack after the bridge structures had been taken down and the material removed from the room, and one group had no experience with the bridge structures, simply working on the hatrack problem alone. Each group included 13 male and 13 female students from an introductory psychology class. Seventy-two per cent of the subjects working with the hatrack in view of the bridge structure solved the problem; 48 per cent of the subjects working with the hatrack and only a memory of the bridge structures solved the problem; and only 24 per cent of the subjects tackling the hatrack problem without previous experience with the bridge structures managed to build the hatrack. There was a strong tendency for men to be better at solving the problem than women in all three groups. Maier continued to use his term 'direction' despite Duncker's criticisms, and argued that a distinction should be made between 'reproductive thinking', where past uses of objects are seen to be equivalent to uses demanded in a new context, and 'productive thinking', where the subject must alter his view of an object. For example, he might re-structure his concept of a clamp as a 'holding device' and see it as a 'hook for a hat'. More generally, the experiment confirms Köhler's original view that if all the elements in the problem are simultaneously visible to the subject, insight is more likely to occur than when some elements are not within the visual field.

Much later, Burke *et al.* (1966) presented the hatrack problem, but without the preliminary step of constructing the bridge structures, to 234 men. The actual attempts at solution were classified into five types (or 'directions'), only one involving the correct solution, and there were two main kinds of hint given after subjects had worked unsuccessfully for 30 minutes. The ceiling hint was 'In the correct solution, the ceiling is part of the construction'; the clamp hint was 'In the correct solution, the clamp is used as the coat hanger'. The ceiling hint was sufficient to stop two false directions (one in which one stick was used as a support to hold the second stick vertically with the clamp joining them, and another in which the sticks were leaned against each other in an X or T shape with the clamp joining them); the clamp hint terminated the former direction only. However, the hints could occasionally set up false directions; and a second experiment showed that hints that were given before the problem-solving began were more useful than hints that were given after the problem-solving attempt was well under way – 'it thus appears that a hint has the best opportunity to initiate a new direction when a problem-solver does not already have one in progress' (p. 399).

Maier also carried out a large number of studies on cooperative problem-solving by groups of subjects and attempted to apply his findings to labour-management relations, marriage counselling, creativity and the study of group leadership. These papers were collected in a single volume by Maier (1970) which also includes the two papers discussed above and others utilizing the two-cord problem.

To summarize: Köhler emphasized that problems are solved when elements in a problem are brought into an 'insightful' relationship that is 'fitting' with respect to the goal. Koffka stressed the same thing but laid more emphasis on the importance of memory retrieval in solving problems, and in his 'grabbing the rope with the teeth' example brought out the importance of unconscious processing and its relationship to stress in the relationship between Ego and environment; Wertheimer showed how problem-solving frequently resulted from a re-structuration of the elements in a problem and emphasized how past habits of thought could blind one to such re-structurations; experimental evidence for such 'functional fixedness' was provided by Maier (in experiments spanning a period from 1930 to 1970), Luchins (with his research on the *Einstellung* effect) and Duncker (1935), who attempted to lay a more formal foundation for the meaning of 're-structuration' in distinguishing between analytic and synthetic evidence as presented by sense-data.

Yet there are two questions that concern us when we consider a summary like the above. First, there is missing a foundational analysis of what is meant by the process of problem-solving – the Gestalt psychologists have told us *how* to solve problems well and poorly but there is no theoretical underpinning to a *formal* science of problem-solving. This might seem a trivial point but in view of the fact that the late twentieth century research of Newell and Simon on 'models of problem-solving' involves *formal* theory, antecedents to this work are to be found, according to their own statements (e.g. Newell *et al.*, 1958), in the work of Otto Selz, who was a contemporary of the Gestalt psychologists but did not emulate the Gestalt line of thinking. Second, the words 'structure', 're-structuration' and 're-organization' can be clearly understood in the context of the study of perception, but in the context of the study of thought, they lack a certain rigour – they are too easy to apply to almost any situation. What justification can be given for extending a metaphor found useful in perception to the much more abstract and cognitive field of problem-solving? If we are to evaluate the Gestalt contributions to our understanding of problem-solving, some kind of answers have to be given to these two questions.

Selz's analysis of problems in terms of goals, and its relation to the work of Newell and Simon

It was the achievement of Otto Selz to have recognized that the cognition that a 'gap' exists between the present situation (the setting of a problem) and the solution of the problem (an internal representation of a possible future event) is indeed a *cognition* that takes the form of an internal representation. To elaborate on this view we must present some background material.

The members of the Würzburg school had initiated the use of verbal reports as a method for studying problem-solving and it is to them that we owe the concepts of 'determining tendency' (a tendency to *stick* to the problem that leads to various solution-attempts or *directions* that are relevant to the problem and do not stray from it) and of 'imageless thought' (ideas that do not obviously have image-form yet which contribute to the solution of the problem - they frequently arise from 'nowhere' in the sense that there is no obvious association aside from the determining tendency linking them to the previous thought). Selz continued in this tradition, but instead of posing difficult conceptual problems as the members of the Würzburg School had done, he asked subjects to find words that had a specific relationship to a word presented by the experimenter. However, these were rarely simple associations such as LIFE–opposite? (answer: DEATH), but could be as difficult as HARBOUR–opposite? To this last one, one subject took 7.6 seconds to respond then reported:

> Then my glance travelled over the expanse of water and reached the sea. Whether I actually got that far visually, I can't say. Anyway, that was the direction and, I thought, I'm coming to the sea. As soon as I had this conscious thought of the sea, I said to myself: stop, that is a good opposite of harbour. Then I gave my response with a pleasant feeling of having found a happy solution. (Selz, 1913, p. 102)

Other tasks involved giving a word and saying what 'whole' that word could be a part of, or vice versa, what 'part' it constituted in a greater whole. So, for example, the question PAINTING–whole? was answered after 10 seconds by one subject as WALL, and in 6.2 seconds by another as GALLERY.

In analyzing hundreds of protocols, each about a paragraph long, Selz concluded that the presentation of the stimulus word allows the subject to form a 'schematic anticipation' of the solution, for example, given PAINTING, the first subject reported 'Tried to find something larger to tie in with the painting, something of which the painting itself forms a spatial part' (p. 134). To this Selz added, 'The schematic anticipation of a whole of which the painting is to form a part is clearly contained in the goal awareness'. That is, the start of a problem involves the subject's having a cognition or 'goal awareness' of the beginning and end of the problem, this cognition being 'schematic' in the sense that it was a general outline to be filled in with detail and with the feeling accompaniment of anticipation. This 'schematic anticipation' is clearly an internal representation. One example that Selz had discussed in detail and that Humphrey (1951) stressed in his account of Selz's theory was taken from history. When Benjamin Franklin wanted to prove that lightning is composed of 'electricity', Selz postulated that he formed a schematic anticipation, with a 'gap' in it as follows:

AIM	X	R_1
to bring thundercloud electricity to earth	The missing 'something'	X would make the cloud-to-earth connection

The solution that eventually occurred to Franklin was that a kite would do the job, so we close the gap as follows:

AIM   KITE R_1

Selz believed that the same format could be applied to Köhler's apes; Sultan had the aim of getting the banana from the ceiling, the 'partial result' would be achieved if the banana could be knocked down, and X would be the use of a stick to do so. This formula, Selz argued, was an advance on associationism because it emphasized that a solution did not flow chain-like according to the Laws of Association from the presentation of a problem, but instead was based on a cognition or internal representation of a total 'something' for which Selz chose the name 'schematic anticipation'. It was also a continuation of the Würzburg tradition because the internal representation need not necessarily take the form of an image (although in the PAINTING–whole? example above, the subject clearly claimed he used an image) and because the schematic anticipation was clearly a sophisticated starting point for the operation of determining tendencies.

Selz wrote up his experiments and his theory in two parts, *Über die Gesetze des geordneten Denkverlaufs (On the laws of ordered thinking*, 1913, 320 pp.) and *Zür Psychologie des produktiven Denkens und des Irrtums (On the psychology of productive thinking or error*, 1922, 688 pp.). This thousand-page treatise has never been translated in its entirety and probably never will be as even German scholars consider it over-elaborate, discursive, and lacking a convenient layout so that the argument can be followed without losing the thread. However, the Dutch psychologist, Adriaan de Groot, who adopted Selz's theory in his analysis of the thought-process of expert chess players (de Groot, 1946), has arranged for passages from the monograph to be translated in his book *Otto Selz: His contributions to psychology* (Frijda and de Groot, 1981) and in that volume will also be found a translation of a short summary of his theory that Selz wrote in 1924.

In that summary, Selz began by defining the associationist account, stressing that associations were often represented as 'diffuse' and with the strongest association winning out at any moment. But for Selz it was difficult to reconcile the notion that a stimulus inevitably elicits the 'strongest' association with the coherence and innovation that we associate with problem-solving. The resolution of the dilemma was to postulate that when a problem is set it elicits a schematic anticipation (Humphrey's translation) or anticipatory schema (Frijda and de Groot's translation) - the German is *antizipierendes Schema*. Selz's example here is the question HUNTING–coordinate? The schema may be represented as

A γ X

where A represents HUNTING and X is to be filled in by something that can be bracketed together with HUNTING as a coordinate concept - a good answer would be FISHING. When we complete the schema, we now have a 'knowledge complex'

HUNTING γ FISHING

Selz went on to categorize these 'actualizations of cognitive (*geistigen*) operations' (p. 43). 'Routine means actualization' operates in cases when a means has to be found relating the problem-as-set to the problem-as-solved but the means is already available as a method. For example, when I intend to write after breakfast, there is a 'routine' available to me from past experience – I do not need to puzzle out how to 'write after breakfast', I just go to my desk and do it. Sometimes such a problem has to be approached by way of 'trying out behaviour' (*probierendes Verhalten*) as when a nine-pins player tries various ways of rolling the ball till he finds a successful one. 'Means abstraction operations' are used when the anticipatory schema cannot be completed by a tried-and-true method but only by the discovery of new solving methods. An example would be Franklin's discovery of the use of a kite to bring electricity from the clouds to the earth. 'Immediate means abstractions', a variant within this category, are used when the solution can be derived directly from the structure of the task itself, and most of Selz's word problems fall in this category. A third major category of actualization of goals involves the utilization of significant means-end relationships 'which, while discovered prior to the present goal setting by accidentally induced or deliberately instigated abstraction processes, are productively exploited only on a later occasion' (p. 67). Many works of creative writing fall in this category, where previous real-life experience colours and guides the craftsmanship of the author.

Selz's work was not particularly appreciated by the Gestalt psychologists. Koffka (1935a) admired Selz for having shown the inadequacy of the associationist view that thought *B* will necessarily be the strongest association of the preceding thought *A*, but he claimed that Selz's theory 'did not make a positive contribution in the right direction' (p. 560). He elaborated on this argument in a separate paper (Koffka, 1927): he felt that Selz's analysis did not really escape from being a mechanistic associationism. At various places Selz talked of the solution of the problem as being in a sense inherent in the framing of the problem; the knowledge-schema that was produced after the anticipatory schema had led to an appropriate chain of attempts at solution was, in Selz's terminology, not necessarily something 'new'. In Selz's model, for example, 'insight' was simply the product of a mechanistic trying out of one or other solution to the problem, whereas for Koffka, insight meant a generally new apprehension of the relationship between elements in a problem. Since the problems that Selz set, involving the finding of coordinate concepts to single words, left little room for insight to show itself, Koffka felt that Selz's tasks were unlikely to reveal much that could be useful in our understanding of problem-solving.

According to Koffka, applying Selz's analysis to the situation of the reversible figure, seen as a vase or two profiles, would lead one to say that when one is seeing the 'vase', the two profiles are in some way already 'contained' in the perception of the vase; whereas for Koffka, the switch-over from seeing the vase to seeing the two profiles was the result of a genuine transformational process operating in the perceptual field. Selz (1922) had written, 'No insight can derive something from a given situation that was not already contained within it.' (p. 614). Koffka (1927) replied, 'When, therefore, I perceive the relationship between the perceptual elements such that the profiles seem to lie on a white background, must I assume that this already belonged to the perceptual situation at a time when I had not yet perceived any profiles?' (p. 177). Extrapolating from this example to problems of a more general kind, Koffka argued that the setting of the problem and its solution were not tied together (*zugeordnet*) in such a way that the solution was like an unknotting (*auslösen*) of the problem; a solution had to grow *out* of the problem, transforming the problem and releasing the tension associated with the problem - 'out of every new cognition (*Erkenntnis*) something new arises, and each new thing that arises makes possible further new events' (Koffka, 1927, p. 181). Koffka saw Selz's theories as formally similar to his own (both involved a denial that solutions follow patterns determined by the 'strongest' associations, and both referred to knowledge-schemata), but claimed that they were different in content because Selz's theory did not refer to transformations in the ways that elements of the problem were seen by the subject to be related to each other. We shall shortly see, however, that in our own time Simon has an answer to Koffka's critique.

Nor was Selz's work overpraised by Humphrey (1951). Humphrey claimed that Selz basically *re-stated* the problem of problem-solving and did not offer a very helpful answer. For Humphrey, the experiments of Köhler with apes and of Duncker and Maier with humans represented an advance on the work of both the Würzburg School and of Selz by suggesting that stresses are set up by the problem which 'work themselves out in organic activity' (p. 184). These activities include perceptual re-organizations (re-structuring, re-centring), which are accomplished by 'insight'. The result of the interaction of problem-stresses is a kind of activity which may be called 'new'.

On the other hand, Newell *et al.* (1958) and Simon (1981a) stress the influence of Selz on their development of computer programs simulating thought processes.

Just how did Selz's work fit better into this historical enterprise than did the Gestalt psychologists? Simon (1981a) has discussed this in detail but as early as 1958, Newell *et al.* had stressed that Selz's notion of a schematic anticipation had an exact counterpart in the Logic Theorist, the program that proved logical theorems: if a schematic anticipation consists of

Find an X that stands in the specified relation R to the given element E

then its counterpart in the Logical Theorist consists of:

Find a *sequence of sentences* (X) that stands in the relation of *proof* (R) to the given *problem expression* (E).

Newell *et al.* carried out their proofs by programming routines in which logical expressions were found that were similar to the logical expressions presented at the beginning or end of a proof. Newell *et al.* defined various alternative ways of defining 'similar' - for example, a proposition such as '*A* implies *B*' can be replaced by 'not–*A* or *B*', or a proposition such as '(*p* or *p*) implies *p*' can be replaced by '[(*p* or *q*) or (*p* or *q*)] implies (*p* or *q*)' - and showed that the computer could pick a given replacement, test to see if it led towards the expression to be proved, and if it did not, try another kind of replacement. This strategy, of trying out one method after another until one is found that is successful, is a counterpart to Selz's sequences of attempts to arrive at a knowledge complex that completes the schematic anticipation.

In his 1981a article, Simon claimed that the method of means-abstraction contains the core of what is nowadays called means-end analysis, a technique that had been incorporated into several programs, notably the General Problem Solver (GPS), the name for a class of programs that can solve logic problems, cryptarithmetic problems, and chess problems. Means-end analysis, as applied in GPS, is used to decide which operator to apply next:

1. It compares current situation with goal situation to detect one or more differences between them.
2. It retrieves from memory an operator that is associated with a difference it has found (i.e., an operator that has the usual effect of reducing differences of this kind).
3. It applies the operator or, if it is not applicable in the current solution, sets up the new goal of creating the conditions that will make it applicable. (p. 36 of the article as reprinted in Simon, 1989)

Simon noted that in GPS solutions can be attained which are generally 'novel' because the computer can generate many combinations of propositions from sets of propositions, and also noted that Selz had discussed 'learning by doing', that is, learning how to solve problems faster by successive applications of solutions which at first are tentative and involve digressions and unsuccessful sub-parts, but which improve as these deficiencies are corrected.

In that article, Simon also indicated that Duncker (1945, p. 8, note 6) had appreciated Selz insofar as Selz had pointed out how problem-solution can frequently take place if the original task is replaced by another problem whose solution is more easily attainable. For example, given 'RAILWAY PLATFORM–coordinate?' one of Selz's subjects transferred the task into 'find another part of the concrete spatial whole which includes a railway station platform' – this rephrasing of the task led to the answer 'railway track'. Duncker had expressed this type of transformation of the schematic anticipation as 'exchange of the original goal for a more specific one'. Generally, Simon believed that Duncker and Selz were the true pioneers of modern research on problem-solving, but 'some of the same flavour comes through in the writings of Köhler and the other Gestaltists'. However, a footnote here indicates that Simon thought the Gestaltists may have gone off-track here, for 'they subordinated the description of process to their interest in sudden "insightful" problem solutions' (Simon, 1981a, as reprinted in Simon, 1989, p. 33).

Simon's explanation of 're-structuring'

This footnote was essentially expanded when Michael Wertheimer (1985) criticized the work of Simon and his collaborators on the grounds that the programs used for problems in logic, cryptarithmetic, chess, and the Tower of Hanoi puzzle did not 'model' the processes of re-structuration and insight on which the Gestalt psychologists had indeed laid so much stress. In an article written in reply, Simon (1987) pointed out that such words as 'insight' are difficult to define, but he also claimed that when re-structuration does occur it can often be shown to be a case of recognition, and that recognition was modelled in various computer programs. In particular, the program known as EPAM (Elementary Perceiver and Memorizer), described by Simon and Feigenbaum (1962) and re-designed into EPAM-III (Simon and Feigenbaum, 1964), models the process that is intermediate between feature detection by the sense organs and the setting up of the vast system of interconnected nodes known as semantic memory. In this intermediate stage of processing, new inputs are first identified by being compared with the content of semantic memory and then built into 'chunks' which constitute the 'learning' of a list of inputs. The initial identification process involves recognition, and it was Simon's contention that the problem of re-structuring can itself be re-structured so as to be perceived as a problem in recognition.

For example, in his book on *Productive Thinking*, Wertheimer (1945) had given extensive discussion to the case of school children solving by themselves the problem of finding the area of a parallelogram (Figure 5.6(a)). By 're-structuring' the parallelogram by mentally chopping off a triangle from one end of the parallelogram and relocating it to the other end subjects can see that the problem can be rephrased as finding the area of a rectangle whose base is the same as one side of the parallelogram and whose height is the altitude of the chopped-off triangle (Figure 5.6(b)). Since subjects already know that the area of a rectangle equals the base times the height, the problem is solved. Simon claimed that this 'insight' involved the ability to recognize a triangle even when one of its boundaries is not marked but must be implied and that such a recognition could be built into a computer program like EPAM-III. Moreover he referred to some research by Tichomirov and Poznyanskaya (1966–67) in which they had observed that chess masters, in the first two seconds of looking at a new chess problem, tend to focus almost exclusively on those squares that were relevant to the chess problem in question – had they holistically 'grasped' the total situation? But Simon and Barenfeld (1969) were able to write a computer program that simulated the saccadic movements of the eyes from one point of focus on a stimulus to another. Simon found that the movements followed an order

(a)

(b)

Figure 5.6 Wertheimer's parallelogram problem: the problem is to find the area of (a). By mentally conceiving (a) in the manner shown in (b), the solution becomes more obvious. (Source: Figures 1 and 2 from Chapter 1 of *Productive Thinking* by Max Wertheimer. Copyright 1959 by Valentin Wertheimer. Copyright renewed 1987 by Michael Wertheimer. Reprinted by permission of HarperCollins Publishers, Inc.)

described by the rules of chess such that each successive saccadic movement focused attention onto one of the squares that stood in an attack or defense relation to the previously attended square. In the problem studied by Tichomirov and Poznyanskaya, the computer program followed the same general paths as had the chess masters in scanning the board. Simon therefore concluded that

> the human performance was simulated by simple recognition processes based upon chess knowledge and did not require any simultaneous or 'holistic' grasp of the entire network. (Simon, 1987, as reprinted in Simon, 1989, p. 487)

Another of Michael Wertheimer's claims was that the Gestalt theory of problem-solving demanded that the subject create an internal representation of elements of the problem, perhaps in the form of visual images, which could then be mentally reassembled to solve the problem – this was particularly true of problems in geometry or problems using tools such as Duncker and Maier had used. Simon's reply was that a program called UNDERSTAND had been developed that first parsed natural-language descriptions of problems and then transferred the parsed description into an 'internal representation' that can be used by GPS. For example, Tower of Hanoi problems could be solved this way – in this problem the computer has an internal representation of the pegs and discs of the problem to work with. Other programs have also created visual pictures from verbally described scenes, notably the ISAAC program of Novak (1977), which can solve physics problems on the basis of schemas stored in memory – it can take a problem written in words about levers, and using its schemas concerning the physics of levers, can draw the problem visually on a cathode ray tube.

The frequent phenomenon of the 'aha' experience after a period of incubation, the phenomenon the Gestalt psychologists attributed to a re-structuring of the elements provided the 'stress' of the problem remained unrelieved, could also be modelled in a program, according to Simon. The 'Aha' experience, he claimed, usually represented a move away from a particular strategy to a new strategy; it was therefore an escape from an *Einstellung* situation. However it need not necessarily result from a conscious abandonment of the *Einstellung*, but from a period of inattention to it. Simon wrote:

> Extracted by this forgetting from the current rut, and on resuming attention to the problem, the problem solver attacks it from a new angle, which happens now to be the correct one. This alternative explanation of the post-incubation 'aha' seems first to have been proposed by Woodworth (1938, pp. 38, 823) and it was later elaborated into a scheme that can be modelled on a computer (Simon, 1966). It has the advantage of parsimony over other explanations in that it employs a well-known mechanism, the *Einstellung* effect, and requires no essentially new hypotheses. (p. 484)

This quotation refers to a paper by Simon (1966) in which he had offered a theory not only of insight but also of incubation. He claimed that by a process of 'familiarization', larger and larger chunks of information became available to long-term memory ready for entry 'fully formed', so to speak, into short-term memory; and at the same time there existed a tendency for the selective forgetting of solution-attempts that had not been successful. While the subject is engaged in various solution attempts, he is also storing features of the environment that can be used in the erection of new sub-goals in the effort at problem-solution. This information is being stored in long-term memory, on what might be called a 'blackboard'. If the problem-solver removes himself from the task for a time, he will forget various sub-goals he had been holding in short-term memory, and, when the time comes to return to the task, he is more likely to avail himself of the information on the 'blackboard' in his long-term memory. He may therefore follow a new path, guided by the improved information on the blackboard:

> Since his blackboard had better information about the problem environment than it did the first time, he has better cues to find the correct path. Under these circumstances (and remembering the tremendous differences a few hints can produce under problem solution), solutions may appear quickly that had previously eluded him in protracted search. (Simon, 1966, p. 35)

In general Simon believes that the various Gestalt words associated with their theory of problem-solving, such as 'insight', 're-structuring', 'aha experience' and 'learning by understanding (as opposed to rote)' can all be simulated by computers. 'Nonoperational' constructs, as he calls them, can be shown to be by-products of an analysis of thinking processes that can be simulated by computer programs. I read Simon's 1987 paper after having met him when he visited Queen's University in 1992 and I asked him then if Gestalt theory had influenced his early work on the computer simulation of human thought processes and he reiterated that Selz's work had a greater influence. His 1987 article indicates that he has seen Gestalt phenomena as human data to be simulated and that the development of GPS, EPAM, and other programs took place relatively independently of his reading of Gestalt psychology.

However I asked another question at the same time. Both the EPAM models of learning serial lists and Newell's SOAR models of skill-learning include the proviso that individual elements in a list or in a series of practised movements gradually become consolidated into larger 'chunks' as learning progresses. The same notion has been incorporated into TODAM2 (Murdock, 1993). My question was whether the notion of 'chunking' was historically influenced by the Gestalt notion of the formation of larger Gestalten. I felt that I could not help noticing the similarity between the notion of increasingly large 'chunks' in which individual elements are subordinated to an increasingly large 'whole', and the general Gestalt work on the 'organization' of lists into fewer and fewer groups that was discussed in Chapter 3. This point will not be pursued here because Simon, at the meeting at Queen's, did not indicate that there was a historical influence of such an analogy on the development of his theories. Miller's (1956) paper on chunking had a much greater direct influence.

This section was written to try to answer two questions, namely, the relationship of Gestalt theory to formal theories of problem-solving, and an evaluation of the theoretical usefulness of the notion of 're-structuring'. To the first question we now have an answer; according to Simon, various phenomena stressed by the Gestalt theorists 'fall out of' a formal theory of problem-solving that owes much to Koffka's rival Selz. The second question we may now approach as follows. If human problem-solving is based on cognitive representations of the problem and its possible solution, it is possible that there can be a shift in the kind of cognitive representation of the problem such that elements of the problem are seen in a new light, pliers being seen as weights, paper-clips as hooks, sticks as devices for knocking bananas down, triangles as parts of parallelograms and so on. According to Simon, these shifts occur during the phase when inputs are accessing long-term memory and can be modelled by a program that 'recognizes'. The question, therefore, is whether 're-structuring' as a hypothetical construct is useful for theories of problem-solving. I prefer to delay answering this question until Chapter 6, where there will be a general discussion of the appropriate terminology to use in cognitive science.

There are, of course, many other branches of enquiry in contemporary research on problem-solving. Johnson-Laird (1983) has stressed that in all problem-solving we make use of 'mental models' that we have built up of the environment; and Gigerenzer *et al.* (1991) have discussed 'probabilistic mental models' in particular. In these models of external reality, relative frequencies of events are stored and used to make probability judgements, and Gigerenzer (1991) has argued that if questions about the probability of an event X are phrased in terms of relative frequency ('how often will X occur in the series of events?'), subjects are less likely to make mistakes than if questions are phrased in the form 'What do you think is the probability that X will occur?' Many of the mistakes made answering the latter kind of question were listed by Kahneman *et al.* (1982) and, just as Köhler criticized Thorndike for setting the wrong kind of task to his cats, and as Koffka criticized Selz for asking questions that were too restrictive to reveal genuine re-structuring, so Gigerenzer (1991) has criticized Kahneman *et al.* for asking questions about subjective probability which are unsuitably phrased for persons whose natural 'probabilistic mental models' include relative frequencies.

Concluding remarks

There is an intense ambitiousness about much of this recent work on problem-solving. Problem-solving is being integrated into such model–classes as GPS (Newell and Simon, 1972), SOAR (Newell, 1990) or ACT (Anderson, 1991); it is being tied in with evolutionary theory (Cosmides and Tooby, 1991); apparent 'errors' in human reasoning are shown not necessarily to be errors at all but the result of the adoption of rational strategies given an ambiguous presentation of the problem (Gigerenzer, 1991); and shifts in strategy, of the kind that Gestalt psychologists might have called 're-structuring' are losing the somewhat mystical flavour they attained under the name 'insight' and are instead seen as predictable events. They are predictors in the sense that they might be translatable into programmable 'production systems' (Simon, 1987); and we might add that Anderson (1991) has shown that some insight solutions might follow from optimization procedures which attempt to minimize the work and effort in pursuit of a plan. The main way in which the Gestalt psychologists anticipated this current research was in their intensely cognitive approach to problem-solving at a time when the behaviourists tried to reduce even human problem-solving to sequences of learned actions. By talking about plans, schemas, and re-structurings of those plans or schemas, and by making use of 'thinking aloud' protocols to study these cognitive entities, the Gestalt psychologists, along with Selz, foreshadowed the modern developments described above in a way that had no parallel in behaviourism or neo-behaviourism.

This chapter has raised a number of important questions about the nature of description and explanation in cognitive science. In particular, it has been suggested that two quite separate kinds of description can co-exist, one that makes no reference to goals (the behaviourist dream) and one that makes references to goals (the formulation of the problem-solver's task by Duncker, Selz, Newell, Simon and others). Since the content of thought plainly includes goals when we formulate an intention, there is a greater *rapprochement* between the descriptions of phenomenological experience espoused by the Gestaltists and the descriptions of problem-solving processes espoused by the cognitive scientists than there is between behaviouristic descriptions and the latter. In the final chapter we shall take certain words that are particularly characteristic of Gestalt psychology, notably 'distinctiveness', 're-structuring', 'goal' and 'Ego', and evaluate their usefulness for cognitive psychology as we now know it.

Chapter 6

Some questions concerning cognitive science raised by Gestalt theory

Four questions raised by the Gestalt approach

We have now examined in detail the theoretical relevance of Gestalt psychology to twentieth century work on memory and problem-solving.

With respect to memory, we examined five sub-areas influenced by Gestalt contributions and found that often it was not so much the experimental evidence for Gestalt theory that was convincing, it was more that certain issues were clearly brought out which had been overlooked in the associationist or behaviourist literature. A study of the time-error revealed the importance of knowing the temporal and spatial surrounds of the stimulus, and anticipated the late twentieth century literature on modality-specific interference and short-term sensory memory. The study of whether memory for forms underwent spon-taneous change in the direction of good figure led to inconclusive results on that issue, but opened up a question of considerable importance in the late twentieth century literature on memory, the nature of the encoding at the time the stimulus material is perceived. The study of organizational processes, first postulated by the Gestalt psychologists, has led to a major research effort in the late twentieth century and studies of von Restorff's isolation effect in particular have a current parallel in the new focus on the concept of 'distinctiveness'. Gestalt theories of retrieval have been complemented by such modern notions as encoding specificity theory, while Koffka's notion of the Ego, which he believed was supported by evidence for the Zeigarnik effect, has a close relation to Tulving's concept of episodic memory. It is also possible that the evidence for implicit memory might be interpreted in terms of memories that are not available to the Ego, which is how Koffka interpreted it.

Gestalt research on problem-solving, because it postulated that subjects build up what we now call 'mental models' of the elements of a problem and then 're-structure' these mental models during the course of the solution to the problem, was ahead of its time in its emphasis on mental representations. Simon's current belief that 'insight' can be reduced to an associationistic series of 'recognition' responses does not detract from the originality of the research of Köhler, Wertheimer, Duncker and Maier and its importance in the development of the psychological theory of mental representations (including the concept of the 'schema'). Moreover the Gestaltists' stress on purposive, goal-directed behaviour was an antecedent to all modern theories of cognition that allow for 'plans' to be mentally represented and executed, theories that were more directly influenced by Miller *et al*.'s *Plans and the Structure of Behaviour* (1960).

On the other hand, the various successes of Gestalt psychology each raise issues of importance in the philosophy of cognitive science which merit extra discussion, and the remainder of the chapter will be devoted to some concluding remarks on each of four questions:

1. How far should 'distinctiveness' be incorporated as a dependent variable into cognitive science?
2. How far should 're-structuring' and 're-organization' be seen as metaphors rather than as referents to indispensable concepts in cognitive science?
3. In what ways does incorporation of the concept of a 'goal' improve (or harm) the progress of cognitive science?
4. Do we need the concept of a 'self' (or a homunculus) in a cognitive science?

Question 1. arose from the work of von Restorff and Köhler on memory; question 2. arose from the work of Wertheimer, Duncker and Maier on problem-solving; question 3. arose from the total corpus of the Gestalt writings claiming that behaviourism (and sometimes associationism) offered an incomplete and mechanistic account of psychology; question 4. was particularly raised by Koffka, who used the Ego as a unifying concept in his *Principles of Gestalt Psychology*.

How far should 'distinctiveness' be incorporated as a dependent variable into cognitive science?

We saw that Köhler's work on the time-error had as its predecessor research on psychophysics, research concerned with the order in which a standard stimulus and a comparison stimulus were presented. We also noted briefly that the notion of an adaptation level against which incoming stimuli are compared, a clear instance of relativistic judgement, arose from research on psychophysics. In the case of the concept of 'distinctiveness' both psychophysicists and researchers on memory have found themselves in recent years forced to re-examine the notion that any stimulus is judged 'on its own merits' so to speak. The case is particularly clear in psychophysics, as was noted by Murray (1993), who offered a discussion of whether in psychophysics it is better to talk of stimulus 'intensity' or of stimulus 'distinctiveness against a background'.

In the commentaries on this target article, many psychophysicists appeared sympathetic to the view that all perception is relativistic, and that attempts to establish a psychophysical law (a law relating physical intensity to subjective intensity) might even be thought of as an ecologically invalid endeavour. The issue of course has not been resolved, but theories of perception since the Gestaltists have often moved in a direction favouring relativistic processing. Such theories include adaptation-level theory, the theory of Brunswik (1956) that visual perception is based on the subject's making correlations between stimuli in the visual field, and even the 'direct' theory of Gibson (1966), which argues that relationships between elements in the visual field are evaluated directly (without much use of Helmholtzian unconscious inferences). In any sort of psychophysics based on theories like these, it is not the absolute intensity of a stimulus which determines its subjective intensity, but its intensity relative to the intensity of neighbouring elements.

The concept of 'distinctiveness' was also implicit in a great deal of theorizing on memory from the 1960s onwards, but was not given much explicit expression until the 1980s. It was implicit when d' was introduced as a measure of memory strength by Wickelgren and Norman (1966): d' reflects a relationship between a signal intensity and a background (noise) intensity. It was implicit in the research of the 1970s on depth-processing, a strategy for enhancing long-term memory; mental activities by the subject that were carried out in the phase where memories were being registered make the memories more 'distinctive' (Craik and Tulving, 1975). It was implicit in distributed memory models of the 1980s, such as TODAM or CHARM, in which weights were assigned to sets of features indicating how much attention those features had received; there were also forgetting parameters in these models that can be interpreted as implying that, if some features of a vector were forgotten, the vector would be less 'distinctive' in memory. However it is only recently that 'distinctiveness' has been dealt with as explicitly as it was in the Gestalt literature, particularly that of von Restorff; Schmidt (1991) has offered a theory of distinctiveness (discussed at the end of Chapter 4), Glenberg (1987) offered a theory of primacy and recency effects in memory, a theory based on 'temporal distinctiveness', Johnson (1991) has offered a formal theory of serial position effects that is based on the idea that items in different serial positions in a list vary in 'distinctiveness', and Neath (1993) has offered an explanation based on the relative 'distinctiveness' of the target items for the fact that as recency decreases, and primacy increases, the longer the retention interval.

Whatever the future usefulness of the term 'distinctiveness', it was the Gestalt psychologists who first stressed it at a time when the Law of Effect and the Law of Frequency were paramount in discussions of both human and animal learning. Current theories of the Law of Effect stress how a reward may enhance the 'distinctiveness' of the previous action in the organism's representation of its own behaviour; this view was anticipated by Guthrie (1935). The Law of Frequency is making a comeback in the guise of a 'power law' of exercise: performance is argued to improve as a power function of the amount of practice at a given motor or cognitive task (see e.g. Anderson, 1991). However it seems to be straining the language to talk of an act based on procedural memory as 'distinctive' in the way that a percept is; it seems to be straining language to say that, if, of two habits, one is 'stronger' than another because of the greater frequency with which is has been exercised, then the stronger habit is more 'distinctive' than the other; and it seems to be straining language to say that if, in a connectionist or network model, one connection has a stronger 'weight' than another, then that connection is more 'distinctive'. To apply the word 'distinctive' to habits, associations and connections is to make the concept of 'distinctiveness' itself less distinctive; it should be reserved for perceptual entities, mental representations and possibly memory traces (so that the trace of an item A in a list might be more 'distinctive' than the trace for another item B in the same list). The school of thought (represented at its most extreme by behaviourism) that makes all cognitive activity a by-product of motor habits would not therefore welcome any use of the word 'distinctiveness' except with respect to stimuli. A dog in a Pavlovian harness may find a circle more 'distinctive' with respect to a square than with respect to an ellipse, and this distinctiveness may be measured by the probability or amplitude of salivation to the circle, but we do not normally say that the conditioned reflex of salivation to the circle is more 'distinctive' than another response.

'Distinctiveness' then is a word of restricted applicability in cognitive psychology. It is most useful when referring to the contents of mental representations which, by analogy with sensory processes, are like perceptions. Schmidt (1991) stressed that the concept of distinctiveness could be made more precise if the concept of incongruity were introduced and von Restorff (1933) had stressed that distinctive items were those that were most different from *several* other items in their environment. A circle is more distinctive from a set of squares than it is from an equally large set of various geometrical shapes. The usefulness of the concept in cognitive science will hinge on how far cognitive science insists that mental representations are part of its domain. In Watsonian behaviourism, there are no centrally excited sensations (images) but modern neuropsychologists are more receptive to the idea of centrally excited sensations, as is clear from a recent review of evidence relating to neurophysiological events apparently correlated with the experiencing of visual images (Farah, 1988). If sensation-like experiences (i.e. images) arise from a central *neurological* event N_1, and this event subsequently leads to another central event N_2 which is associated with its own sensation-like experience, then the chain of events N_1N_2 will be associated with a unique set of mental representations (sensation-like events) whose contents are directly predictable from N_1 and N_2.

A cognitive science in which the contents of a sequence of mental representations can (in theory) be mapped onto a unique sequence of neurological events can safely assert that the contents of those mental events are part of the domain of its science. To attempt to say that 'I have an image of myself posting a letter in the future' is reducible to a sequence of purely speech-motor responses is not feasible in such a cognitive science. Once it is admitted that mental representations can be uniquely mapped onto neurological events, and are not mere verbal shorthand for an act of internal speech, then the concept of 'distinctiveness' is a potential dependent variable in such a science. Its operational definition, admittedly, is more difficult to specify. When the Gestalt psychologists stressed that a stimulus would be easier to retain and retrieve if it were isolated from its surrounding elements, they opened the door to a cognitive science in which mental representations, grounded on discrete central neurological events, were the *data* to be described and explained. In such a science a 'trace' or 'schema' might have a unique neurological specification and the execution of a plan on the basis of an image representation of the plan could not then be completely described if the description were only in terms of a chain of motor responses. The validity of such a science therefore depends crucially on evidence for centrally excited sensations, such as is being provided by Farah and others.

How far should 're-structuring' and 're-organization' be seen as metaphors rather than as referents to indispensable concepts in cognitive science?

This issue was discussed in Chapter 5, where it was argued that Simon maintained that, in the ordinary course of events, the associative response to a given stimulus element A that is part of a problem-setting might at one time be R_1, a response determined by previous experience with A, whereas at a different time A might give rise to R_2, a new response that might be helpful in solving the problem. However, when A arouses R_1, and later, A arouses R_2, both R_1 and R_2 can, according to Simon, be seen as 'recognition' responses related to different aspects of A. Thus, if A is a pair of pliers, R_1 might be the recognition of A *as* a gripping device, and later, R_2 might be the recognition of A *as* a weight to be hung on a cord. As hinted on p. 162, it is a subtle question as to whether the associations pliers → gripping device and pliers → weight should be called 'recognition' responses as opposed to 'associations'. In Chapter 4, we made the claim that all responses of the kind we call 'recognition responses' have to be qualified by an 'as' – a word flashed in a tachistoscope can be recognised *as* a word in the English language or *as* a word that was seen in a list presented shortly beforehand. But when the pliers are seen in a new light *as* a weight, this is not necessarily a *re*-cognition, it is a *new* cognition. The pliers are *cognized*, not re-cognized, as weights. A computer program purporting to model 'insight' would have to have built into it a large set of statements to deal with a variety of contingencies (e.g. pliers cognized as being weights rather than gripping devices).

Moreover, all cases of re-structuring, including the computer program case, require that a second stimulus or response element initiate the transition from A's leading to R_1 to A's leading to R_2. Subjects conceived of the pliers → weight association (or 'cognition') by being given an extra stimulus (seeing the experimenter brush against the cord from which the pliers were to hang as a weight) or by conceiving of it themselves through a train of thought (i.e. 'mediating responses'). In almost all cases the 'new look' at A is inspired by a new stimulus, or, alternatively, the arousal of an old memory in the new context of the problem. The apes of Birch (1945) were more likely to use sticks as devices for knocking down a banana if they had had previous experience of using sticks this way. When Gauss solved the problem of adding the first n numerals, he did so by bringing to mind a new kind of sum: instead of adding the first two numerals, he added the first and the last numeral, leading to a solution. Re-structurings and re-organizings of mental problems therefore hinge heavily on the introduction of a new element which, so to speak, arouses a new context in which the stimulus element A can be 'cognized' *as* R_2 rather than as R_1.

How do 're-structuring' and 're-organization' as applied to problem-solving differ then from 're-structuring' and 're-organization' as applied to perceptual situations? In the perceptual situation, re-structuring might come about through what Dodwell (1993) calls 'level 2' processes, direct brain effects determined by the contents of the total visual field. The Gestalt psychologists wished to extend this notion to problem-solving, but, as Katz (1942) had noted, the extension may have been inappropriate because problem-solving involves the use of *learned* associations and memory. In Pylyshyn's (1984) terms, much of the re-structuring that takes place when a problem is solved is 'cognitively penetrable' whereas at least some of the re-structuring that takes place in perception might be the result of unlearned physiological processing of a total visual field (a processing that is at least in part 'top-down' processing). If these arguments are true, then the words 're-structuring' and 're-organization' as applied to problem-solving are essentially metaphors, shorthand for giving a vivid description for what is in fact the normal unravelling of a chain of associations given that a new element provokes a context in which A is cognized as R_2 rather than as R_1.

Yet I am not sure that Wertheimer would have been happy with this conclusion because he might have argued that when a new element introduces a new context in which A is cognized as R_2 rather than R_1, the physiological events underlying the 'new cognition' are as uninfluenced by learning as are the Gestalt laws of organization in perception. The brain was designed to 'group' and 'organize' the contents of consciousness, whether these contents are derived from external stimuli or from a revival of some contents of long-term memory. It was Köhler and von Restorff who specifically asserted what they argued was itself an insight, namely that grouping-by-similarity in spatial perception and grouping-by-similarity in the temporal domain of memory are mediated by the same kind of unlearned brain-processes. This is a strong claim that is not easy to disprove if one admits to memory activation by resonance, as so many models do. It is also a simplification insofar as cognition of A *as* R_2 can be modelled by specifying the context in which A is seen as R_2, a context that may be different from that in which A is seen as R_1. It seems to me that the memory models popular in the early 1990s, such as SAM, TODAM or CHARM, could be adapted to model Gestalt re-structuring by specifying the role of the context in determining the associations inspired by individual stimulus-elements in a problem. As context changed, so would these associations. If the context remained relatively stable, there would be the risk of functional fixedness. If a new context were inspired by a hint, then there would be a new set of associations which could be experienced as a sudden 'insight' if the hint set up a context which, by resonance (temporal grouping by similarity) aroused memories of a similar context in which the stimulus-element had a role different from its previous role. Seeing the cord brushed would arouse a mental context of 'things swinging', which would arouse the memory that 'things swinging' swing more widely if there is a weight on the bottom and this aroused memory might lead to the insight that the pliers, visible right there to the subject, could serve as such a weight.

Note that this 'insight' will probably involve the experiencing of a visual image, in which the pliers are imaged as being attached to the cord and acting as a weight for the cord if the latter is set into motion and it might have been preceded by an image of a wavering cord that needs to be *set* swinging by the addition of a weight. If the image sequence includes a rapid switch from an image involving a loosely moving cord to one involving a satisfactorily swinging cord, with the 'switch' involving the moving of the pliers from their previous resting-place to a position where they are attached to the bottom of the cord, this 'switch' may also be dependent on unconscious processing, such as is implicated in a perceptual re-organization like a figure-ground reversal. But is the switch in the pliers situation due to Dodwell's level 2 processing (cognitively impenetrable) or to level 3 processing (cognitively penetrable)? I suspect the latter. If this is the case, then 're-structuring' in the context of problem-solving is not analogous to *all* cases of perceptual re-organization, such as figure-ground reversals, which may come about because of innate principles of brain functioning. The problem is that an extreme Gestaltist might claim that, since the arousal of an association by a stimulus is itself the result of an innate principle of brain functioning, even mental representations that are cognitively penetrable may be prone to the same kind of 're-structuring' as goes on in perceptual re-organization like figure-ground reversals. So the question of whether re-structuring in problem-solving is equivalent to re-structuring in perception can only be answered positively if we decide that 'associating' involves level 2 processing. Some Gestalt psychologists like Wertheimer and Köhler probably thought it did; others like Katz were more cautious about asserting this; and Simon probably felt that, since association processes can be described without recourse to analogies with perception or with brain functioning, the question is peripheral when it comes to computer simulation.

This wide spectrum of opinion is understandable given the tasks that these various psychologists set themselves. Wertheimer and Köhler were always looking for a few fundamental principles of brain operation that would account for as wide a range of psychological phenomena as possible; they ran the risk of being *too* general, building a psychological theory like an inverted pyramid on one or two assumptions, as Titchener remarked (Henle, 1984, p. 14). Simon was looking for a model (a program) that would simulate psychological phenomena. He found he could do without such concepts as 're-structuring' that were based on descriptions, not of psychological processes (the steps involved in solving a problem) but on psychological experience (the subjective experiences of rapidly changing images). The question therefore of whether we need 're-structuring' as a fundamental concept in cognitive psychology is related to the question of a certain *arbitrariness* inherent in the choice of terms to be defined in a cognitive science. A concept that is useful at the level of the description of psychological experience (e.g. the concept of 're-structuring') may be questionable in the description of underlying brain processes (which may be level 2 or level 3) and superfluous in the description of a program that simulates the behaviour of a person solving problems (as in Simon's computer models). But we have also learned from the above argument that if centrally excited sensations (images) play a concrete role in certain problem-solving situations, then there is *prima facie* evidence that an account of those changing images in terms of perceptual re-structuring is an informative and effective means whereby one scientist can communicate with another concerning the psychological processes of problem-solving.

In what ways does incorporation of the concept of 'goals' improve (or harm) the progress of cognitive science?

When the Gestalt psychologists came to North America they were surprised to discover that the behaviourists thought that incorporation of the word 'goal' into the description of animal behaviour was scientifically suspect. In part, this was because the behaviourists wanted a 'bottom-up' psychology in which a systematic account of behaviour was based on $S–R$ associations, both learned and acquired; in part it was because, even though humans described their own behaviour in terms of their goals, it seemed anthropomorphic to assert that a rat had a mental representation of a goal when it found itself in the start-box of a maze. The work of Tolman did much to break down resistance to this latter notion, and even Hull had recourse to what he called 'fractional anticipatory goal responses', the production by the rat of eating responses shortly before it actually arrived in the goal-box. But I believe that the main reason for the resistance of the behaviourists to the incorporation of 'goals' into their scientific accounts of a behaviour was their profound belief that a description of even complex behaviour in terms of $S–R$ associations was parsimonious, adequate and accurate; if any movement M is determined by the preceding movement, why incorporate mention of a future movement in a mechanistic description of why M was produced? In turn, this reflected the fact that the behaviourism had its ancestry in the associationistic tradition going back to Locke.

The Gestaltists had emerged from a different tradition, going back to Leibniz, one in which the aim of psychology was to explain how the organism, human or animal, built up a representation of reality. In such a mental framework, it was easy to extend the 'representation of reality' to cover a representation of a possible 'future reality'. The Gestaltist has no trouble in believing that a dog in a Pavlovian harness, when it hears a tone previously paired with food, forms an internal representation of a possible future event, namely, the arrival of food. Indeed, the 'expectancy' view of classical conditioning, which has now been widely taught thanks to textbooks like that of Gleitman (1980), both corresponds to Gestalt views and may have been influenced by them, because Gleitman was a pupil of Tolman, and Tolman at one time worked in Germany with Koffka. The reasons for the clash between the behaviourists and the Gestaltists concerning the need for 'goals' to be irreducible entities in a systematic psychological science include a historical factor.

But it is more than that. In the late twentieth century psychologists with an interest in the philosophy of science are coming more and more to realize that the question of whether we need to talk about 'goals' is a central issue in psychology. Even in the Middle Ages, St Thomas Aquinas (1273) argued that one major difference between humans and animals was that humans had an exact knowledge of what would happen if they executed particular plans or intentions (they had a 'perfect' apprehension of what would happen if they used their will) whereas animals had only an 'imperfect' apprehension; animals were motivated by instinct, humans were motivated by mental representations of possible future events. Over the succeeding centuries it became clear that as the human brain evolved it became increasingly capable of representing events that were not directly present to sensations; it became increasingly capable of planning to bring about events that it inferred would result if it executed particular activities in the present (an account of the possible time-course of the evolution of planning capabilities has been offered by Donald, 1991).

In his book *The Sciences of the Artificial*, Simon (1981b) has argued that the scope of science should include not only natural events and the description of the behaviour of natural objects (including living things) but should also include the description of objects that have been created (usually by humans), objects such as tilled fields, roads, household utensils, computers, etc. The main difference between natural objects like rocks and animals and 'artificial' objects like tools and computers is that the latter were created to serve particular 'goals'; tilled fields served the goal of providing food, grown under conditions more favourable than those occurring in the wild, roads served transportation goals, household utensils served the goals of the cook, and computers the goals of the scientists. Simon insisted that human thought and language, while not necessarily having evolved as a device for achieving a goal laid down by some 'external' entity such as a god (as cooking pots evolved to fulfil the goals of cooks) nevertheless can be seen as having evolved as a solution to a problem. The problem is that of adapting to obstacles preventing the complete adaptation of the organism to its environment. Generally speaking, the special senses, individual colouring, individual movement-patterns and so on of a given species have evolved so that the species can continue to survive and breed in its natural environment. The scientific laws that governed this process of evolution, Simon believes, are relatively simple. But the environment itself is not simple; an animal seeking food is repeatedly faced with obstacles to progress such as natural barriers, bad weather, predators, illness and so on. To cope with the complexity of the environment, various species, notably humans, evolved the ability to cope with short-term obstacles to progress; essentially human intelligence, with its 'foresight' or ability to make plans and formulate goals, evolved as an adaptation suitable for the overcoming of problems set by a complex environment. Similarly, humans have in turn invented machines that can behave in a manner that can be described as 'goal-seeking'. As Simon (1981b) notes,

> Some years ago Grey Walter built an electromechanical 'turtle' capable of exploring a surface and periodically seeking its nest, where its batteries were recharged. More recently, goal-seeking automata have been under construction in several laboratories, including Professor Marvin Minsky's in Cambridge, Massachusetts. Suppose we undertook to design such an automaton with the approximation dimensions of an ant, similar means of locomotion, and comparable sensory activity. Suppose we provided it with a few simple adaptive capabilities: when faced with a steep slope, try climbing it obliquely; when faced with an insuperable obstacle, try detouring; and so on... How different would its behaviour be from the behaviour of the ant?...
>
> An ant, viewed as a behaving system, is quite simple. The apparent complexity of the behaviour over time is largely a reflection of the complexity of the environment is which it finds itself. (p. 64)

Human rationality is, for Simon, essentially a simple solution to the problem of adapting to short-term obstacles, but which exhibits complexity because the environment is complex. In the development of his theory of cognitive psychology, Simon has suggested that there are a few basic constants underlying complex thought behaviour, including a limit on the capacity of short-term memory (it only holds a few 'chunks'), a limit on the time it takes to process information from short-term memory into long-term memory (a few seconds for most lists of verbal material, probably less for visual material like pictures), and limits on the development of skills at organizing complex inputs into manageable units (as when a chess player can reproduce a chessboard with 24 men on it, provided it is part of an actual game so that the positions of the men are 'organized' with respect to the rules of chess). Allan Newell, in his *Unified Theories of Cognition* (1990), has greatly elaborated on this basic theme, included the analysis of cognitive processes into different 'levels', some operating in timeframes of hundredths of a second, some within tenths of a second and so on. But in all of this kind of theorizing, 'goals' are taken as unifying factors facilitating theory construction. Whether we are talking of humans having the goals of memorizing nonsense syllables or solving chess problems, or machines having the goals of proving logic theorems or, like humans, solving chess problems, *theory* construction is facilitated by the incorporation of the concept of goals.

Moreover, Simon himself points to a problem underlying all the above, one which I believe applies not only to the sciences of the artificial, but also to the differing stances of the behaviourists and the Gestaltists with respect to the desiderata for a learning theory. The successful solution of a problem in science depends in part on tackling the problem at the right level. We are usually only interested in a particular *aspect* of an event in nature. As Simon (1981b) notes,

We are seldom interested in explaining or presenting phenomena in all their particularities; we are usually interested only in a few properties abstracted for the complex reality. . .

It is fortunate that this is so, for if it were not, the topdown strategy that built the natural sciences over the last three centuries would have been infeasible. We knew a great deal about the gross physical and chemical behaviour of matter before we had a knowledge of molecules, a great deal about molecular chemistry before we had an atomic theory and a great deal about atoms before we had any theory of elementary particles – if indeed we have such a theory today.

This skyhook – skyscraper construction of a science from the roof down to the yet constructed foundation was possible because the behaviour of the system at each level depended on only a very approximate, simplified, abstracted characterization of the system at the level next beneath. (p. 20)

Let us distinguish between the 'representation of reality' that is unique to each organism (including each human) and the *scientific* representation of reality, shared by many, which consists of a set of propositions about both natural and artificial objects; a set of propositions that can be communicated between scientists. In discussing 're-structuring', we noted that whether or not that term was useful in a psychological science in part depended on an 'arbitrary' decision. We now wish to qualify this; the choice of terminology in a science is 'arbitrary' in the sense that there is no pre-existing necessity determining the choice of terms; the choice of terms is the result of human decision. But it is not 'arbitrary' in the sense of being 'random'; the decisions as to what terms are used in the science are based on sound reasons. Among the qualities that are devised in such a terminology are parsimoniousness, adequacy, and accuracy. We need discuss no further the question of accuracy; it is a given that any scientific assertions should correspond to reality. But 'parsimoniousness' and 'adequacy' do need further qualification. As is obvious from the quotations above, a description of the behaviour of objects at a *lower* level than the level that is being aimed at may not be parsimonious, but may be cumbersome; furthermore it may, in an important sense, be inadequate. If we describe the behaviours of a goal-setting automaton in terms of the electrochemical events in its internal computer, the description would not only be cumbersome in the sense of being long-winded, it may also be inadequate for communicating an important property of this automaton, namely, its goal-seeking property. A long set of propositions about the electrochemical events at a molecular level may never even mention the word 'goal', and this would be inadequate for communication at a higher level, that of describing the automaton's behaviour. Similarly, a description of events in the myriad synapses of a human brain that occur during the thinking and subsequent execution of the plan 'I intend to write after breakfast' would be orders of magnitude less parsimonious than a description of (inner speech and image) processes involving the setting up of the plan, the reminding of oneself of the plan throughout breakfast, and the execution of the writing after breakfast. It would also be inadequate for the purposes of another scientist who wished to understand the causes of my action of writing at a particular time, namely, after breakfast.

It is clear, therefore, that in the scientific representation of reality, goal-terminology is parsimonious and adequate at one level of description but may be absent at a lower level. With respect to the representation of psychological reality in a psychological science, the Gestaltists clearly considered goal-terminology to be essential. The behaviourists, influenced perhaps by their envy of the success of physicists at basing their science on events at a molecular or atomic level, thought they could use a lower-level description of behaviour in terms of S–R associations that would be parsimonious (only one basic kind of unit, the S–R association) and adequate (the successful development of a theory like Hull's would lead one to infer there was no need to refer to 'goals', 'plans' or 'purposes'). In fact the behaviourist's dream remained unfulfilled because (1) S–R association terminology is parsimonious only in the sense of involving few variables; it is not parsimonious in describing human behaviours because it involves too many propositions to describe a behaviour sequence that can be much more broadly described in terms of goals; and (2) S–R association terminology is inadequate because it leaves out internal representations such as images, which in turn are subject to the contextual influences in space and time that the Gestalt psychologists emphasized.

But behaviourism left a mark on psychology which will never fade, because behaviourism was a branch of associationism, and associationistic models cannot be said to be 'failures' in our own time. The SAM model can handle contexts and images in terms of associations and the connectionist models can simulate learning, including classical conditioning (Kehoe, 1988). However it is noteworthy that the most successful connectionist models use something equivalent to a 'goal' when they assert that the output of a network on trial n is compared to an 'ideal' with the weights in the network being adjusted so that on trial $n+1$ the output provides a better match to the unchanged ideal. It is rather unnerving, however, to realize that the success of Simon, Newell and their colleagues in modelling both inferential and memory processes with computer programs is based on a view of psychology that does include goal-terminology and has no programmed equivalent of internal scalable magnitudes such as 'habit strength', 'memory strength' or 'associative strength'. When Simon visited my Department in 1992, he acquiesced when I suggested that Newell (1990) seemed to dislike internal scalable magnitudes, to judge by Newell's scattered negative references to 'strength' concepts; and both Simon (1981b) and Newell (1990) lay more stress on numerical constants affecting short-term and long-term memory in their theory of how a basically simple nervous system can adapt itself to a complex environment.

Historically, then, the Gestalt psychologists had ideas about the usefulness of goal-terminology in psychological science that correspond to those of such major pioneers of cognitive science as Simon and Newell. They also insisted that internal representations by organisms of external reality need not be re-described in terms of movements but could consist of images. Possibly the most important difference between the views of the majority of cognitive psychologists and the views of the behaviourists concerns the role of words in cognitive science; for Watson, 'words' were represented by speech-movements, whereas for many cognitive psychologists words can be represented not only at the low-level discourse of speech-movements but at the higher-level discourse of 'symbols' that can be manipulated in 'lists'. At this level goals formulated in words cannot be 'reduced' to speech-movements any more than the instructions in a computer program can be 'reduced' to electrochemical events. The Gestalt psychologists acted as if they thought along these lines, although so far as I know, they did not discuss the fact that the language we use to describe a natural event (a human action) may also be suited to the description of the behaviour of an artificial object (a computer executing a program). They believed in goal-terminology because it provided an appropriate context within which any individual actions could be discussed; when Köhler's apes stood on a box to reach a banana, their actions could not only be described, but *explained*, in the context of a goal, namely getting their banana. However, I feel that a lower-level explanation of goal-directed behaviour in terms of a mechanical unwinding of a series of actions, each determined by the previous, may not be inaccurate, any more than a description of a computer's execution of a program in terms of electrochemical events is inaccurate; it is simply unparsimonious and inadequate at the level of explanations with which the psychologist is concerned, namely, the level concerned with molar actions, conscious motivations and the experiencing of internal representations of external reality in the form of words and images.

More generally, Köhler, in his book, *The Place of Values in the World of Facts*, had stressed that the subject-matter of science should be expanded to include not only non-living objects like rocks and living objects like animal bodies, but also mental experiences which, he argued, were determined by the goals individuals were thinking about at the time of those experiences. He argued that all thought-experiences were determined by what he called 'requiredness'; what we attend to and what we ignore is a function of how the stimuli in question 'fit' into the ongoing *mental* framework at the time of perception. Goal-terminology fits naturally into a philosophical viewpoint that includes mental experiences as *data* in a natural science.

Do we need the concept of a 'self' (or a homunculus) in cognitive science?

According to Koffka, the Ego represented a particular memory schema and other phenomena of memory, such as the memorizing of material with the aim of recalling it at a particular time later, or the non-forgetting of material if it represents an unfinished task (Zeigarnik effect), can be explained in terms of it. But for a very large number of other psychologists, the self was simply an abstraction, a mental concept derived from the most common element of mental experiences unique to an individual, namely the element of their all belonging to that same individual. This view had its origins in Locke's analysis of personal identity (Locke, 1690); it received further support in Hume's contention that whenever he tried to find a 'self' by examining his own mind, all he found were individual experiences (Hume, 1739–1740); and, reflecting the main opinion current in North America at the time Koffka was writing, for the behaviourists the 'self' was simply a superfluous concept.

The most interesting criticism of this view that I have come across was written by the American psychologist Calkins (1915) at a time when the introspectionist technique was being widely used on the continent of Europe. Mary W. Calkins (1863–1930) is a heroine in the literature on women in psychology because she was one of the first women to teach psychology (at Wellesley College near Boston), having been encouraged by William James. She became the first woman President of the American Psychological Association in 1905. In 1894 she reported studies using the paired-associates technique independently of G.E. Müller's invention of the closely related method of hits (see Chapter 3). She also conducted a survey of her own dreams showing how events from the previous day were often incorporated into dreams (Calkins, 1893); Freud integrated this discovery into his theory of the dream-work and acknowledged Calkins' contribution. Yet her writings on the self, while frequently referred to in biographies of her life such as that of Furumoto (1990), remain little known. She considered her self-psychology to be her most important contribution to psychology even though her commitment to it ran against the streams both of Titchenerian structuralism and of Watsonian behaviourism. Essentially Calkins believed that experimentalists who studied individual facets of sensation, perception, and even problem-solving were missing the importance of the self. For her the self was not just a philosophical abstraction but a phenomenally observable presence in conscious experience; it was a datum as much as any sensation or image.

Her evidence for this belief was presented in detail in her 1915 paper. She believed that the introspections obtained in various kinds of experiments confirmed her notion that the description of mental events is impossible without involving the notion of a self or an 'I' that determined behaviour. For example, she referred to some experiments on recognition by the Frenchman D. Katzaroff (1911). Katzaroff presented 18 geometrical drawings as a series to subjects, then asked them to pick these 18 out of a group of 36 drawings, 18 of which were old and 18 of which were new. He studied the reaction times associated with making these recognition responses, but here we shall focus on the introspections he obtained. He observed that recognition was probably based on a *direct* feeling of familiarity; it was not based on a mental comparison between the probe drawing and a memory image of the target drawing. Calkins translated one of Katzaroff's remarks as follows:

> The feeling of the familiar, the 'seen before' which accompanies a repeated sensation arises from the fact that this very sensation has *connected itself with the very feeling of our 'self' and has been enveloped by this feeling of self*. (Calkins, 1915, p. 507; Katzaroff's italics)

In another study using introspections, Michotte and Prüm (1911) showed subjects two numerals, and the subject could choose between two arithmetical operations to carry out upon them (e.g. multiplication and division). However he did not have actually to do the arithmetic. Instead he touched a key to signal he had made his choice and then 'devoted himself as painstakenly as possible to introspection, reviewing everything from the moment of the appearance to the stimulus. As soon as this observation was concluded and the different states fixed in his memory he gave a signal to the experimenter working in the next room' and dictated to him the results of the introspection (Calkins, 1915, p. 208). The gist of these introspections was that when the problem was presented the subject frequently had muscular sensations suggestive of stress or agitation but these sensations were quite separate from what Michotte and Prüm called a 'consciousness of activity'. In this state there was a strong feeling that there was a self who directed the decision as to what arithmetical operation to use. Various quotations from subjects included 'there was an awareness that it was *I* who acted' and 'the consciousness of acting, of doing, of determining, was clearly presented, though there was no representation of the *I* and though the *I* was present in no other explicit way'.

And finally there was the work of Ach (1910), ostensibly devoted to an introspective analysis of 'willing'. He had subjects learn paired-associates (nonsense syllables) to a very high degree; after learning these, the subject, given a stimulus-syllable, could give the appropriate response-syllable almost automatically. But sometimes he was asked to give a *new* syllable (e.g. a syllable that was a reversal of the stimulus-syllable, when the overlearned response had been a syllable that rhymed with the stimulus-syllable). In the original learning, syllables had been paired with unrelated syllables, rhyming syllables (e.g. zup tup) or reversed syllables (e.g. dus sud). So, for example, having learned 'zup tup' to a high level, the subject might unexpectedly be asked to produce the reversal 'zup-puz'. Ach believed that the effort involved in producing 'zup-puz', after having overlearned 'zup-tup', was an index of 'will' or 'volition'; and certainly many subjects reported muscular sensations in various parts of the body, particularly the forehead, when they were confronted with having to make a response that 'went against the grain' of their previous learning. Ach analyzed the experiences reported by his subjects as having four phases, a perceptual phase made of the strain-sensations that characterized attention, a consciousness (sometimes verbal, sometimes an 'imageless awareness') of the end or aim of will, an activity or consciousness that could be labelled 'I will', and finally, a consciousness of difficulty or exertion. In this sequence the sense of the self, or the I is prominent – the end of will is to perform an action, but the start-point is the self.

Calkins, having presented this (now forgotten) evidence that a sense of self plays a crucial part in recognition, decision-making, and the execution of actions in which one must overcome a previous habit, contended that cognitive psychology could not do without the concept of a 'self'. She admitted that the self cannot be observed in the way that an external object can be observed; she did not discuss the question of whether the self was necessarily unitary; but she pointed out that even diehard psychologists who denied we needed the self as a concept in a scientific psychology could not avoid using terms referring indirectly to the self in their own writings:

> [The self psychologist] finds that the technical writings of selfless psychologists are full of terms of self psychology; that they bristle with references to experience, of which 'I take note', or in which 'I am concerned' or with definitions of psychical reality as 'that which is experienced by a single subject'. In a word, selfless psychologists are constantly implying a subject, or self, and are perpetually distinguishing it from its experiences. To the self-psychologists it seems futile to explain this inveterate habit of referring to the self by the convention of language, for the convention of acknowledging a self is precisely the fact to be explained. (p. 520)

From the claim that the self is a 'verbal abstraction', and therefore useful for communication purposes between scientists but not really essential to cognitive science, Calkins has moved to the claim that the self is an entity that should be treated in its own right. Koffka's evidence for a 'self' that was not just a verbal abstraction rested on his believing that the 'self' was the name for a vast system of memory traces. Under *both* of these views, it is possible to assert that not everybody has a unitary self, and the evidence from multiple personality disorder that individuals have separate 'selves', in which one 'self' cannot necessarily recall what is in another 'self', supports the notion that the 'self' can be reduced to sets of memories. This idea is expounded on by Dennett (1991) in his book entitled *Consciousness Explained*, who refers to the 'reality of selves'; but he claims that

> A self, according to my theory, is not any old mathematical point, but an abstraction defined by the myriads of attributions and interpretations (including self-attributions and self-interpretations) that have composed the biographies of the living body whose Center of Narrative Gravity it is. As such, it plays a singularly important role in the ongoing cognitive economy of that living body, because of all the things in the environment an active body must make mental models of, none is more crucial than the model the agent has of itself. (pp. 426–7)

By 'Center of Narrative Gravity' Dennett meant that whenever I am reporting my experiences, it is myself that forms the kernel of my reports; just as the description of the behaviour of a physical object is simplified by the assumption that it has a centre of gravity, the description of the experiences of a human being can be thought of as having a centre of 'narrative gravity'.

So Calkins claimed we needed the 'self' for an adequate description not only of planned actions and decisions but also of memory retrieval (particularly recognition); Koffka claimed that the 'self' was a name for a set of memories whose arousal was reflected in a sense of 'me-ness'; Dennett claims that it is an abstraction, albeit a crucial one, in the description of phenomenological experience. Calkins claimed that many experiments on psychology failed to single out the 'self' as a factor because the tasks were not designed to explore the characteristics of selfhood; 76 years later, Dennett claimed that if we *did* design experiments to explore the nature of the 'self', these would probably be unethical – we cannot ethically conduct an experiment to determine the conditions under which more than one self emerges, but 'we can avail ourselves of the data generated by some of the terrible experiments nature conducts, cautiously drawing conclusions' (p. 419) – such an experiment is exemplified by multiple personality disorder, which Dennett claims is often related to the subjects' having been sexually abused in childhood. To top off the growing consensus that the 'self' can no longer be neglected by psychologists, Donald (1991) argues that the evidence for a central processor controlling the interpretation of sensory inputs (including written inputs) and the emission of planned actions obliges us to believe in a homunculus:

> Fear of the homunculus begets irrational behaviour in cognitive scientists. They dread the truth: in a tiny slab of brain there resides a consciousness capable of all we have achieved and experienced; and obviously, on one level, *there is a homunculus.* The homunculus is synonymous with the reflective, conscious mind, and somehow, somewhere in the protean parenchyma of mind, it must reside. *It cannot be explained away as an epiphemonenon, 'reduced' to algorithms or neural events, or simply denied existence.* It is *the* mainstream problem, the principal problem under investigation. It is no help to call it a central processor, when the central processor possesses virtually the same properties as the homunculus. (p. 365)

It is obvious from the above quotation that the concept of 'self' or a 'homunculus' is popular in the 1990s in the way that it was not in the 1930s, and of course this is a clear case where Koffka anticipated later trends. At the same time I believe that the argument concerning 'goal'-terminology is applicable also to the case of 'self'-terminology. At a low level of discourse, one involving nervous events or even *S–R* chains, it is probable that a scientist could do without a 'self'; at a higher level the 'self' is a useful concept. Nevertheless, there may be brain centres particularly concerned with 'self-monitoring', and Frith (1992) has argued that the various cognitive deficits in schizophrenia may be subsumed under a general heading of a disorder in self-monitoring – instead of being in control of movements, speech, ordered thinking and imaging, the schizophrenic patient is no longer in control: rather than willing images to happen, the schizophrenic patient is overwhelmed by images of which he is not in control, as when he hears hallucinated 'voices'. I believe that research on psychotic thinking may do more to bring back talk of the 'self' in cognitive psychology than will any of the reasoning of the earlier part of this section.

There is also a large amount of late twentieth century research on implicit memory, some of which was reviewed in Chapter 4. For Claparède and Koffka, implicit memory represented memory for information that had been retained but had not been linked up to the Ego-schema. The notion of an Ego can also be found in Ribot's early book *Diseases of Memory* (1881), in which he claimed that the laws of retention, like the laws determining the *feeling* of emotional responses, represented properties of the nervous system but the actual execution of retrieval plans demanded the operation of a large connected mass of traces Ribot called the Ego. When conscious retrieval fails, but retention can be demonstrated, as in most experiments on implicit memory, the reason is not that 'implicit memory' is some special kind of 'memory system'; according to Koffka, the reason is that it involves a special kind of retrieval, one that is not determined by the provision of conscious retrieval cues appropriate to the elicitation of memories forming part of the Ego. Tulving (1994) has recently also insisted that 'implicit memory' is not a kind of memory system, but recent researchers on implicit memory, so far as I know, have not focused on the question of the role of the self in determining retrieval performance. Moreover, Freud's idea that memories that threaten one's self-esteem are particularly difficult to retrieve (are 'repressed') needs closer examination in the context of Tulving's classification of memory systems (Figure 4.2). Hence, the 'self' may be revived in the near future at a high level of discourse in which retrieval behaviour is discussed. It may be remarked that Freud wrote a manuscript in which he tried to explain repression at a *lower* level of discourse, the neurological level; it is the final part of his *Project for a Scientific Psychology* (1954) and has, alas, been lost.

It seems, then, that at relatively high levels of discourse the concept of a 'self' or 'homunculus' may not be simply a gratuitous simplification but may be indispensable in a scientific explanation. At low levels, such as the neurological or the level of *S–R* associations, it may not be necessary. Because the issue of whether we need a 'self', in psychological explanation, has only rarely been discussed in the context of levels of explanation, it has not always been appreciated that the apparent clash between behaviourists and Gestaltists on the question is one which can be resolved by stressing that behaviourists were arguing at a low level that talked only of 'habits', a level that might have been inadequate for the full description of such phenomena as decision-making, mental illness and implicit memory. It is also fair to point out that the majority of laboratory tasks given to subjects in psychology experiments rarely use conditions in which the involvement of the 'self' is a *variable*; hence, there is little reason to distrust most accounts of psychological experiments that make no mention of the 'self'. As for the behaviourist views on the 'self', Watson (1928a) would probably have made it an epiphenomenon at his level of discourse, but he uses the word 'personality' rather than 'self': he believed that one's so-called 'personality' was simply a set of habits and that so-called 'double personality' referred to separate sets of habits that could be evoked in one and the same person.

Concluding remarks

The above discussion of whether psychology needs the concepts of distinctiveness, re-structuring, goals and the self has led, by a rather natural line of argument, to a position close to that of Herbert Simon in which scientific propositions that are judged to be acceptable at one level of discourse are not necessarily acceptable at a higher level. Like physics, whose history shows a progression from discussion of high level objects (planets, billiard balls), through middle level objects (molecules) to low level objects (atomic particles), the history of psychology has also shown a tendency for different levels of discourse to be popular at different times. At the highest level, behaviour can be said to be explicable in terms of goals, including the goal of attaining a 'self' or 'personality' which is to be desired; at a lower level, behaviour might be said to consist of a relatively deterministic chain of habits; at a lower level still, it may be said to be dependent on neurological events. It has always been an ambition of psychologists to explain higher level behaviour in terms of lower level concepts; Watson's attempt to explain 'multiple personality' in terms of 'habits' is a good example. The Gestaltists were not immune to this temptation; witness Köhler's unceasing attempts to explain memory and perception phenomena in terms of events concerning molecules in the brain. But the Gestaltists shared with late twentieth century cognitive psychologists the belief that an explanation of behaviour in terms of higher level concepts such as goals and the Ego was a valid type of explanation; and in stressing that the learning of an 'item' was always a function of how that item related to its context (e.g. was an item in a list to be learned isolated from its companions?) they made it difficult to base a model of psychological events on stimulus characteristics alone. Furthermore, the distinction between a level of discourse involving goal-terminology and a level of discourse involving habits becomes blurred if it is allowed that centrally excited sensations (images) exist; an image allows a goal to be represented but it is also not reducible to motor habits, even though, over the course of evolution, imagery may have evolved in some way from movements (Washburn, 1916). Perhaps a level involving images is necessary if this argument is to be refined. At any rate, the Gestaltists anticipated the views of many late twentieth century psychologists when they argued that goals could be set as a result of imaging, that lists of words could be more easily memorized with the use of images, and that problem-solving could be described in some cases as involving a re-structuring of a mental representation of a situation, a re-structuring probably involving images in which familiar objects are viewed as having new properties.

It seems reasonable to me that much of the apparent conflict between the behaviourists and the Gestaltists can be resolved if we adopt this view. Whether Köhler's chimpanzees or Duncker's human subjects were 're-structuring' perceptions with a view to the goal of solving the problem, or, alternatively, demonstrating earlier habitual behaviour until a particular behaviour-pattern solving the problem occurred, is a matter of deciding at which level of discourse we are going to make more headway in developing a scientific psychology. Because *novel* behaviour is easier to describe in the language of re-structuring than it is in the language of habits, because *persistent* behaviour in problem-solving is easiest to describe in terms of goal-directed actions, and because *successful* behaviours in problem-solving often seemed to be the result of a mental manipulation by the subject of images, the Gestalt psychologists thought that the incorporation of goals and images into a scientific psychology was appropriate. This view seems to be shared by late twentieth century writers such as Simon (1981b) who has emphasized that successful simulation of human behaviours by computer programs includes statements about goals, and Farah (1988) who has obtained evidence that visual images are accompanied by identifiable events in the brain. Nevertheless, the behaviourists' dream of reducing psychology to a sequence of statements about habits is by no means dead, as is indicated by the popularity of associationist models such as SAM (which nevertheless shares with the Gestaltists a concern for contextual variables), connectionist models (which, however, nearly always involve a mechanism for correcting a response so that it more nearly approximates an ideal response or 'goal'), and TODAM and CHARM (which allow memory representations to be blended in with each other, a feature shared with less formally expressed Gestalt theories of memory). It seems to me that people who would come heavily down on the side of behaviourism as opposed to Gestalt psychology, or vice versa, have not sufficiently pondered the consequences of a viewpoint according to which both are 'right' but at different levels of discourse.

We may recapitulate, then, the historical record leading to the present state of affairs as follows. When Wertheimer wrote his pioneering paper on apparent movement in 1912, the introspectionists of Germany and France were extending their researches to encompass actions in which the individual *felt* that he or she controlled the next action they executed; and the Würzburg group in particular were writing about the determining tendencies that dictated that a flow of cognitive events should be directed by the nature of the problem that had been set. This kind of research was quickly dismissed by Watson, whose influence, after a delay, ensured that North American experimental psychologists focused their researches on conditioning theory and 'habits' to the exclusion of cognitive processes – an influence that lasted until the 1950s. However, the Gestalt psychologists readily adopted the vocabulary for dealing with cognitive events that had been present in everyday language and in the writings of the introspectionists. Köhler's work on problem-solving in apes brought the notion of 're-structuring' to the fore – a concept that implies that even apes have some general schema for cognizing that a problem *is* a problem to be solved in the future. Köhler, Wulf, Lauenstein, von Restorff and I. Müller stressed the importance of distinctiveness in memorizing and made the suggestion that grouping-by-similarity in spatial perception had an analog in the temporal realm of memory. Koffka introduced the notion of schemata, in particular the Ego-schema, into memory theory and presented a systematic discussion of retrieval processes that has a modern counterpart in Tulving's theory. At a time when the behaviourists saw lists of nonsense syllables as serial chains to be memorized by brute rote learning, the Gestalt psychologists stressed that learning was largely a matter of organizing the material by the use of appropriate encoding strategies and appropriate imagery and that brute rote learning should only be used as a last resort. More generally, Gestalt psychologists stressed the goal-directedness of behaviour. In North America this attitude was eschewed by most of the behaviourists, except for Tolman, and the gradual conversion of North American psychologists to the view that behaviour should be described (and even explained) in terms of the goals of the behaviour is one of the major achievements of the cognitive revolution.

There is little point in belabouring the issue further here. The Gestalt psychologists anticipated the cognitive revolution with respect to the four issues discussed in this chapter (distinctiveness, re-structuring, goal-directedness, the self), but in addition made invaluable discoveries about memorizing, retrieving and problem-solving that clearly foreshadowed modern research on these areas. But the fact that the Gestalt psychologists *anticipated* late twentieth century science does not mean that they *influenced* it very much. This is in part because the contributions of the Gestalt theorists to cognitive psychology have been underknown (in comparison with their contributions to perception), and it is hoped that this book will help to make their insights on cognitive psychology better appreciated.

Appendix

A chronological list of the main events in the development of Gestalt ideas about cognition

1890	Von Ehrenfels' paper on Gestalt quality
1904	Wertheimer obtains PhD from Würzburg
1908	Koffka obtains PhD from Berlin
1909	Köhler obtains PhD from Berlin
1910	Wertheimer hires Köhler and Koffka as assistants at Frankfurt
1911	Koffka leaves Frankfurt to teach at Giessen
1912	Wertheimer's paper on apparent motion
1913	Köhler's paper attacking the constancy hypothesis (the notion that to every stimulus there corresponds a particular sensation)
1913	Köhler goes to Tenerife to study behaviour in apes
1913	J.B. Watson's first paper on behaviourism
1913, 1922	Selz's books on thinking, introducing the concept of an 'anticipatory schema'
1915	Rubin's paper in Danish on figure-ground organization (translated into German in 1921)
1916	Wertheimer leaves Frankfurt to teach at Berlin
1917	Köhler's *The Mentality of Apes* (translated into English in 1927)
1918	Köhler's paper on relational responding in apes and chickens
1920	Sir Henry Head's *Studies in Neurology* in which the concept of a memory schema is introduced. This concept was taken up both by Koffka (1935a) and by Bartlett (1932)
1920	Köhler's *Die physischen Gestalten in Ruhe und im stationären Zustand*
1922	Köhler joins Wertheimer at Berlin
1922	Koffka's paper in English on Gestalt theories of perception
1922	Wulf's paper on memory for nonsense forms: emphasis on what we now call 'verbal encoding'
1923	Wertheimer's paper on principles of organization in perception (similarity, closure, etc.)
1923	Köhler's paper on the time-error
1924	Schulte's paper on paranoia as a result of 'we-crippledness'
1925	Wertheimer's first paper on productive thinking (problem-solving)
1926	Gottschaldt's paper on hidden figures
1926	Lewin's paper on quasi-needs as determining sequences of thoughts and actions
1927	Koffka goes to the United States to teach at Smith College

1927	Zeigarnik's paper on the superior retention of unfinished tasks
1927	Koffka's paper criticizing Selz's analysis of thought
1928	Koffka's *Growth of the Mind*
1929	Köhler's *Gestalt Psychology*
1929	Duncker's paper on induced motion
1930	Maier's first paper on human problem-solving
1933	Wertheimer goes to the United States to teach at the New School for Social Research, New York City
1933	Harrower's paper on memory for jokes
1933	Von Restorff's paper on the superior retrieval of isolated items
1934	Köhler goes to United States to teach at Swarthmore College
1935	Duncker's book on productive thinking (translated into English in 1945 with the title *On Problem-solving*)
1935	Koffka's *Principles of Gestalt Psychology*
1936-41	The period of Wertheimer's seminars in New York that were summarized by Luchins and Luchins (1970)
1937	Köhler and von Restorff's paper on recognition as influenced by the contents of the material seen in the retention interval
1938	Köhler's *The Place of Value in a World of Facts*
1938	Ellis's *A Source Book of Gestalt Psychology*
1938	Ilse Müller's paper on retroactive and proactive inhibition seen as cases exemplifying von Restorff's isolation effect
1940	Katona's *Organizing and Memorizing*
1941	Koffka dies
1942	Köhler's *Dynamics in Psychology*
1942	Katz's *Gestalt Psychology* (in Swedish; translated into English in 1951)
1943	Wertheimer dies
1944	Köhler and Wallach's paper on figural after-effects
1945	Wertheimer's *Productive Thinking*
1953	Köhler's account of how Americans criticized the Gestalt emphasis on goal-directedness in behaviour
1956	Year commonly accepted as marking the beginning of the cognitive revolution
1961	Henle's *Documents of Gestalt Psychology*
1964	Helson's *Adaptation Level Theory*
1967	Köhler dies
1969	Köhler's *The Task of Gestalt Psychology*
1970	Maier's *Problem Solving and Creativity*
1971	Henle's *The Selected Papers of Wolfgang Köhler* (including Köhler's bibliography)
1986	Metzger's *Gestalt-Psychologie*

References

Aall, A. (1913), Ein neues Gedächtnisgesetz? Experimentelle Untersuchung über die Bedeutung der Reproduktionsperspektive. *Zeitschrift für Psychologie*, **66**, 1–50.

Ach, N. (1910), *Über den Willensakt und das Temperament*. Leipzig: Quelle & Meyer.

Allport, G.W. (1930), Change and decay in the visual memory image. *British Journal of Psychology*, **21**, 138–48.

American Psychiatric Association (1987), *Diagnostic and Statistical Manual of Mental Disorders* (3rd edition, revised). Washington, DC: American Psychiatric Association.

Anderson, J.R. (1983), *The Architecture of Cognition*. Cambridge, MA: Harvard University Press.

Anderson, J.R. (1991), Is human cognition adaptive? *Behavioral and Brain Sciences*, **14**, 471–517.

Anderson, J.R. and Bower, G. (1973), *Human Associative Memory*. Washington, DC: Winston.

Asch, S.E. (1968a), Wolfgang Köhler: 1887–1967. *American Journal of Psychology*, **81**, 110–19.

Asch, S.E. (1968b), The doctrinal tyranny of associationism: or what is wrong with rote learning. In T.R. Dixon and D.L. Horton (eds), *Verbal Behavior and General Behavior Theory*. Englewood Cliffs, NJ: Prentice Hall, pp. 214-28.

Ash, M.G. (1981), Academic politics in the history of science: Experimental psychology in Germany. *Central European History*, **13**, 255–86.

Ash, M.G. (1982), *The Emergence of Gestalt Theory: Experimental psychology in Germany, 1890–1920*. Unpublished PhD thesis, Harvard University.

Ashby, W.R. (1952), *Design for a Brain*. New York: John Wiley.

Atkinson, R.C. and Shiffrin, R.M. (1968), Human memory: A proposed system and its control processes. In K.W. Spence (ed.), *The Psychology of Learning and Motivation: Advances in research and theory*, Vol. 2. New York: Academic Press, pp. 89–195.

Baars, B.J. (1986), *The Cognitive Revolution in Psychology*. New York: Guilford Press.

Baddeley, A.D. (1990), *Human Memory: Theory and practice*. London: Allyn & Bacon.

Baddeley, A.D. and Hitch, G. (1974), Working memory. In G.A. Bower (ed.), *Recent Advances on Learning and Motivation*, Vol. 8. New York: Academic Press.

Baddeley, A.D., Thomson, N. and Buchanan, M. (1975), Word length and the structure of short-term memory. *Journal of Verbal Learning and Verbal Behavior*, **14**, 575–89.

Barnes, J.M. and Underwood, B.J. (1959), 'Fate' of first-list associations in transfer theory. *Journal of Experimental Psychology*, **58**, 97–105.

Bartel, H. (1938), Über die Abhängigkeit spontaner Reproduktionen von Feldbedingungen. *Psychologische Forschung*, **22**, 1–25.

Bartlett, F.C. (1932), *Remembering*. Cambridge: Cambridge University Press.

Bateson, G. (1974), *Perceval's Narrative: A patient's account of his psychosis*. New York: Morrow Paperback.

Beck, J. (ed.) (1982), *Organization and Representation in Perception*. Hillsdale, NJ: Lawrence Erlbaum.

Beers, C.W. (1908), *A Mind that Found Itself*. New York: Longmans, Green. Reprinted: Garden City, NY: Doubleday, 1953.

Behrens, P.J. (1980), The first dissertation in experimental psychology: Max Friedrich's study of apperception. In W.G. Bringmann and R.D. Tweney (eds), *Wundt studies*. Toronto: C.J. Hogrefe.

Benussi, V. (1914), Referat über Koffka-Kenkel 'Beiträge zur Psychologie der Gestalt- und Bewegungserlebnisse'. *Archiv für die gesamte Psychologie*, **32**.

Bergen, A. van (1968), *Task Interruption*. Amsterdam: North-Holland.

Birch, H.G. (1945), The relation of previous experience to insightful problem-solving. *Journal of Comparative Psychology*, **38**, 367–83.

Bleuler, E. (1916), *Lehrbuch der Psychiatrie*, Berlin: Springer. English translation (1924), *Textbook of Psychiatry*. New York: Macmillan.

Boas, F. (1882), Über die verschiedenen Formen des Unterschiedsschwellenwertes. *Pflügers Archiv für Physiologie*, **27**, 214–22.

Bolles, R.C. (1993), *The Story of Psychology: A thematic history*. Pacific Grove, CA: Brooks/Cole.

Boring, E.G. (1950), *A History of Experimental Psychology* (2nd edition). Englewood Cliffs, NJ: Prentice Hall.

Bower, G.H. (1970), Imagery as a relational organizer in associative learning. *Journal of Verbal Learning and Verbal Behavior*, **9**, 529–33.

Bower, G.H. and Clark, M.C. (1969), Narrative stories as mediators for serial learning. *Psychonomic Science*, **14**, 181–2.

Bower, G.H. and Winzenz, D. (1969), Group structure, coding and memory for digit series. *Journal of Experimental Psychology Monograph*, **80**, No. 2, Part 2.

Bower, G.H., Lesgold, A.M. and Tieman, D. (1969), Grouping operations in free recall. *Journal of Verbal Learning and Verbal Behavior*, **8**, 481–93.

Bower, G.H., Clark, M.C., Lesgold, A.M. and Winzenz, D. (1969), Hierarchical retrieval schemes in recall of categorized word lists. *Journal of Verbal Learning and Verbal Behavior*, **8**, 323–43.

Brentano, F. (1874), *Psychologie vom empirischen Standpunkt*. Leipzig: Duncker. Trans. (1973), A.C. Rancurello, D.B. Terrell and L.L. McAlister, *Psychology from an empirical standpoint*. London: Routledge & Kegan Paul.

Breuer, J. and Freud, S. (1895), *Studien über Hysterie*. Leipzig and Vienna: Franz Deuticke. Trans. J. and A. Strachey in A. Richards (ed.) (1974), *Studies on Hysteria*. London: Penguin.

Broadbent, D.E. (1958), *Perception and Communication*. New York: Pergamon.

Broadbent, D.E. and Broadbent, M.H.P. (1981), Recency effects in visual memory. *Quarterly Journal of Experimental Psychology*, **33A**, 1–15.

Broadbent, D.E., Cooper, P.J. and Broadbent, M.H. (1978), A comparison of hierarchical matrix retrieval schemes in recall. *Journal of Experimental Psychology: Human Learning and Memory*, **4**, 486–97.

Brooks, L. (1967), The suppression of visualization by reading. *Quarterly Journal of Experimental Psychology*, **19**, 289–99.

Brown, J.F. (1928), Über gesehene Geschwindigkeiten. *Psychologische Forschung*, **10**, 84–101.

Brown, J.F. (1931), The visual perception of velocity. *Psychologische Forschung*, **14**, 199–232.

Bruner, J. (1993), Meaning-making as central to a cognitive revolution. Talk given at a conference entitled *Reassessing the Cognitive Revolution*, York University, Toronto, 22–4 October.

Bruner, J.S., Goodnow, J.J. and Austin, G.A. (1956), *A Study of Thinking*. New York: John Wiley.

Brunswik, E. (1956), *Perception and the Representative Design of Psychological Experiments*. Los Angeles: University of California Press.

Burke, R.J., Maier, N.R.F. and Hoffman, L.R. (1966), Functions of hints in individual problem-solving. *American Journal of Psychology*, **79**, 389–99.

Buskirk, W.L. van (1932), An experimental study of vividness in learning and retention. *Journal of Experimental Psychology*, **15**, 563–73.

Calkins, M.W. (1893), Statistics of dreams. *American Journal of Psychology*, **5**, 311–43.

Calkins, M.W. (1894), Association (Part 1). *Psychological Review*, **1**, 476–83.

Calkins, M.W. (1915), The self in scientific psychology. *Psychological Review*, **26**, 495–524.

Cantor, J. and Engle, R.W. (1989), The influence of concurrent load on mouthed and vocalized modality effects. *Memory and Cognition*, **17**, 701–11.

Carmichael, L., Hogan, H.P. and Walter, A.A. (1932), An experimental study of the effect of language on the reproduction of visually perceived form. *Journal of Experimental Psychology*, **15**, 73–86.

Cartwright, D. (1938), On visual speed. *Psychologische Forschung*, **22**, 320–42.

Ceraso, J. (1967), The interference theory of forgetting. *Scientific American*, **317**, October, 117–24.

Ceraso, J. and Tendler, M. (1968), Pair vs. list interference. *American Journal of Psychology*, **81**, 47–52.

Christianson, S-Å. and Loftus, E.F. (1987), Memory for traumatic events. *Applied Cognitive Psychology*, **1**, 225–39.

Claparède, E. (1911), Récognition et moïté. *Archives de Psychologie*, **11**, 79–90. English translation (1951), Recognition and me-ness, in D. Rapaport (ed.), *Organization and Pathology of Thought*. New York: Columbia University Press, pp. 58–75.

Cosmides, L. and Tooby, J. (1991), Reasoning and natural selection. In R. Dulbecco (ed.), *Encyclopedia of Human Biology* (8 vols). San Diego: Academic Press.

Craik, F.I.M. (1991), Peace pipes around the TODAM pole: A puff for short-term memory. In W.E. Hockley and S. Lewandowsky (eds), *Relating Theory and Data: Essays on human memory in honour of Bennet B. Murdock*. Hillsdale, NJ: Lawrence Erlbaum, pp. 195–203.

Craik, F.I.M. and Tulving, E. (1975), Depth of processing and the retention of words in episodic memory. *Journal of Experimental Psychology: General*, **104**, 268–94.

Crannell, C.W. (1970), Wolfgang Köhler. *Journal of the History of the Behavioral Sciences*, **6**, 267.

Crowder, R.G. and Neath, I. (1991), The microscope metaphor in human memory. In W.E. Hockley and S. Lewandowski, *Relating Theory and Data: Essays on human memory in honour of Bennet B. Murdock*. Hillsdale, NJ: Lawrence Erlbaum, pp. 111–25.

Crumbaugh, J.C. (1954), Temporal changes in the memory of visually perceived form. *American Journal of Psychology*, **67**, 647–58.

Dain, N. (1980), *Clifford W. Beers: Advocate for the insane*. Pittsburgh: University of Pittsburgh Press.

Danziger, K. (1990), *Constructing the Subject: Historical origins of psychological research*. New York: Cambridge University Press.

Darley, J.M., Glucksberg, S., Kamin, L.J. and Kinchla, R.A. (1984), *Psychology*. Englewood Cliffs, NJ: Prentice Hall.

Den Heyer, K. and Barrett, B. (1971), Selective loss of visual and verbal information in STM by means of visual and verbal interpolated tasks. *Psychonomic Science*, 25, 100–2.

Dennett, D.C. (1991), *Consciousness Explained*. Boston: Little, Brown.

Diamond, S. (1972), The debt of Leibniz to Pardies. *Journal of the History of the Behavioral Sciences*, 1, 10–23.

Dodwell, P.C. (1993), From the top down. *Canadian Psychology*, 34, 137–51.

Dodwell, P.C. and Humphrey, G.K. (1990), A functional theory of the McCollough effect. *Psychological Review*, 97, 78–89.

Donald, M. (1991), *Origins of the Modern Mind*. Cambridge, MA: Harvard University Press.

Duncker, K. (1929), Über induzierte Bewegung (Ein Beitrag zur Theorie optisch wahrgenommener Bewegung), *Psychologische Forschung*, 12, 180–259. Abridged English translation in W.D. Ellis (ed.) (1938), *A Source Book of Gestalt Psychology*. London: Routledge & Kegan Paul, pp. 161–72.

Duncker, K. (1935), *Zur Psychologie des produktives Denkens*. Berlin: Julius Springer. Trans. L.S. Lees (1945), On problem-solving, *Psychological Monographs*, 58, No. 5 (Whole No. 270).

Dutta, S. and Kanungo, R.N. (1967), Retention of affective material: A further verification of the intensity hypothesis. *Journal of Personality and Social Psychology*, 5, 476–81.

Ebbinghaus, H. (1885), Über das Gedächtnis. Leipzig: Duncker & Humblot. Trans. H.A. Ruger and C.E. Bussenius in H. Ebbinghaus (1964), *Memory: A contribution to experimental psychology*. New York: Dover.

Ehrenfels, C. von (1890), Über Gestaltqualitäten. *Vierteljahrschrift für wissenschaftliche Philosophie und Soziologie*, 14, 249–92.

Ehrenfels, C. von (1937), On Gestalt-qualities. *Psychological Review*, 44, 521–4.

Eich, J.E. (1980), The cue-dependent nature of state-dependent retrieval. *Memory and Cognition*, 8, 157–73.

Eich, J.M. (1982), A composite holographic associative recall model. *Psychological Review*, 89, 627–61.

Ellenberger, H.F. (1970), *The Discovery of the Unconscious*. New York: Basic Books.

Ellis, W.D. (1938), *A Source Book of Gestalt Psychology*. London: Routledge & Kegan Paul.

Epstein, W. (1988), Has the time come to rehabilitate Gestalt theory? *Psychological Research*, 50, 2–6.

Epstein, W., Rock, I. and Zuckerman, C.B. (1960), Meaning and familiarity in associative learning. *Psychological Monographs*, 74, No. 4 (Whole No. 491).

Ericksen, R.L. (1963), Relational isolation as a means of producing the von Restorff effect in paired–associate learning. *Journal of Experimental Psychology*, 66, 111–19.

Ericsson, K.A. and Polson, P.G. (1988), An experimental analysis of the mechanisms of a memory skill. *Journal of Experimental Psychology: Learning, memory and cognition*, 14, 305–16.

Ericsson, K.A. and Simon, H.A. (1980), Verbal reports as data. *Psychological Review*, 87, 215–51.

Ericsson, K.A. and Simon, H.A. (1984), *Protocol Analysis: Verbal reports as data*. Cambridge, MA: MIT Press.

Ericsson, K.A., Chase, W.G. and Faloon, S. (1980), Acquisition of a memory skill. *Science*, 208, 1181–2.

Farah, M.J. (1988), Is visual imagery really visual? Overlooked evidence from neuropsychology. *Psychological Review*, **95**, 307–17.

Fechner, G.T. (1860), *Elemente der Psychophysik* (2 vols). Leipzig: Breitkopf & Härtel. Reprinted: Amsterdam: E.J. Bonset, 1964. Trans. H.E. Adler in G.T. Fechner (1966), *Elements of Psychophysics*, Vol. 1. New York: Holt, Rinehart & Winston.

Forrin, B. and Cunningham, K. (1973), Recognition time and serial position of probed item in short-term memory. *Journal of Experimental Psychology*, **99**, 272–9.

Freud, S. (1954), *Project for a Scientific Psychology*. Trans. C. Mosbacher and J. Strachey in S. Freud, *The Origins of Psychoanalysis: Letters to Wilheim Fliess, drafts and notes, 1887–1902* (ed. M. Bonapart, A. Freud and E. Kries). New York: Basic Books. (Originally written in 1895.)

Fraser, J.B. (1908), A new visual illusion of direction. *British Journal of Psychology*, **2**, 307–20.

Frick, R.W. (1988a), Issues of representation and limited capacity in the auditory short-term store. *British Journal of Psychology*, **29**, 213–40.

Frick, R.W. (1988b), Issues of representation and limited capacity on the visuospatial scratchpad. *British Journal of Psychology*, **79**, 289–308.

Friedrich, M. (1883), Über die Apperceptionsdauer bei einfachen und zusammengesetzten Vorstellungen. *Philosophische Studien*, **1**, 39–77.

Frijda, N.C. and Groot, A.D. de (eds) (1981), *Otto Selz: His contribution to psychology*. New York: Mouton.

Frings, G. (1914), Über den Einfluss der Komplexbildung auf die effektuelle und generative Hemmung. *Archiv für die gesamte Psychologie*, **30**, 415–79.

Frith, C.D. (1992), *The Cognitive Neuropsychology of Schizophrenia*. Hove, Sussex: Lawrence Erlbaum.

Furumoto, L. (1990), Mary Whiton Calkins (1863–1930). In N. O'Connell and N.F. Russo (eds), *Women in Psychology: A bio-bibliographic sourcebook*. New York: Greenwood Press, pp. 57–65.

Gardner, H. (1985), *The Mind's New Science: A history of the cognitive revolution*. New York: Basic Books.

Gernsbacher, M.A., Hargreaves, D.J. and Beeman, M. (1989), Building and accessing clausal representations: The advantage of first mention versus the advantage of clause recency. *Journal of Memory and Language*, **28**, 735–55.

Gibson, J.J. (1929), The reproduction of visually perceived forms. *Journal of Experimental Psychology*, **12**, 1–39.

Gibson, J.J. (1966), *The Senses Considered as Perceptual Systems*. Boston: Houghton Mifflin.

Gigerenzer, G. (1991), How to make cognitive illusions disappear: Beyond heuristics and biases. In E. Stroebe and M. Hewstone (eds), *European Review of Social Psychology*, Vol. 2. New York: John Wiley, pp. 83–115.

Gigerenzer, G. and Murray, D.J. (1987), *Cognition as Intuitive Statistics*. Hillsdale, NJ: Lawrence Erlbaum.

Gigerenzer, G., Hoffrage, U. and Kleinbölting, H. (1991), Probabilistic mental models: A Brunswikian theory of confidence. *Psychological Review*, **98**, 506–28.

Gleitman, H. (1980), *Psychology*. New York: W.W. Norton.

Glenberg, A.M. (1987), Temporal context and memory. In D.S. Gorfein and R.R. Hoffman (eds), *Memory and Learning: The Ebbinghaus Centennial Conference*. Hillsdale, NJ: Lawrence Erlbaum, pp. 173–90.

Glenberg, A.M. and Swanson, N.C. (1986), A temporal distinctiveness theory of recency and modality effects. *Journal of Experimental Psychology: Learning, Memory and Cognition*, **12**, 3–24.

Gottschaldt, K. (1926), Über den Einfluss der Erfahrung auf die Wahrnehmung der Figuren, I; Über den Einfluss gehäufter Einprägung von Figuren auf ihre Sichtbarkeit in umfassenden Konfigurationen. *Psychologische Forschung*, **8**, 261–317. Abridged English translation in W.D. Ellis (ed.) (1938), *A Source Book of Gestalt Psychology*. London: Routledge & Kegan Paul, pp. 109–22.

Greeno, J.G., James, C.T., DaPolito, F.S. and Polson, P.G. (1978), *Associative Learning: A cognitive analysis*. Englewood Cliffs, NJ: Prentice Hall.

Gregg, V. (1976), Word frequency, recognition and recall. In J. Brown (ed.), *Recall and Recognition*. Chichester: John Wiley.

Groot, A.D. de (1946), *Het denken van den schaker*. Amsterdam: North-Holland. Trans. A.D. de Groot (1965), *Thought and Choice in Chess*. The Hague: Mouton.

Guthrie, E.R. (1935), *The Psychology of Learning*. New York: Harper.

Harcum, E.R. and Skrzypek, G. (1965), Configuration determinants in visual perception of binary patterns: Supplementary report. *Perceptual and Motor Skills*, **21**, 860–2.

Harper, R.S., Newman, E.B. and Schwab, F.R. (1985), Gabriele Gräfin von Wartensleben and the birth of *Gestaltpsychologie*. *Journal of the History of the Behavioural Sciences*, **21**,118–23.

Harrower, M.R. (1932), Organization in higher mental processes. *Psychologische Forschung*, **17**, 56–120.

Harrower-Erickson, M.R. (1942), Kurt Koffka: 1886–1941. *American Journal of Psychology*, **55**, 278–81.

Hartmann, G.W. (1935), *Gestalt Psychology*. New York: Ronald Press.

Head, H. (1920), *Studies in Neurology* (2 vols). London: Oxford University Press.

Hebb, D.O. (1961), Distinctive features of learning in the higher animal. In J.F. Delafresnaye (ed.), *Brain Mechanisms and Learning*. London: Oxford University Press, pp. 37–46.

Hebb, D.O. and Foord, E.N. (1945), Errors of visual recognition and the nature of the trace. *Journal of Experimental Psychology*, **35**, 335–48.

Heijden, A.H.C. van der (1992), *Selective Attention in Vision*. London: Routledge.

Hellström, A. (1985), The time-order error and its relatives: Mirrors of cognitive processes in comparing. *Psychological Bulletin*, **97**, 35–61.

Helson, H. (1925, 1926), The psychology of Gestalt. *American Journal of Psychology*, **36**, 342–70, 494–526; **37**, 25–62, 189–216.

Helson, H. (1933), The fundamental propositions of Gestalt psychology. *Psychological Review*, **40**, 13–32.

Helson, H. (1947), Adaptation-level as frame of reference for prediction of psychophysical data. *American Journal of Psychology*, **60**, 1–29.

Helson, H. (1964), *Adaptation-level Theory: An experimental and systematic approach to behavior*. New York: Harper & Sons.

Henle, M. (1955), Some effects of motivational processes on cognition. *Psychological Review*, **62**, 423–32. Reprinted in M. Henle (ed.) (1961), *Documents of Gestalt Psychology*. Los Angeles, CA: University of California Press, pp. 172–86.

Henle, M. (ed.) (1961), *Documents of Gestalt Psychology*. Los Angeles, CA: University of California Press.

Henle, M. (ed.) (1971), *The Selected Papers of Wolfgang Köhler*. New York: Liveright.

Henle, M. (1978), One man against the Nazis – Wolfgang Köhler. *American Psychologist*, **33**, 939–44.

Henle, M. (1984), Robert M. Ogden and Gestalt psychology in America. *Journal of the History of the Behavioural Sciences*, **20**, 9–19.

Henle, M. (1985), Rediscovering Gestalt psychology. In S. Koch and D.E. Leary (eds), *A Century of Psychology as Science*. New York: McGraw Hill, pp. 100–20.

Henle, M. (1987), Koffka's *Principles* after fifty years. *Journal of the History of the Behavioural Sciences*, **23**, 14–21.

Herbart, J.F. (1816), *Lehrbuch der Psychologie*. Königsberg: A.W. Unzer. Trans. M.K. Smith (1891), *A Textbook in Psychology*. New York: D. Appleton

Hick, W.E. (1952), On the rate of gain of information. *Quarterly Journal of Experimental Psychology*, **4**, 11–26.

Hintzman, D.L. (1984), MINERVA2: A simulation model of human memory. *Behavioral Research Methods, Instruments and Computers*, **1**, 96–101.

Hirshman, E. (1988), The expectation-violation effect: Paradoxical effects of semantic relatedness. *Journal of Memory and Language*, **27**, 40–58.

Hirshman, E., Whelley, M.M. and Palij, M. (1989), An investigation of paradoxical memory effects. *Journal of Memory and Language*, **28**, 594–609.

Hoffman, W.C. and Dodwell, P.C. (1985), Geometric psychology generates the visual Gestalt. *Canadian Journal of Psychology*, **39**, 491–528.

Hollingworth, H.L. (1910), The central tendency of judgment. *Journal of Philosophy, Psychology and Scientific Method*, **7**, 461–9.

Hornbostel, E.M. von and Wertheimer, M. (1920), Über die Wahrnehmung der Schallrichtung. *Berliner Berichte*, **20**, 388–96.

Hull, C.L. (1935), The conflicting psychologies of learning – a way out. *Psychological Review*, **42**, 491–516.

Hull, C.L. (1943), *Principles of Behavior*. New York: Appleton-Century-Crofts.

Hull, C.L., Hovland, C.I., Ross, R.T., Hall, M., Perkins, D.T. and Fitch, F.B. (1940), *Mathematico-deductive Theory of Rote Learning*. New Haven: Yale University Press.

Hulme, C., Thomson, M., Muir, C. and Lawrence, A. (1984), Speech rate and the development of short-term memory span. *Journal of Experimental Child Psychology*, **38**, 241–53.

Hume, D. (1739–1740), *A Treatise of Human Nature* (ed. L.A. Selby-Bigge, 1955). Oxford: Clarendon Press, 1955.

Humphrey, G. (1951), *Thinking: An introduction to its experimental psychology*. London: Methuen.

Irwin, F.W. and Seidenfeld, M.A. (1937), The application of the method of comparison to the problem of memory change. *Journal of Experimental Psychology*, **21**, 343–81.

James, W. (1890), *The Principles of Psychology* (2 vols). New York: Henry Holt. (Reprinted: New York: Dover, 1950.)

James, W. (1902), *The Varieties of Religious Experience*. London: Longmans, Green. (Reprinted: New American Library, 1958.)

Jersild, A. (1929), Primacy, recency, frequency and vividness. *Journal of Experimental Psychology*, **12**, 58–70.

Johnson, D. (1993), Introductory: What is the cognitive revolution? Why does it need to be reassessed at the present moment? Talk given at a conference entitled *Reassessing the Cognitive Revolution*, York University, Toronto, 22–4 October.

Johnson, G.J. (1991), A distinctiveness model of serial learning. *Psychological Review*, **98**, 204–17.

Johnson-Laird, P.N. (1983), *Mental Models: Towards a cognitive science of language, inference and consciousness*. Cambridge, MA: Harvard University Press.

Kahneman, D., Slovic, P. and Tversky, A. (eds) (1982), *Judgments under Uncertainty: Heuristics and biases*. Cambridge: Cambridge University Press.

Kant, I. (1783), *Prolegomena to any Future Metaphysic*. Trans. (1889) J.P. Mahaffy and J.H. Bernard. London: Macmillan.

Kant, I. (1798), *Anthropology from a Pragmatic Point of View*. Trans. (1974) M.J. Gregor. The Hague: Martinus Nijhoff.

Kaplan, R.M. and Pascoe, G.C. (1977), Humorous lectures and humorous examples: Some effects upon comprehension and retention. *Journal of Educational Psychology*, **69**, 61–5.

Karier, C.J. (1989), Review of B.J. Baars, *The Cognitive Revolution in Psychology*. *Journal of the History of the Behavioural Sciences*, **25**, 77–81.

Karlin, L. and Brennan, G. (1957), Memory for visual figures by the method of identical stimuli. *American Journal of Psychology*, **70**, 248–53.

Katona, G. (1940), *Organizing and Memorizing: Studies in the psychology of learning and teaching*. New York: Columbia University Press.

Katz, D. (1911), Die Erscheinungsweisen der Farben und ihre Beeinflüssung durch die individuelle Erfahrung. *Zeitschrift für Psychologie (Ergänzungsband)*. Leipzig: Barth.

Katz, D. (1942), *Gestaltpsychologie*. Basel: Schwabe. Trans R. Tyson (1951), *Gestalt Psychology: Its nature and significance*. London: Methuen.

Katzaroff, D. (1911), Contribution à l'étude de la récognition. *Archives de Psychologie*, **11**, 1–78.

Kehoe, E.J. (1988), A layered network model of associative learning: Learning to learn and configuration. *Psychological Review*, **95**, 411–33.

Kenkel, F. (1913), Untersuchungen über den Zusammenhang zwischen Erscheinungs-grösse und Erscheinungsbewegung bei einigen sogenannten optischen Täuschungen. *Zeitschrift für Psychologie*, **67**, 358–449.

Kess, J.F. (1992), *Psycholinguistics: Psychology, linguistics and the study of natural language*. Philadelphia: John Benjamins.

Koffka, K. (1915), Zur Grundlegung der Wahrnehmungspsychologie. Eine Auseinan-dersetzung mit V. Benussi. *Zeitschrift für Psychologie*, **73**, 11–90. Abridged English translation in W.D. Ellis (ed.) (1938), *A Source Book of Gestalt Psychology*. London: Routledge & Kegan Paul, pp. 371–8.

Koffka, K. (1921), *Die Grundlagen der psychischen Entwicklung*. Osterwieck am Harz: Zickfeldt. Second edition trans. R.M. Ogden (1925), *The Growth of the Mind*. New York: Harcourt, Brace.

Koffka, K. (1922a), Perception, an introduction to the Gestalt-theorie. *Psychological Bulletin*, **19**, 531–85.

Koffka, K. (1922b), Die Prävalenz der Kontur. *Psychologische Forschung*, **2**, 147–8.

Koffka, K. (1927), Bemerkungen zur Denk-Psychologie. *Psychologische Forschung*, **9**, 163–83.

Koffka, K. (1935a), *Principles of Gestalt Psychology*. London: Routledge & Kegan Paul.

Koffka, K. (1935b), The ontological status of value. In H.M. Kallen and S. Hook (eds), *American Philosophy Today and Tomorrow*. New York: Lee Furman Inc.

Köhler, W. (1909), Akustiche Untersuchungen, I. *Zeitschrift für Psychologie*, **54**, 241–89.

Köhler, W. (1910), Akustiche Untersuchungen, II. *Zeitschrift für Psychologie*, **58**, 59–140.

Köhler, W. (1913), Über unbemerkte Empfindungen und Urteilstäuschungen. *Zeitschrift für Psychologie*, **66**, 51–80. Trans. H.E. Adler in M. Henle (ed.) (1971), *The Selected Papers of Wolfgang Köhler*. New York: Liveright, pp. 13–39.

Köhler, W. (1915), Optische Untersuchungen am Schimpansen und am Haushuhn. *Abhandlungen der Königlich Preussischen Akademie der Wissenschaften*. (Berlin) physikalisch-mathematische Klasse (Whole No. 3).

Köhler (W.) (1917a), Intelligenzprüfungen an Anthropoiden. I. *Abhandlungen der Königlich Preussichen Akademie der Wissenschaften*. (Berlin) physikalisch-mathematische Klasse (Whole No.1). Trans. E. Winter (1925), *The Mentality of Apes*. New York: Harcourt, Brace and World, Inc. (Reprinted: Penguin Books, 1957.)

Köhler, W. (1917b), Die Farbe der Sehdinge beim Schimpansen und beim Haushuhn. *Zeitschrift für Psychologie*, **77**, 248–55.

Köhler, W. (1918), Nachweis einfacher Strukturfunctionen beim Schimpansen und beim Haushuhn. Über eine neue Methode zur Untersuchung des bunten Farbensystems. *Abhandlungen der Königlich Preussichen Akademie der Wissenschaften*. (Berlin) physikalisch-mathematische Klasse (Whole No. 2). Abridged English translation in W.D. Ellis (ed.) (1938), *A Sourcebook of Gestalt Psychology*. London: Routledge & Kegan Paul, pp. 217–27.

Köhler, W. (1920), *Die physischen Gestalten in Ruhe und im stationären Zustand. Eine naturphilosophische Untersuchung*. Braunschweig: Vieweg. Abridged English translation in W.D. Ellis (ed.) (1938), *A Sourcebook of Gestalt Psychology*. London: Routledge & Kegan Paul, pp. 17–54.

Köhler, W. (1923), Zur Theorie des Sukzessivvergleichs und der Zeitfehler. *Psychologische Forschung*, **4**, 115–75.

Köhler, W. (1929), *Gestalt Psychology*. 2nd edition 1947. New York: Liveright. (Reprinted: New York: Meridian, 1980.)

Köhler, W. (1938), *The Place of Value in a World of Facts*. New York: Liveright.

Köhler, W. (1940), *Dynamics in Psychology*. New York: Liveright. (Reprinted: London: Faber and Faber, 1942; New York: Grove Press, 1960.)

Köhler, W. (1942), Kurt Koffka 1886–1941. *Psychological Review*, **49**, 97–101.

Köhler, W. (1944), Max Wertheimer 1880–1943. *Psychological Review*, **51**, 145–6.

Köhler, W. (1953), The scientists from Europe and their new environment. In F.L. Neumann, H. Peyre, E. Panofsky, W. Köhler and P. Tillich (eds) (1953), *The Cultural Migration: The European scholar in America*. Philadelphia: University of Pennsylvania Press, pp. 112–37. (Reprinted in M. Henle (ed.) (1971), *The Selected Papers of Wolfgang Köhler*. New York: Liveright, 413–35.)

Köhler, W. (1958), The present situation in brain physiology. *American Psychologist*, **13**, 150–4. (Reprinted in N. Henle (ed.) (1961), *Documents of Gestalt Psychology*. Berkeley and Los Angeles: University of California Press, pp. 97–106.)

Köhler, W. (1969), *The Task of Gestalt Psychology*. Princeton, NJ: Princeton University Press.

Köhler, W. and Restorff, H. von (1937), II. Analyse von Vorgängen im Spurenfeld. Zur Theorie der Reproduktion. *Psychologische Forschung*, **21**, 56–112.

Köhler, W. and Wallach, H. (1944), Figural after-effects: An investigation of visual processes. *Proceedings of the American Philosophical Association*, **88**, 269–357.

Köhler, W. and Wegener, J. (1955), Currents of the human auditory cortex. *Journal of Cellular and Comparative Physiology*, **45** (Suppl.1), 25–54.

Korte, A. (1915), Kinematopische Untersuchungen. *Zeitschrift für Psychologie*, **72**, 194–296.

Kraepelin, E. (1909–1913), *Psychiatrie*. 8th edition. Leipzig: Barth. English translation of parts of this: *Manic-depressive Insanity and Paranoia*. New York: Arno Press, 1976.

Kries, J. von (1882), Ueber die Messung intensiver Grössen und über das sogenannte psychophysische Gestez. *Vierteljahrschrift für wissenschaftliche Philosophie*, **6**, 257–94.

Kubovy, M. and Pomerantz, J.R. (eds) (1981), *Perceptual Organization*. Hillsdale, NJ: Lawrence Erlbaum.

Kuhlmann, F. (1906), On the analysis of the memory consciousness: A study of mental imagery and memory of meaningless visual forms. *Psychological Review*, **13**, 316–48.

Laming, D. and Scheiwiller, P. (1985), Retention in perceptual memory: A review of models and data. *Perception and Psychophysics*, **37**, 189–97.

Lange, K. (1894), *Apperception: A monograph on psychology and pedagogy* (ed. C. de Garmo, with 13 translators). Boston: D.C. Heath.

Lashley, K.S., Chow, K.L. and Semmes, J. (1951), An examination of the electrical field theory of cerebral integration. *Psychological Review*, **58**, 123–36.

Lauenstein, O. (1933), Ansatz zu einer physiologischen Theorie des Vergleichs und der Zeitfehler. *Psychologische Forschung*, **17**, 130–77.

Lazarus, R.S., Yousem, H. and Arenberg, D. (1953), Hunger and perception. *Journal of Personality*, **21**, 312–28.

Leahey, T.H. (1992), *A History of Psychology*. 3rd edition. Englewood Cliffs, NJ: Prentice Hall.

Leary, D.E. (1980), The historical foundation of Herbart's mathematization of psychology. *Journal of the History of the Behavioral Sciences*, **16**, 150–63.

Lecours, A.R. and Joanette, Y. (1980), Linguistic and other aspects of paroxysmal aphasia. *Brain and Language*, **10**, 1–23.

Leibniz, G.W. (1765, actually written in 1700–1705), *New Essays concerning Human Understanding*. Trans. A.G. Langley (1949), LaSalle, ID: Open Court.

Lewandowsky, S. and Murdock, B.B. (1989), Memory for serial order. *Psychological Review*, **96**, 25–57.

Lewin, K. (1922), Das Problem der Willensmessung und der Assoziation. *Psychologische Forschung*, **1**, 191–302; **2**, 294–329.

Lewin, K. (1926), Vorsatz, Wille und Bedürfnis. *Psychologische Forschung*, **7**, 330–85. English translation in D. Rapaport (ed.) (1951), *Organization and Pathology of Thought*. New York: Columbia University Press, pp. 95–153.

Ley, R. (1990), *A Whisper of Espionage: Wolfgang Köhler and the Apes of Tenerife*. Garden City, NY: Avery.

Light, L.L. and Carter-Sobell, L. (1970), The effects of changed semantic context on recognition memory. *Journal of Verbal Learning and Verbal Behavior*, **9**, 1–11.

Locke, J. (1690), *An Essay concerning Human Understanding*. (Reprinted: London: J.M. Dent, 1961.)

Loftus, E. (1979), *Eyewitness Testimony*. Cambridge, MA: Harvard University Press.

Luce, A.D. (1986), *Response Times: Their role in inferring elementary mental organization*. New York: Oxford University Press.

Luchins, A.S. (1939), The Einstellung effect in learning by repetition. Unpublished thesis, New York University. In *New York University's Abstracts of PhD Theses*.

Luchins, A.S. (1942), Mechanization in problem solving. *Psychological Monograph*, **54**, no. 6 (Whole No. 248).

Luchins, A.S. and Luchins, E.H. (1970), *Wertheimer's Seminars Revisited: Problem solving and thinking* (3 vols). Albany, NY: Faculty Student Association, State University of New York at Albany, Inc.

MacColl, S.A. (1939), *A Comparative Study of the Systems of Lewin and Koffka with Special Reference to Memory Phenomena*. Durham, NC: Duke University Press.

Maccurdy, J.T. (1928), *Common Principles in Psychology and Physiology*. Cambridge: Cambridge University Press.

Mach, E. (1866), Über den psychologischen Effect räumlich vertheilter Lichtreize. *Sitzungberichte der Kaiserlichen Akademie der Wissenschaft in Wien, Mathematisch-Naturwissenschaftliche Classe*. Abth. II, **54**, 131–44.

Mach, E. (1886), *Die Analyse der Empfindungen und das Verhältnis des Physischen zum Psychischen*. Trans. C.M. Williams and S. Waterlow (1914), *The Analysis of Sensations and the Relation of the Physical to the Psychical*. Chicago: Open Court.

Maier, N.R.F. (1930), Reasoning in humans: I. On direction. *Journal of Comparative Psychology*, **10**, 115–43.

Maier, N.R.F. (1931), Reasoning in humans: II. The solution of a problem and its appearance in consciousness. *Journal of Comparative Psychology*, **12**, 181–94.

Maier, N.R.F. (1945), Reasoning in humans: III. The mechanics of equivalent stimuli and of reasoning. *Journal of Experimental Psychology*, **35**, 349–60.

Maier, N.R.F. (1970), *Problem Solving and Creativity in Individuals and Groups*. Belmont, CA: Brooks/Cole.

Mandler, G. (1991), Your face looks familiar but I can't remember your name: A review of dual process theory. In W.E. Hockley and S. Lewandowsky, *Relating Theory and Data: Essays on human memory in honor of Bennet B. Murdock*. Hillsdale, NJ: Lawrence Erlbaum, pp. 207–25.

Mandler, G. and Mandler, J. (1969), The diaspora of Gestalt psychology: The Gestaltists and others. In D. Fleming and B. Bailyn (eds), *The Intellectual Migration: Europe and America, 1930–1960*. Cambridge, MA: Harvard University Press, pp. 371–419.

Marcel, A.J. (1983), Conscious and unconscious perception: Experiments on visual masking and word recognition. *Cognitive Psychology*, **15**, 197–237.

McClelland. J.L., Rumelhart, D.E. and the PDP Research Group (1986), *Parallel Distributed Processing: Explorations in the microstructures of cognition*. Vol. 2. *Psychological and Biological Models*. Cambridge, MA: MIT Press.

McCulloch, W. and Pitts, W. (1943), A logical calculus of the ideas immanent in nervous activity. *Bulletin of Mathematical Biophysics*, **5**, 115–33.

McDaniel, M.A. and Einstein, D.O. (1986), Bizarre imagery as an effective memory: the importance of distinctiveness. *Journal of Experimental Psychology: Learning, Memory and Cognition*, **12**, 54–65.

McDougall, W. and McDougall, K. (1927), Notes on instinct and intelligence in rats and cats. *Journal of Comparative Psychology*, **7**, 145–76.

Meissner, W.W. (1978), *The Paranoid Process*. New York: Jason Aronson.

Melton, A.W. and Irwin, J.McQ. (1940), The influence of degree of interpolated learning on retroactive inhibition and the overt transfer of specific responses. *American Journal of Psychology*, **53**, 173–203.

Melton, A.W. and von Lackum, W.J. (1941), Retroactive and proactive inhibition in retention: evidence for a two-factor theory of retroactive inhibition. *American Journal of Psychology*, **54**, 157–73.

Mensink, G.J. and Raaijmakers, J.G.W. (1988), A model for interference and forgetting. *Psychological Review*, **95**, 434–55.

Metcalfe, J. (1990), Composite holographic associative recall model (CHARM) and blended memories in eyewitness testimony. *Journal of Experimental Psychology: General*, **119**, 145–60.

Metcalfe, J. (1991), Composite memories. In W.E. Hockley and S. Lewandowsky, *Relating Theory and Data: Essays on human memory in honor of Bennet B. Murdock*. Hillsdale, NJ: Lawrence Erlbaum, pp. 399–423.

Metzger, W. (1963), Zur Geschichte der Gestalttheorie in Deutschland. *Psychologia*, **6**, 11–21. (Reprinted in M. Stradler and H. Crabus (eds) (1986), *Gestalt-psychologie*, Frankfurt am Main: Verlag Waldemar Kramer.)

Meudell, P.R. (1972), Short-term visual memory: comparative effects of two types of visually presented material and nonverbal material. *Journal of Experimental Psychology*, **94**, 244–7.

Mewhort, D.J.K., Merikle, P.M. and Bryden, M.P. (1969), On the transfer from iconic to short-term memory. *Journal of Experimental Psychology*, **81**, 89–94.

Michotte, A. and Prüm, E. (1911), Etude expérimentale sur le choix voluntaire et ses antecédents immédiats. *Archives de Psychologie*, **10**, 113–320.

Miller, G.A. (1956), The magical number seven, plus or minus two: Some limits on our capacity for processing information. *Psychological Review*, **63**, 81–97.

Miller, G.A., Galanter, E. and Pribram, K. (1960), *Plans and the Structure of Behavior*. New York: Holt, Rinehart & Winston.

Montague, W.E., Adams, J.A. and Kiess, H.O. (1966), Forgetting and natural language mediation. *Journal of Experimental Psychology*, **72**, 829–33.

Morgan, M.J. and Moulden, B. (1986), The Münsterberg figure and twisted cords. *Vision Research*, **26**, 1793–800.

Müller, G.E. (1911, 1913, 1917), Zur Analyse der Gedächtnistätigkeit und des Vorstellungsverlaufes Part I. *Zeitschrift für Psychologie Ergänzungsband*, No. 5, 1911; Part III: No. 8, 1913; Part II: No. 9, 1917.

Müller, G.E. and Pilzecker, A. (1900), Experimentelle Beiträge zur Lehre vom Gedächtniss. *Zeitschrift für Psychologie, Ergänzungsband*, No.1.

Müller, G.E. and Schumann, F. (1893), Experimentelle Beiträge zur Untersuchung des Gedächtnisses. *Zeitschrift für Psychologie*, **6**, 81–190, 257–339.

Müller, G.E. and Schumann, F. (1898), Über die psychologischen Grundlagen der Vergleichung gehobener Gewichter. *Pflügers Archiv für die gesamte Physiologie*, **45**, 37–112.

Müller, I. (1938), Zur Analyse der Retentionsstörung durch Häufung. *Psychologische Forschung*, **22**, 180–210.

Murdock, B.B. Jr. (1960), The distinctiveness of stimuli. *Psychological Review*, **67**, 16–31.

Murdock, B.B. Jr. (1982), A theory for the storage and retrieval of item and associative information. *Psychological Review*, **89**, 609–26.

Murdock, B.B. (1993), TODAM2: A model for the storage and retrieval of item, associative and serial-order information. *Psychological Review*, **100**, 183–203.

Murray, D.J. (1966), Vocalization-at-presentation and immediate recall, with varying recall methods. *Quarterly Journal of Experimental Psychology*, **18**, 9–18.

Murray, D.J. (1967), The role of speech responses in short-term memory. *Canadian Journal of Psychology*, **21**, 263–76.

Murray, D.J. (1968), Articulation and acoustic confusability in short-term memory. *Journal of Experimental Psychology*, **78**, 679–84.

Murray, D.J. (1975), Graphemically cued retrieval of words from long-term memory. *Journal of Experimental Psychology: Human Learning and Memory*, **106**, 65–70.

Murray, D.J. (1976), Research on human memory in the nineteenth century. *Canadian Journal of Psychology*, **2**, 1263–76.

Murray, D.J. (1982), Rated associability and episodic memory. *Canadian Journal of Psychology*, **36**, 420–34.

Murray, D.J. (1986), Characteristics of words determining how easily they will be translated into a second language. *Applied Psycholinguistics*, **7**, 353–72.

Murray, D.J. (1987), A perspective for viewing the integration of probability theory into psychology. In L. Krüger, G. Gigerenzer and M.S. Morgan (eds), *The Probabilistic Revolution*. Vol. 2. *Ideas in the Sciences*. Cambridge, MA: MIT Press.

Murray, D.J. (1988), *A History of Western Psychology* (2nd edition). Englewood Cliffs, NJ: Prentice Hall.

Murray, D.J. (1993), A perspective for viewing the history of psychophysics. *Behavioral and Brain Sciences*, **16**, 115–86.

Murray, D.J. and Hitchcock. C.H. (1973), The nature of the memory deficit in Korsakoff's psychosis. *Canadian Journal of Psychology*, **27**, 414–21.

Murray, D.J. and Newman, F.M. (1973), Visual and verbal coding in short-term memory. *Journal of Experimental Psychology*, **100**, 58–62.

Murray, D.J., Rowan, A.J. and Smith, K.H. (1988), The effect of articulatory suppression on short-term recognition. *Canadian Journal of Psychology*, **42**, 424–36.

Murray, D.J., Ward, R. and Hockley, W.E. (1975), Tactile short-term memory in relation to the two-point threshold. *Quarterly Journal of Experimental Psychology*, **27**, 303–12.

Naveh-Benjamin, M. and Ayres, T.J. (1986), Digit span, reading rate and linguistic relativity. *Quarterly Journal of Experimental Psychology*, **38**, 739–51.

Neath, I. (1993), Distinctiveness and serial position effects in recognition. *Memory and Cognition*, **21**, 689–98.

Neath, I. and Crowder, R.G. (1990), Schedules of presentation and temporal distinctiveness in human memory. *Journal of Experimental Psychology: Learning, Memory and Cognition*, **16**, 316–27.

Neisser, U. (1967), *Cognitive Psychology*. New York: Appleton-Century-Crofts.

Neisser, U. (1982), *Memory Observed*. San Francisco: Freeman.

Neisser, U. (1993), Ecological and representational approaches to cognitive science. Talk given at a conference entitled *Reassessing the Cognitive Revolution*, York University, Toronto, 22–4 October.

Newell, A. (1990), *Unified Theories of Cognition*. Cambridge, MA: Harvard University Press.

Newell, A. and Simon, H.A. (1972), *Human Problem Solving*. Englewood Cliffs, NJ: Prentice Hall.

Newell, A., Shaw, J.C. and Simon, H.A. (1958), Elements of a theory of human problem solving. *Psychological Review*, **65**, 151–66.

Newman, E.B. (1944), Max Wertheimer: 1880–1943. *American Journal of Psychology*, **57**, 428–35.

Newman, S.E. and Saltz, E. (1958), Isolation effect: Stimulus and response generalization as explanatory concepts. *Journal of Experimental Psychology*, **55**, 467–72.

Nisbet, B.C. (1975), Grace Roads: An account of a 'drop-in' communicator. *Journal of the Society for Psychical Research*, **48**, 148–58; 197–208.

Norman, D.A. (ed.) (1970), *Models of Human Memory*. New York: Academic Press.

Novak, G.S. (1977), Representations of knowledge in a program for solving physics problems. *Proceedings of the Fifth International Joint Conference on Artificial Intelligence*. Cambridge, MA: UJCAI.

O'Brien, E.J. and Myers, J.L. (1985), When comprehension difficulty improves memory for text. *Journal of Experimental Psychology: Learning, Memory and Cognition*, **11**, 12–21.

Osgood, C.E. (1949), The similarity paradox in human learning: A resolution. *Psychological Review*, **56**, 132–43.

Osgood, C.E. (1953), *Method and Theory in Experimental Psychology*. New York: Oxford University Press.

Osgood, C.E. and Heyer, A.W. (1952), A new interpretation of figural after-effects. *Psychological Review*, **59**, 98–118.

Paivio, A. (1971), *Imagery and Verbal Processes*. New York: Holt, Rinehart & Winston.

Paivio, A. (1986), *Mental Representations: A dual coding approach*. New York: Oxford University Press.

Parkin, A.J. (1987), *Memory and Amnesia*. New York: Blackwell.

Parkin, A.J. (1993), *Memory: Phenomena, experiment and theory*. Oxford: Blackwell.

Penney, C.G. (1989), Modality effects and the structure of short-term verbal memory. *Memory and Cognition*, **17**, 398–422.

Perkins, F.T. (1932), Symmetry in visual recall. *American Journal of Psychology*, **44**, 473–90.

Pillsbury, W.B. and Raush, H.L. (1943), An extension of the Köhler-Restorff inhibition phenomenon. *American Journal of Psychology*, **56**, 293–8.

Postman, L. (1971), Organization and interference. *Psychological Review*, **78**, 290–302.

Postman, L. and Brown, D. (1952), Perceptual consequences of success and failure. *Journal of Abnormal and Social Psychology*, **47**, 213–221.

Postman, L. and Phillips, L.W. (1954), Studies in incidental learning: I. The effect of crowding and isolation. *Journal of Experimental Psychology*, **48**, 48-56.

Postman, L. and Underwood, B.J. (1973), Critical issues in interference theory. *Memory and Cognition*, **1**, 19–40.

Poulton, E.C. (1989), *Bias in Quantifying Judgments*. Hillsdale, NJ: Lawrence Erlbaum.

Pratt, C.C. (1933), The time-error in psychophysical judgments. *American Journal of Psychology*, **45**, 292–7.

Pratt, C.C. (1967), Introduction to W. Köhler, *The Task of Gestalt Psychology*. Princeton, NJ: Princeton University Press.

Preyer, W. (1882), *Die Seele des Kindes*. Trans. H.W. Brown (1909), *Mind of the Child*. New York: Appleton.

Pylyshyn, Z.W. (1984), *Computation and Cognition: Toward a foundation for cognitive science*. Cambridge, MA: MIT Press.

Raaijmakers, J.G.W. and Shiffrin, R.M. (1981), Search of associative memory. *Psychological Review*, **88**, 93–134.

Ranschburg, P. (1905), Über die Bedeutung der Ähnlichkeit beim Erlernen, Behalten und bei der Reproduktion. *Journal für Psychologie und Neurologie*, **5**, 93–127.

Ratcliff, R. (1978), A theory of memory retrieval. *Psychological Review*, **85**, 59–108.

Rescorla, R.A. (1967), Pavlovian conditioning and its proper control procedures. *Psychological Review*, **74**, 71–80.

Restorff, H. von (1933), Über die Wirkung von Bereichsbildung im Spurenfeld. *Psychologische Forschung*, **18**, 299–342.

Rhetorica ad Herennium, trans. M. Caplan (1958). The Loeb Classical Library. London: Heinemann.

Ribot, T. (1881), *Diseases of Memory*. Trans. W.H. Smith (1882). New York: Appleton.

Riley, D.A. (1962), Memory for form. In L. Postman (ed.), *Psychology in the Making: Histories of selected research problems*. New York: Alfred A. Knopf.

Roediger, H.L. III (1980), Memory metaphors in cognitive psychology. *Memory and Cognition*, **8**, 231–46.

Rubin, E. (1915), *Synsoplevede Figuere*. Copenhagen: Gyldendalsde Boghandel. Translated into German (1921) as *Visuell wahrgenommene Figuren* (same publisher).

Rumelhart, D.E., McClelland, J.L. and the PDP Research Group (1986), *Parallel Distributed Processing: Explorations in the microstructures of cognition*. Vol. 1. *Foundations*. Cambridge, MA: MIT Press.

Rundus, D. (1971), Analysis of rehearsal processes in free recall. *Journal of Experimental Psychology*, **89**, 63–77.

Russell, B. (1945), *A History of Western Philosophy*. New York: Simon & Schuster.

Ryan, J. (1969a), Grouping and short-term memory: Different means and patterns of grouping. *Quarterly Journal of Experimental Psychology*, **21**, 137–47.

Ryan, J. (1969b), Temporal grouping, rehearsal and short-term memory. *Quarterly Journal of Experimental Psychology*, **21**, 148–55.

Samelson, F. (1981), Struggle for scientific authority: The reception of Watson's behaviourism, 1913–1920. *Journal of the History of the Behavioural Sciences*, **17**, 399–425.

Samelson, F. (1985), Organizing for the kingdom of behaviour: Academic battles and organizational policies in the twenties. *Journal of the History of the Behavioural Sciences*, **21**, 33–47.

Saul, E.V. and Osgood, C.E. (1950), Perceptual organization of material as a factor influencing ease of learning and degree of retention. *Journal of Experimental Psychology*, **40**, 372–9.

Schacter, D.L. (1987), Implicit memory: History and current status. *Journal of Experimental Psychology: Learning, Memory and Cognition*, **13**, 501–18.

Schacter, D.L., Wang, P.L., Tulving, E. and Freedman, M. (1982), Functional retrograde amnesia: A quantitative case study. *Neuropsychologia*, **20**, 523–32.

Scheerer, E. (1987), The unknown Fechner. *Psychological Research*, **49**, 197–202.

Schmidt, S.R. (1985), Encoding and retrieval processes in the memory for conceptually distinctive events. *Journal of Experimental Psychology: Learning, Memory and Cognition*, **11**, 565–78.

Schmidt, S.R. (1991), Can we have a distinctive theory of memory? *Memory and Cognition*, **19**, 523–42.

Schulte, M. (1924), Versuch einer Theorie der paranoischen Eigenbeziehung und Wahnbildung. *Psychologische Forschung*, **5**, 1–23. Abridged English translation in W.D. Ellis (ed.) (1938), *A Source Book of Gestalt Psychology*. London: Routledge & Kegan Paul, pp. 362–9.

Sechenov, I.M. (1863), *Reflexes of the Brain*. Trans. S. Belsky (1965). Cambridge, MA: MIT Press.

Selz, O. (1913), *Über die Gesetze des geordneten Denkverlaufs. Eine experimentelle Untersuchung*. Stuttgart: W. Spemann. English translation in N.H. Frijda and A.D. de Groot (eds) (1981), *Otto Selz: His contribution to psychology*. New York: Mouton, pp. 76–146.

Selz, O. (1922), *Über die Gesetze des geordneten Denkverlaufs. Zweiter Teil. Zur Psychologie des produktiven Denkens und des Irrtums*. Bonn: Friedrich Cohen. English translation of selected passages in N.H. Frijda and A.D. de Groot (eds), *Otto Selz: His contribution to psychology*. New York: Mouton, pp. 76–146.

Selz, O. (1924), *Die Gesetze der produktiven und reproduktiven Geistestätigkeit. Kurzgefasste Darstellung*. Bonn: Friedrich Cohen. English translation of selected passages in N.H. Frijda and A.D. de Groot (eds) (1981), *Otto Selz: His contribution to psychology*. New York: Mouton, pp. 20–75.

Semon, R.W. (1904), *Die Mneme als erhaltendes Prinzip im Wechsel des organischen Geschehens*. Leipzig: Engelmann. Trans. L. Simon in R.W. Semon (1921), *The Mneme*. London: George Allen & Unwin.

Shipley, T. (ed.) (1961), *Classics in Psychology*. New York: Philosophical Library.

Simon, H.A. (1966), Scientific discovery and the psychology of problem solving. In R. Colodny (ed.), *Mind and Cosmos*. Pittsburgh: Pittsburgh University Press, pp. 22–40.

Simon, H.A. (1981a), Otto Selz and information-processing psychology. In N.H. Frijda and A.D. de Groot (eds) (1981), *Otto Selz: His contribution to psychology*. New York: Mouton, pp. 147–63.

Simon, H.A. (1981b), *The Sciences of the Artificial*. 2nd edition. Cambridge, MA: MIT Press. (First edition, 1969.)

Simon, H.A. (1987), The information-processing explanation of Gestalt phenomena. *Computers in Human Behavior*, **2**, 241–55.

Simon, H.A. (1989), *Models of Thought*, Volume II. New Haven: Yale University Press.

Simon, H.A. and Barenfeld, M. (1969), Information processing analysis of perceptual processes in problem solving. *Psychological Review*, **76**, 473–83.

Simon, H.A. and Feigenbaum, E.A. (1962), A theory of the serial position effect. *British Journal of Psychology*, **53**, 307–20.

Simon, H.A. and Feigenbaum, E.A. (1964), Effects of similarity, familiarization and meaningfulness in verbal learning. *Journal of Verbal Learning and Verbal Behavior*, **3**, 385–96.

Skinner, B.F. (1938), *The Behaviour of Organisms. An Experimental Analysis*. New York: Appleton-Century-Crofts.

Slak, S. (1970), Phonemic recoding of digital information. *Journal of Experimental Psychology*, **86**, 398–406.

Slamecka, N.J. and Graf, P. (1978), The generation effect: Delineation of a phenomenon. *Journal of Experimental Psychology: Human Learning and Memory*, **4**, 592–604.

Sokal, M. (1984), The Gestalt psychologists in behaviourist America. *American Historical Review*, **89**, 1240–63.

Stern, W. (1914), *Psychologie der frühen Kindheit bis zum sechsten Lebensjahre*. Leipzig: Quelle und Meyer.

Stevens, J. (1988), An activity theory approach to practical memory. In M.M. Grueneberg, P.E. Morris and R.N. Sykes (eds), *Practical Aspects of Memory: Current research and issues Vol. I: Memory in Everyday Life*. Chichester: John Wiley, pp. 335–41.

Stout, G.F. (1888), The Herbartian psychology. *Mind*, **13**, 473–98.

Sullivan, J.J. (1968), Franz Brentano and the problem of intentionality. In B.B. Wolman (ed.), *Historical Roots of Contemporary Psychology*. New York: Harper & Row.

Tate, J.D. and Springer, R.M. (1971), Effects of memory time on successive judgments. *Psychological Bulletin*, **76**, 394–408.

Ternus, J. (1926), Experimentelle Untersuchung über phänomenale Identität. *Psychologische Forschung*, **7**, 81–136. Abridged English translation in W.D. Ellis (ed.) (1938), *A Source Book of Gestalt Psychology*. London: Routledge & Kegan Paul, pp. 149–60.

Thigpen, C.H. and Cleckley, H. (1957), *The Three Faces of Eve*. New York: McGraw-Hill.

Thomas Aquinas, St (1273), On the voluntary and involuntary. *Summa Theologica* I–II. English translation in A.C. Pegis (1945), *The Basic Writings of Saint Thomas Aquinas*, Vol. 2. New York: Random House, pp. 225–38.

Thomson, D.M., Robertson, S.L. and Vogt, R. (1982), Person recognition: The effect of context. *Human Learning*, **1**, 137–54.

Thorndike, E.L. (1898), Animal intelligence. *Psychological Review Monograph*, 1898, Supplement 2. (Reprinted in E.L. Thorndike (1911), *Animal Intelligence*. New York: Macmillan.)

Thorndyke, E.L. (1913–1914), *Educational Psychology*, 3 vols. New York: Teachers College, Columbia University.

Tichomirov, O.K. and Poznyanskaya, E.D. (1966–67), An investigation of visual search as a means of analyzing heuristics. *Soviet Psychology*, **5**, 2–15.

Titchener, E.B. (1910), *A Text-book of Psychology*. New York: Macmillan.

Titchener, E.B. (1914), On psychology as the behaviourist views it. *Proceedings of the American Philosophical Society*, **53**, 1–17.

Tolman, E.C. (1932), *Purposive Behavior in Animals and Man*. New York: Appleton-Century-Crofts.

Tolman, E.C. (1948), Cognitive maps in rats and men. *Psychological Review*, **55**, 189–208.

Tulving, E. (1962), Subjective organization in free recall of 'unrelated' words. *Psychological Review*, **69**, 344–54.

Tulving, E. (1983), *Elements of Episodic Memory*. New York: Oxford University Press.

Tulving, E. (1994), Memory processes and memory systems. 21st Bartlett Lecture. *Quarterly Journal of Experimental Psychology* (in press).

Tulving, E. and Donaldson, W. (1972), *Organization and Memory*. New York: Academic Press.

Tulving, E. and Schacter, D.L. (1990), Priming and human memory systems. *Science*, **247**, 301–6.

Underwood, B.J. (1948), 'Spontaneous recovery' of verbal associations. *Journal of Experimental Psychology*, **38**, 429–39.

Underwood, B.J. (1957), Interference and forgetting. *Psychological Review*, **64**, 49–60.

Viney, W. (1993), *A History of Psychology: Ideas and context*. Boston: Allyn & Bacon.

Walk, H.A. and Johns, E.E. (1984), Interference and facilitation in short-term memory for odors. *Perception and Psychophysics*, **36**, 508–14.

Walker, E.L. and Veroff, J. (1956), Changes in the memory-trace for perceived forms with successive reproductions. *American Journal of Psychology*, **69**, 395–402.

Wallace, W.P. (1965), Review of the historical, empirical and theoretical status of the von Restorff phenomenon. *Psychological Bulletin*, **63**, 410–24.

Wallach, H. (1949), Some considerations concerning the relation between perception and cognition. *Journal of Personality*, **18**, 6–13.

Wallach, H. (1963), The perception of neutral colors. *Scientific American*, **208**, 107–16.

Wartensleben, G. Gräfin von (1913), Über den Einfluss der Zwischenzeit auf die Reproduktion gelesener Buchstaben. *Zeitschrift für Psychologie*, **64**, 321–85.

Washburn, M. (1916), *Movement and Mental Imagery: Outlines of a motor theory of the complexer mental processes*. Boston: Houghton Mifflin.

Watkins, M.J., Ho, E. and Tulving, E. (1976), Context effects in recognition memory for faces. *Journal of Verbal Learning and Verbal Behavior*, **15**, 505–17.

Watson, J.B. (1913), Psychology as the behaviorist views it. *Psychological Review*, **20**, 158–77.

Watson, J.B. (1924), *Behaviorism*. 2nd edition, 1930. Chicago: Chicago University Press.

Watson, J.B. (1928a), *The Ways of Behaviorism*. New York: Harpers.

Watson, J.B. (with the assistance of R.R. Watson) (1928b), *Psychological Care of Infant and Child*. New York: W.W. Norton.

Watson, J.B. and Rayner, R. (1920), Conditioned emotional responses. *Journal of Experimental Psychology*, **3**, 1–14.

Wertheimer, Max (1912), Experimentelle Studien über das Sehen von Bewegungen. *Zeitschrift für Psychologie*, **61**, 161–265. Abridged English translation: W. Wertheimer, Experimental studies on the seeing of motion in T. Shipley (ed.) (1961), *Classics in Psychology*. New York: Philosophical Library, pp. 1032–89.

Wertheimer, Max (1920), Über Schlussprozesse im produktiven Denken. Berlin: Weltkreisverlag. Reprinted in Max Wertheimer, *Drei Abhandlungen zur Gestalttheorie*. Erlangen: Verlag der philosophischen Akademie 1925. Abridged English translation in W.D. Ellis (ed.) (1988), *A Source Book of Gestalt Psychology*. London: Routledge & Kegan Paul, pp. 274–82.

Wertheimer, Max (1922a), Untersuchungen zur Lehre von der Gestalt. I. Prinzipielle Bemerkungen. *Psychologische Forschung*, **1**, 47–58. Abridged English translation in W.D. Ellis (ed.) (1988), *A Source Book of Gestalt Psychology*. London: Routledge & Kegan Paul, pp. 12–16.

Wertheimer, Max (1922b), Untersuchungen zur Lehre von der Gestalt. II. *Psychologische Forschung*, **4**, 301–50. Abridged English translation in W.D. Ellis (ed.) (1938), *A Source Book of Gestalt Psychology*. London: Routledge & Kegan Paul, pp. 71–88.

Wertheimer, Max (1925), Über Schlussprozesse im produktiven Denken. In *Drei Abhandlungen zur Gestalttheorie*. Erlangen: Verlag der Philosophischen Akademie. Abridged English translation in W.D. Ellis (ed.) (1938), *A Source Book of Gestalt Psychology*. Routledge & Kegan Paul, pp. 274–82.

Wertheimer, Max (1945), *Productive Thinking*. New York: Harper.

Wertheimer, Michael (1985), A Gestalt perspective on computer simulations of cognitive processes. *Computers in Human Behavior*, **1**, 29–33.

West, D.J. (1962), *Psychical Research Today*. London: Pelican Books.

Whitely, P.L. and Blankenship, A.B. (1936), The influence of certain conditions prior to learning upon subsequent recall. *Journal of Experimental Psychology*, **19**, 496–504.

Wickelgren, W.A. (1966), Consolidation and retroactive interference in short-term recognition memory for pitch. *Journal of Experimental Psychology*, **72**, 250–9.

Wickelgren, W.A. (1969), Associative strength theory of recognition memory for pitch. *Journal of Mathematical Psychology*, **6**, 13–61.

Wickelgren, W.A. and Norman, D.A. (1966), Strength models and serial position in short-term memory. *Journal of Mathematical Psychology*, **3**, 316–47.

Wiener, N. (1948), *Cybernetics, or Control and Communication in the Animal and the Machine*. Cambridge, MA: MIT Press.

Wispé, L.G. and Drambarean, N.C. (1953), Physiological need, word frequency and visual duration thresholds. *Journal of Experimental Psychology*, **46**, 25–31.

Witasek, S. (1918), Assoziation und Gestalteinprägung. *Zeitschrift für Psychologie*, **79**, 161–210.

Woodworth, R.S. (1938), *Experimental Psychology*. New York: Holt.

Wolff, C. (1734), *Psychologia Rationalis*. Reprinted in J. Ecole (ed.) (1972), Christian Wolff. *Gesammelte Werke*, Part II, Vol. 6. Hildesheim: Georg Olms.

Wolford, G. and Hollingsworth, S. (1974), Lateral masking in visual information processing. *Perception and Psychophysics*, **16**, 315–20.

Wright, A.A., Santiago, H.C., Sands, S.F., Kendrick, D.F. and Cook, R.G. (1985), Memory processing of serial lists by pigeons, monkeys and people. *Science*, **229**, 287–9.

Wulf, F. (1922), Über die Veränderung von Vorstellungen (Gedächtnis und Gestalt). *Psychologische Forschung*, **1**, 333–73. Abridged English translation in W.D. Ellis (ed.) (1938), *A Source Book of Gestalt Psychology*. London: Routledge & Kegan Paul, pp. 136–48.

Wundt, W. (1874), *Grundzüge der physiologischen Psychologie* (1st edition). Leipzig: W. Engelmann.

Wundt, W. (1894), Über psychiche Causalität und das Princip des psychophysischen Parallelismus. *Philosophische Studien*, **10**, 1–124.

Wundt, W. (1896), *Grundriss der Psychologie*. Leipzig: W. Engelmann. The 4th revised edition trans. C.M. Judd (1902), *Outlines of Psychology*. New York: Gustav E. Stechart.

Zangwill, O.L. (1937), An investigation of the relationship between the process of reproducing and recognizing simple figures with special reference to Koffka's trace theory. *British Journal of Psychology*, **27**, 250–76.

Zeigarnik, B. (1927), Über das Behalten von erledigten und unerledigten Handlungen. *Psychologische Forschung*, **9**, 1–85. Abridged English translation in W.D. Ellis (ed.) (1938), *A Source Book of Gestalt Psychology*. London: Routledge & Kegan Paul, pp. 300–14.

Zeki, S. (1992), The visual image in mind and brain. *Scientific American*, **267**, 68–76.

Index